First World War

and Army of Occupation

War Diary

France, Belgium and Germany

15 DIVISION
44 Infantry Brigade
Gordon Highlanders
5th Battalion
1 June 1918 - 28 February 1919

WO95/1938/1

The Naval & Military Press Ltd
www.nmarchive.com
Published in association with The National Archives

Published by

The Naval & Military Press Ltd

Unit 10 Ridgewood Industrial Park,

Uckfield, East Sussex,

TN22 5QE England

Tel: +44 (0) 1825 749494

www.naval-military-press.com

www.nmarchive.com

This diary has been reprinted in facsimile from the original. Any imperfections are inevitably reproduced and the quality may fall short of modern type and cartographic standards.

Contents

Document type	Place/Title	Date From	Date To
Heading	WO95/1938 44 Infantry Bde 15 Division 5 Btn Gordon Highlanders June 1918-Feb 1919		
Heading	15th Division 44th Infy Bde 5th Bn Gordon Hors Jun 1918-Feb 1919		
Heading	5th Gordon Hrs. June 1918 & July 1918 44 Bde 15 Div		
Heading	5th Bn The Gordon Highrs. War Diary. For June 1st To June 30th. 1918. Volume 38		
War Diary	La Miquellerie	01/06/1918	01/06/1918
War Diary	Maroeuil	02/06/1918	02/06/1918
War Diary	Y Huts Near Maroeuil	03/06/1918	06/06/1918
War Diary	Y Huts Maroeuil.	07/06/1918	07/06/1918
War Diary	In The Field	08/06/1918	15/06/1918
War Diary	(In The Field) Wakefield Camp.	20/06/1918	25/06/1918
War Diary	In The Field	26/06/1918	30/06/1918
Miscellaneous	Strength		
Heading	Appendices Confidential Vol. 38		
War Diary			
Operation(al) Order(s)	Operation Order No. 16A. By Lieut. Col. G.A. Smith D.S.O. Comdg. 1/5th Battn. Gordon Highlanders. Appendix No. 1	31/05/1918	31/05/1918
Miscellaneous	Addendum 16 O.O. Le 16a Of 31.5.1918 Appx. 1	31/05/1918	31/05/1918
Operation(al) Order(s)	Battalion Orders No. 22A. by Lieut. Col. G.A. Smith D.S.O. Comdg 1/5th Battn. Gordon Highlanders. Appendix No. 2	31/05/1918	31/05/1918
Miscellaneous	Reference 15th Division G.S. 446. dated 14.5.18. Appendix No 3	14/05/1918	14/05/1918
Heading	War Diary		
Operation(al) Order(s)	Battalion Orders, No 22A By Lt Colonel G A Smith, D S O, Commanding 1/5th Battalion Gordon Highlanders, Appendix No. 4	02/06/1918	02/06/1918
Heading	War Diary Battalion Orders 3rd June 1918		
Operation(al) Order(s)	5th. Battalion, The Gordon Highlanders. Operation Orders No. 1. By Lieut-Colonel G.A. Smith, D.S.O., Comdg. Appendix No. 5	11/06/1918	11/06/1918
Operation(al) Order(s)	Operation Orders No. 1 Appx No. 5		
Operation(al) Order(s)	5th Battalion, The Gordon Highlanders. Operation Order No. 3 by Lieut-Colonel G.A. Smith, D.S.O., Comdg. Appendix No. 6	16/06/1918	16/06/1918
Operation(al) Order(s)	5th Battalion, The Gordon Highlanders. Operation Order No. 4 by Lieut-Colonel G.A. Smith, D.S.O., Appendix No. 7	16/06/1918	16/06/1918
Miscellaneous	5th Gordon Highlanders Appendix No. 8		
Heading	RSM		
Operation(al) Order(s)	2nd Gordon Highlanders. Operation Orders No. 2. By Lieut-Colonel G.A. Smith, D.S.O. Comdg. Appendix No. 9	20/06/1918	20/06/1918
Heading	War Diary		
Miscellaneous	G.H./S/21. Appendix No. 10	20/06/1918	20/06/1918
Map	From Maroeuil Appendix No 11		

Operation(al) Order(s)	The Gordon Highlanders. Battalion Order No. 35. By Lieut-Colonel G.A. Smith, D.S.O. Comdg. Appendix No. 12	23/06/1918	23/06/1918
Miscellaneous	Second Sheet No. 35 Apex 12	23/06/1918	23/06/1918
Heading	263 B		
Miscellaneous	To O.C.-Coy & R.S.M. Appendix 13	24/06/1918	24/06/1918
Heading	War Diary 24.6.18		
Operation(al) Order(s)	The Gordon Highlanders. Battalion Order No. 36. By Lieut-Colonel G.A. Smith, D.S.O. Comdg. Appendix No. 14	24/06/1918	24/06/1918
Miscellaneous	Second Sheet No. 36. Apex 14	24/06/1918	24/06/1918
Operation(al) Order(s)	5th Battalion, The Gordon Highlanders. Operation Order No. 4. By Lieut-Colonel G.A. Smith, D.S.O. Comdg. Appendix No. 15	25/06/1918	25/06/1918
Operation(al) Order(s)	5th Battalion, The Gordon Highlanders. Operation Order No. 6. By Lieut-Colonel G.A. Smith, D.S.O. Comdg. Appendix No. 16	29/06/1918	29/06/1918
Miscellaneous	Distribution.		
Miscellaneous	5th Bn Gordon Highlanders. Appendix 17A		
Miscellaneous	Extract from B.O. No. 27A Appendix 18		
Miscellaneous	Honours and Awards. Appendix 19		
Miscellaneous	Military Cross Appendix 20		
Miscellaneous	Casualties, Appendix 21		
Map	Appendix 22		
Map	Appendix 23		
Map	Trenches Corrected To 11.5.18 Appendix 24		
Map	Appendix 25		
Map	Trench Map 51B N.W. E S W 1:20,000		
Heading	5th. Bat. Gordon Hdrs. War Diary From 1st July To 31st July 1918. Volume 39		
War Diary	In The Field. R. Bn. R. Bde (From Scarpe S To Broken Mill)	01/07/1918	03/07/1918
War Diary	In The Field	04/07/1918	31/07/1918
Heading	Appendices July 18		
Operation(al) Order(s)	5th Battalion, The Gordon Highlanders Operation Order No. 7 By Lieut-Colonel G.A. Smith, D.S.O. Comdg.	04/07/1918	04/07/1918
Miscellaneous	Not To Be Taken Beyond Art. Or Inf. Brigade H.Q. XVIII Corps Intelligence Summary. Appendix 2	09/07/1918	09/07/1918
Operation(al) Order(s)	The Gordon Highlanders. Operation Order No. 8. By Lieut-Colonel G.A. Smith, D.S.O. Comdg.	09/07/1918	09/07/1918
Miscellaneous	44th 'Highland' Brigade Intelligence Summary, For Period From 7 A.M. 10th To 7 A.M., 11th July, 1918	11/07/1918	11/07/1918
Miscellaneous	The Gordon Highlanders. Administrative Instructions (Issued in conjunction with c.o. No. 9.)	12/07/1918	12/07/1918
Operation(al) Order(s)	The Gordon Highlanders. Operation Order No. 9. By Lieut-Colonel G.A. Smith, D.S.O. Comdg.	13/07/1918	13/07/1918
Heading	Secret O.C.-Signals O.O. No. 9		
Miscellaneous	A Form. Messages And Signals.		
Operation(al) Order(s)	5th Gordon Highrs Operation Order No. 11	16/07/1918	16/07/1918
Operation(al) Order(s)	5th Gordon Highlanders Operation Order No. 12. By Lieut-Colonel G.A. Smith, D.S.O. Comdg.	19/07/1918	19/07/1918
Miscellaneous	44th Brigade G.34-19.7.18	19/07/1918	19/07/1918
Operation(al) Order(s)	5th Gordon Highrs Operation Order No. 13	21/07/1918	21/07/1918
Operation(al) Order(s)	5th Gordon Highrs Operation Order No. 14	21/07/1918	21/07/1918
Operation(al) Order(s)	5th Gordon Highrs Operation Order No. 15 By Lt. Col. G.A. Smith D.S.O. Comdg.	22/07/1918	22/07/1918

Operation(al) Order(s) Miscellaneous	44th Highland Brigade Operation Order No. 287	23/07/1918	23/07/1918
Operation(al) Order(s)	5th Gordon Highrs Operation Order No. 15 By Lieut-Col G.A. Smith, D.S.O.	25/07/1918	25/07/1918
Miscellaneous	5th Gordon Highrs Operation Order No. 16 Lieut Colonel G.A. Smith, D.S.O. Comdg.	27/07/1918	27/07/1918
Miscellaneous	Headquarters 44th Infantry Brigade.	28/07/1918	28/07/1918
Miscellaneous	Copy Of Telegrams Received From C.O.C. 15th Division.	29/07/1918	29/07/1918
Operation(al) Order(s)	5th Gordon Hdrs. Operation Order No. 17 By Major J.B. Wood. D.S.O., M.C. Comdg.	29/07/1918	29/07/1918
Diagram etc	Appendix A		
Miscellaneous	Casualties From 24th To 31st July.		
Miscellaneous	Strength During Month Of July, 1918		
Miscellaneous	Casualties July 1918		
Heading	5th Gordon Hrs. August 1918 44th Bde 15th Div		
Heading	5th Battn. The Gordon Highlanders. War Diary For The Month Of August. Volume 40		
War Diary	In The Field	01/08/1918	31/08/1918
Miscellaneous	Casualties From 5th To 31st August 1918		
Miscellaneous	Strength During August 1918		
Miscellaneous	General Headquarters. British Armies In France 11th. August, 1918	11/08/1918	11/08/1918
Operation(al) Order(s)	The Gordon Highrs Operation Order No. 20 by Major T.B Wood DSO MC Comdg.	01/08/1918	01/08/1918
Operation(al) Order(s)	5 Gordon Highrs Operation Order No. 21 By Major Wood DSO. Comdg.	04/08/1918	04/08/1918
Miscellaneous	Casualties From 1st To 4th August 1918		
Miscellaneous	Ordre General No. 343	05/08/1918	05/08/1918
Operation(al) Order(s)	The Gordon Highlanders. Operation Order No. 22. By Major J.B. Wood, D.S.O. M.C. Comdg.	06/08/1918	06/08/1918
Miscellaneous	Arrangements for Move (issued in Conjunction with Operation Order No. 22)	06/08/1918	06/08/1918
Operation(al) Order(s)	The Gordon Highlanders. Battalion Order No. 51 By Major J.B. Wood, D.S.O., M.C. Cmdg.	12/08/1918	12/08/1918
Operation(al) Order(s)	5th Battn. The Gordon Highlanders. Operation Order No. 24. By Lt. Col. J.B. Wood, D.S.O., M.C. Cmdg.	15/08/1918	15/08/1918
Operation(al) Order(s)	5th Battalion. The Gordon Highlanders. Operation Order No. 25. By Lt. Col. J.B. Wood, D.S.O., M.C. Cmdg.	20/08/1918	20/08/1918
Operation(al) Order(s)	5th Battn. The Gordon Highlanders. Operation Order No. 26. By Lt. Col. J.B. Wood, D.S.O., M.C. Cmdg.	20/08/1918	20/08/1918
Operation(al) Order(s)	5th Battn. The Gordon Highlanders. Operation Order No. 27. By Lt. Col. J.B. Wood, D.S.O., M.C. Cmdg.	22/08/1918	22/08/1918
Miscellaneous	Sheet 2 No. 54	23/08/1918	23/08/1918
Operation(al) Order(s)	5th Battn. The Gordon Highlanders. Operation Order No. 28. By Lt. Col. J.B. Wood, D.S.O., M.C., Cmdg.	24/08/1918	24/08/1918
Operation(al) Order(s)	5th Battn. The Gordon Highlanders. Operation Order No. 29 By Lieut-Colonel J.B. Wood, D.S.O., M.C. Comdg.	27/08/1918	27/08/1918
Miscellaneous	Sheet 2 No. 55	29/08/1918	29/08/1918
Miscellaneous	O.C. "A", "B", "C" & "D" Coys., Q.M. & R.S.M.	30/08/1918	30/08/1918
Heading	Lieut. Colonel.		
Heading	War Diary For The Month Of September 1918 Volume No. 41		
War Diary	In The Field	01/09/1918	30/09/1918

Miscellaneous	Second Army No. A1496/39. VII Corps.	15/08/1918	15/08/1918
Miscellaneous	Special Order By General Sir H.S. Horne, K.C.B., K.C.M.G., Commanding First Army.	15/09/1918	15/09/1918
Heading	105 Lieut D S McDonald		
Miscellaneous	Effective Strength.		
Miscellaneous	Casualties For September 1918		
Operation(al) Order(s)	5th Battn. The Gordon Highlanders. Operation Order No. 30. By Lt. Col. J.B. Wood, D.S.O., M.C. Cmdg.	01/09/1918	01/09/1918
Operation(al) Order(s)	5th Battn. The Gordon Highlanders. Battalion Order No. 30. Part II By Lt. Col. J.B. Wood, D.S.O., C. Cmdg.	01/09/1918	01/09/1918
Operation(al) Order(s)	5th Battn. The Gordon Highlanders, Operation Order No. 31 By Lieut. Col. J.B. Wood, D.S.O. M.C. Cmdg.	04/09/1918	04/09/1918
Operation(al) Order(s)	Sheet E O.O. No. 31	04/09/1918	04/09/1918
Diagram etc	Operation Order No. 31		
Operation(al) Order(s)	Moge Operation Order No. 32, Lt Col, J.B. Wood 1 D.S.O. M.C.	05/09/1918	05/09/1918
Operation(al) Order(s)	Operation Order No. 33 Moge	08/09/1918	08/09/1918
Operation(al) Order(s)	44th Highland Brigade Order No. 305	10/09/1918	10/09/1918
Operation(al) Order(s)	Operation Order No. 38 By 5th Battn. The Gordon Highlanders.	11/09/1918	11/09/1918
Miscellaneous			
Operation(al) Order(s)	13 Bn The Royal Scots. Operation Order No. 100	11/09/1918	11/09/1918
Miscellaneous	Table "A"		
Miscellaneous	Table "B"		
Heading	Appx VIIIA		
Map	Quarries (5)		
Miscellaneous	5th Gordon Highrs. Reference Map. Sheet 44.A.	15/09/1918	15/09/1918
Operation(al) Order(s)	5th Battalion, The Gordon Highlanders. Operation Order No. 38. By Lieut-Colonel, The Lord Dudley Gordon, D.S.O. Cmdg.	15/09/1918	15/09/1918
Miscellaneous	Special Order.	15/09/1918	15/09/1918
Operation(al) Order(s)	5th Battn, The Gordon Highlanders. Operation Order No. 38A.	16/09/1918	16/09/1918
Heading	I.O		
Operation(al) Order(s)	44th Infantry Brigade Order No. 311	20/09/1918	20/09/1918
Miscellaneous	O.C. "A", "B", "C" & "D" Coys.	22/09/1918	22/09/1918
Operation(al) Order(s)	5th Battn. The Gordon Highlanders. Operation Orders No. 40	26/09/1918	26/09/1918
Miscellaneous	O.C. "A", "B", "C" & "D" Coys, Q.H., T.O., I.O. & R.S.H.	29/09/1918	29/09/1918
Heading	War Diary. For The Month Of October. 1918. Volume 42. Vol 44		
War Diary	In The Field	01/10/1918	17/10/1918
War Diary	Carvin	18/10/1918	18/10/1918
War Diary	Bois D' Epinoy	18/10/1918	19/10/1918
War Diary	Merignies	20/10/1918	20/10/1918
War Diary	Cappelle	21/10/1918	21/10/1918
War Diary	Deroderie	22/10/1918	31/10/1918
Miscellaneous	Strength October 1918		
Miscellaneous	Casualties October 1918		
Operation(al) Order(s)	5th Battalion, The Gordon Highlanders. Operation Order No. 41	01/10/1918	01/10/1918
Operation(al) Order(s)	5th Battn, The Gordon Highlanders. Operation Order No. 43	07/10/1918	07/10/1918

Operation(al) Order(s)	5th Battn. The Gordon Highlanders. Operation Order No. 44	10/10/1918	10/10/1918
Operation(al) Order(s)	5th Battn. The Gordon Highlanders. Operation Order No. 45	13/10/1918	13/10/1918
Map	Meurchin 1		
Map	Wingles 1		
Miscellaneous	Reference Sketch On Back.		
Operation(al) Order(s)	5th Battn. The Gordon Highlanders. Operation Order No. 47	16/10/1918	16/10/1918
Miscellaneous	5th Battn. The Gordon Highlanders. Operation Order.	17/10/1918	17/10/1918
Miscellaneous	5th Battalion. The Gordon Highlanders. Warning Order.	17/10/1918	17/10/1918
Operation(al) Order(s)	5th Battalion The Gordon Highlanders. Operation Orders No. 48	18/10/1918	18/10/1918
Miscellaneous	Warning Order.	20/10/1918	20/10/1918
Operation(al) Order(s)	5th Battalion The Gordon Highlanders. Operation Order No. 52	29/10/1918	29/10/1918
Operation(al) Order(s)	Administrative Instructions. (In Conjunction With Operation Orders. No. 52)	29/10/1918	29/10/1918
Heading	War Diary. For The Month Of November. 1918 Volume 43 5 Gordon Hrs Vol 45		
War Diary	Deroderie	01/11/1918	09/11/1918
War Diary	Hollain	09/11/1918	10/11/1918
War Diary	Tourpes	11/11/1918	11/11/1918
War Diary	Chievres	12/11/1918	30/11/1918
Miscellaneous	O.C. All Coys, L.G.O., T.O & Q.M., Signals & R.S.M. App. No I	01/11/1918	01/11/1918
Miscellaneous	C Form. Messages And Signals. App No. II	08/11/1918	08/11/1918
Miscellaneous	C Form. Messages And Signals. App No. III	08/11/1918	08/11/1918
Miscellaneous	O.C. All Coys. R.S.M. App. No IV	08/11/1918	08/11/1918
Miscellaneous	C Form. Messages And Signals. App. V		
Miscellaneous	C Form. Messages And Signals.		
Miscellaneous	O.C. Coys Z 96 App. VI	09/11/1918	09/11/1918
Miscellaneous	O.C. A.B.C.D. Coys T. OIO Sigls & RSM App. VII	11/11/1918	11/11/1918
Operation(al) Order(s)	5 Battn. Gordon. Highlanders. Operation Order No. 1 App. No. 9	12/11/1918	12/11/1918
Miscellaneous	O.C. All Coys. R.S.M	12/11/1918	12/11/1918
Miscellaneous	C Form. Messages And Signals. App X	13/11/1918	13/11/1918
Miscellaneous			
Miscellaneous	OC 8/10 Battn Gordon. Highlanders.	16/08/1918	16/08/1918
Map	Map To Accompany 44th Bde "C" Notes No. 34		
Heading	War Diary For The Month Of December 1918 Volume No. 44 5 Gordon Hrs Vol 46		
War Diary	Chievres	01/12/1918	17/12/1918
War Diary	Soignies	18/12/1918	19/12/1918
War Diary	Ittre	20/12/1918	22/12/1918
War Diary	Hivelles	23/12/1918	31/12/1918
Miscellaneous	Effective Strength.		
Miscellaneous	Orders For Royal Visit Of 7th December, 1918. App. No. I	05/12/1918	05/12/1918
Heading	App No. I		
Miscellaneous	All Officers R.S.M. App. No. I.	06/12/1918	06/12/1918
Operation(al) Order(s)	5th Battn. The Gordon Highlanders. Operation Order No. 1. Appendix No. 2	16/12/1918	16/12/1918
Operation(al) Order(s)	5th Battalion, The Gordon Highlanders. Operation Order, No. 2 Appendix No. 3	16/12/1918	16/12/1918

Operation(al) Order(s)	5th Battn. The Gordon Highlanders. Administrative Instructions Issued In Conjunction With O.O., No. 1		
Operation(al) Order(s)	5th Battn. The Gordon Highlanders. Operation Order No. 3. Appendix No. 4	21/12/1918	21/12/1918
Miscellaneous	44th Brigade No. G.6. 14.12.18	14/12/1918	14/12/1918
Map			
Heading	War Diary January 1919. Volume. 45. Vol 47, Vol 47		
War Diary	Nivelles	01/01/1919	31/01/1919
Miscellaneous	Effective Strength.		
Heading	Cover for Documents. Nature of Enclosures. Confidential War Diary of 5th Bn. the Gordon Highlanders. form. 1st Feby. 1919 to 28th Feby. 1919. Volume 46. Vol 48		
War Diary	Nivelles	01/02/1919	19/02/1919
War Diary	Halle	20/02/1919	20/02/1919
War Diary	Mechernich	21/02/1919	21/02/1919
War Diary	Roggandorf and Strempt	22/02/1919	28/02/1919
Miscellaneous	Strength During Month Of Feb. 1919. Appendix I		

WO 95 | 1938

44 INFANTRY BDE
15 DIVISION

5 BTN GORDON HIGHLANDERS

June 1918 - Feb 1919

15TH DIVISION
44TH INFY BDE

5TH BN GORDON HDRS

JUN 1918 - FEB 1919

From 61 DIV 183 BDE

44 Bde
15th Div

5th Gordon Hrs.
JUNE 1918
+
July 1918

CONFIDENTIAL

5TH. BTN. THE GORDON HIGHRS.

44/15 Vol 38

44 Inf Bde 15

WAR DIARY

FOR

JUNE 1ST. TO JUNE 30TH.

1918

June '18 – Feb '19

VOLUME 38.

6 Brig

Instructions regarding War Diaries and Intelligence Summaries are contained in F. S. Regs., Par. II. and the Staff Manual respectively. Title pages will be prepared in manuscript.

WAR DIARY
or
INTELLIGENCE SUMMARY.
(*Erase heading not required.*)

Army Form C. 2118.

Place	Date	Hour	Summary of Events and Information	Remarks and references to Appendices
LA MIQUELLERIE	1 June		The battalion left billets at LA MIQUELLERIE at 5.30 a.m and marched by road to AIRE station, arriving there at 9.45 a.m. 100x interval was maintained between companies. The train left an hour later, and was delayed at various places en route, the longest halt being at PERNES for nearly 4 hours, caused by the line being torn up by a shell.	APPENDICES 1, 2 + 3.
MAROEUIL	2 June		Arrived at MAROEUIL station at 1 a.m. The battalion detrained, and marched to "Y" huts, situated about 1½ miles from the station, on the ARRAS - St POL road. The day was spent in cleaning up, and the new officers who joined the battalion at AIRE station on 1 June were posted to companies. C.O attended a conference between Brig. Gen. Thomson 44 INF. Bde. + Col. Berkeley AA+QMG + Lord Dudley Gordon commanding 8/10th GORDON Hdrs. re amalgamation.	GB.
"Y" huts near MAROEUIL	3 June		The day was spent in inspections and training, gas drill, saluting drill, physical training and musketry all receiving attention. See	APPENDIX 4.
	4 June		The battalion received talks at AGNEZ-les-DUISANS, ~~and~~ by companies, and on returning to camp carried on with training under company arrangements. The establishment of Transport + Ordnance Stores was adjusted today.	

A6945 Wt. W11422/M1160 35,000 12/16 D. D. & L. Forms/C./2118/14.

Army Form C. 2118.

Instructions regarding War Diaries and Intelligence Summaries are contained in F. S. Regs., Part II, and the Staff Manual respectively. Title pages will be prepared in manuscript.

WAR DIARY
or
INTELLIGENCE SUMMARY.
(Erase heading not required.)

Place	Date	Hour	Summary of Events and Information	Remarks and references to Appendices
"Y" huts near MAROEUIL	5 June		2 Coy Commdrs + S.O. visited 8/10th Gordon Hdrs in line re adjustment of personnel	
			The battalion carried on training. "C" Coy proceeded to the range and fired musketry practice, while "A" "B" and "D" Coys devoted their attentions to trench duties, relieving of sentries in the line and musketry. 7 men were inoculated, who had not been done for over 12 months.	
	6 June		The battalion carried on training under company arrangements in the forenoon. At 12 noon the battalion was inspected by Capt. A. G. Cameron (2nd in command). 57 more men were inoculated, who had not been done for over 12 months. The Commanding Officer visited the 8/10th Bn. THE GORDON HIGHLANDERS. in the line 8/10 was RIGHT FRONT Bn in the LEFT Bde. Sector ~~with Bn Hqrs in~~ + were relieved tonight for the amalgamation taking up positions as Res. Bn. for the Bde with Hqs in Railway Cutting H14a 05.70.	

A6945 Wt. W11422/M1160 35,000 12/16 D. D. & L. Forms/C./2118/14.

Instructions regarding War Diaries and Intelligence Summaries are contained in F. S. Regs., Part II. and the Staff Manual respectively. Title pages will be prepared in manuscript.

WAR DIARY
or
~~INTELLIGENCE SUMMARY.~~
(*Erase heading not required.*)

Army Form C. 2118.

Place	Date	Hour	Summary of Events and Information	Remarks and references to Appendices
'Y' HUTS MAROEUIL	7.6.18		Training went on under company arrangements in the forenoon & at 9.30 am the C.O had all the officers in conference regarding the details of amalgamation with 8/10th Gordon Hdrs. & Trench Duties etc etc. During the afternoon preparations were made for the move. At 7.30 pm the Battn paraded ready to move off. The Bn. marched up the ARRAS–St Pol Road by companies at 100 yds interval followed by Hqrs Personnel each had a piper & a drummer who accompanied them until opposite the N.W gate of ARRAS. thence the companies moved by ST. NICOLAS & BLANGY to the various platoon positions held by 8/10th GORDON HDRS (RES. BN. LEFT BRIGADE SECTOR). The 1/5th GORDON HDRS marched up to the amalgamation with 17 Officers & 218 O.R. (parade state)	
IN THE FIELD	8.6.18		During the day the business of the amalgamation was carried on. About 5 am the amalgamation of the 8/10th & 1/5th GORDON HDRS was completed the combined battalion to be known as 5th Battalion The GORDON HDRS. Bn. Hqrs. H14 a 05 70. in Railway Cutting. Situation quiet weather good.	
"	9.6.18		A conference by C.O. and Company Commdrs was held at Bn. Hqrs. on trench discipline & tactical dispositions. Situation quiet warm weather. Work done. Trench Improvement.	
"	10.6.18		Situation quiet. Weather pleasant. Work done in improving trenches etc.	
"	11.6.18		Weather continued warm & pleasant & a considerable amount of work was done by Bn in carrying parties & in trench improvements. O.O. No 4 APPENDIX 5. was issued for relief of 4/5th BLACK WATCH during the night of 12/13th June.	O.O. No 1. APPENDIX 5. [initials]

D. D. & L., London, E.C. (10340) Wt W5300/P713 250,000 3/18 E 2688 Forms/C2118/16.

Army Form C. 2118.

WAR DIARY
or
INTELLIGENCE SUMMARY.
(*Erase heading not required.*)

Instructions regarding War Diaries and Intelligence Summaries are contained in F. S. Regs., Par. II. and the Staff Manual respectively. Title pages will be prepared in manuscript.

Place	Date	Hour	Summary of Events and Information	Remarks and references to Appendices
In the field.	12.6.18.		The day passed peacefully at night the bn relieved the 4/5th Black Watch as per attached operation order. "D" & "B" coys occupied the front line, "A" coy the support on MAC trench & "C" coy in MISSOURI – the Reserve line. Relief completed by 12 mn.	Operation order no: 1 attached. APPENDIX 5.
	13.6.18.		Day very warm & pleasant the whole front very quiet. T.M's & 4.5 Hows busy cutting the wire in front of the German lines in preparation for the raid to be made by the Black Watch. A patrol of 1 N.C.O & 3 O.R's left our lines at 11 P.M. but returned without hearing anything. A great deal of work was done during the night (13/14) TRIPOLI trench being continued towards TOWY alley shelters being built where necessary in the line. Orders for the evacuation of the apex of the SNOUT were received the front line now being what was formerly the base of the salient known as SNOUT trench. The snout is however to be patrolled & temporary blocks introduced.	
	14.6.18		There was the usual artillery activity on the part of the enemy on our lines, this T.M's showed a little aggression during the 24 hrs. Our R.E.S's were busy from dawn to dusk patrolling the lines being continually	

A6945 Wt. W11422/M1160 35,000 12/16 D. D. & L. Forms/C./2118/14.

Instructions regarding War Diaries and Intelligence Summaries are contained in F. S. Regs., Part II. and the Staff Manual respectively. Title pages will be prepared in manuscript.

WAR DIARY
or
INTELLIGENCE SUMMARY.
(Erase heading not required.)

Army Form C. 2118.

Place	Date	Hour	Summary of Events and Information	Remarks and references to Appendices
14.6.18.	14.6.18		harassed by hostile A.A. & M.Gs. No E.A. seen the whole day. Our artillery & T.Ms were as before busy destroying enemy wire preparatory to the raid. At night TRIPOLI trench was worked on and the sap SNOUT trench wired. An officer & sergeant of the Black Watch went out from our position at night to examine the wire cut for their raid. A patrol of 7 belonging to the [illegible] left our lines but no enemy were seen.	
	15.6.18		An operation order concerning the discharge of gas from the front was received for the following night to take place if not suitable on the night of the 15/16th the first favourable night following. Front & support lines to be evacuated during discharge. This a new method of projecting gas is said to be very effective. It is a secret which has puzzled the enemy & in consequence is jealously safeguarded.	
	16.6.18.		A quieter day than usual, though hostile T.M's showed greater activity firing on STOKES, Sunken Rd, & TRIPOLI trenches. Our artillery effectively retaliated & gave great assurance to our front line garrisons. Our air-craft busy patrolling the whole day, & no doubt doing very good work. Enemy A.A. shooting fairly good but our machines quite fearless. More work was done at night on TRIPOLI trench which when completed will constitute a valuable asset to our defences. Gas beam attack postponed at the last minute, because of absence of wind. All ranks very disappointed.	B. Thwaites

2/Lt. R. Parsons "D" Coy slightly wounded.

D. D. & L., London, E.C. (A5001) Wt. W1771/M2031 750,000 5/17 Sch. 52 Forms/C2118/14.

Army Form C. 2118.

Instructions regarding War Diaries and Intelligence Summaries are contained in F. S. Regs., Part II. and the Staff Manual respectively. Title pages will be prepared in manuscript.

WAR DIARY
or
~~INTELLIGENCE SUMMARY.~~
(Erase heading not required.)

Place	Date	Hour	Summary of Events and Information	Remarks and references to Appendices
(IN THE FIELD) WAKEFIELD CAMP.	26.6.18		Training. Musketry Competitions were carried out on Range. See APPENDIX Nº 12. Work party to Bury Cable to parade at 4 30 pm. See APPENDIX 13.	B.O. 35. APPENDIX 12. WORK PARTY G.H.W/11.
"	25.6.18		Lewis Gun Team + Revolver Competitions were carried out. Prizes for previous days competitions were presented by C.O. SEE APPENDIX 14	B.O. 36 APPENDIX 14
			Battn moved to Reserve Bn Right Sector as per operation orders No. 4(A) APPENDIX Nº 15.	B.O. 4(A) APPENDIX 15

D. D. & L., London, E.C.
(10340) Wt W5300/P713 750,000 3/18 E 2688 Forms/C2118/16.

Instructions regarding War Diaries and Intelligence Summaries are contained in F. S. Regs., Part II. and the Staff Manual respectively. Title pages will be prepared in manuscript.

WAR DIARY
or
~~INTELLIGENCE SUMMARY.~~
(Erase heading not required.)

Army Form C. 2118.

Place	Date	Hour	Summary of Events and Information	Remarks and references to Appendices
IN THE FIELD	26.6.18		The relief of the 10th Bn. Scottish Rifles, reserve Bn. of the RIGHT Bde. was completed & reported by code wire at 12.25 a.m. & the Bn. was then in the following dispositions:- A Coy lay in front of the debris of ATHIES, company Hqs. at H 14 d 8.7. No. 3 Platoon on the RIGHT astride the RIVER SCARPE billeted in the buildings of ATHIES MILL which is situated partly on an islet & partly on the RIGHT bank of the river where the SOUTH road from ATHIES crosses the SCARPE. (H 21 a 25.50) No. 2 Platoon occupied ATHIES TRENCH during "STAND TO" between the ATHIES – FAMPOUX N & S. Roads (H 15. c 7.2. & H 15 c 7.5) but were billeted in dugouts (H 15 c 4 4) Nos. 4 & 1. Platoons lay in EFFIE SWITCH NORTH of ATHIES – FAMPOUX NORTH Road from H 15 a 0.2 to H 15 a 5 4. No. 1 Platoon had orders in case of attack to occupy HOLLINS LANE ~~H 14 b 2.5 – H 14 b 3.7~~ H 15 central. D. Coy., in support, had in front No. 16 platoon & 2 sections of No. 15 in HOLLINS LANE H 14 b 2.5 – H 14 b 3.7. as battle positions & were accomodated in shelters in TRAMWAY VALLEY. No. 14 Platoon & 2 sections of 15 Platoon in TILLOY TRENCH from H 14 a 0.5 – H 14 a 6.6. C. & B Coys were in Reserve & were accomodated in huts on the WESTERN face of the ARRAS – LENS Railway embankment, which rises here 65 feet above the SCARPE, from the river to the ~~ARRAS~~ BLANGY – FAMPOUX road & known as STIRLING CAMP. The situation was quiet during the period except for a bombardment by "Yellow Cross" (Mustard Gas) shells between 3.30 am. – 5 am. in area H 14 b H 15 a & H 15 c	J.S.R.

A6945 Wt. W11422/M1160 35,000 12/16 D. D. & L. Forms/C./2118/14.

Instructions regarding War Diaries and Intelligence Summaries are contained in F. S. Regs., Part II. and the Staff Manual respectively. Title pages will be prepared in manuscript.

WAR DIARY
or
~~INTELLIGENCE~~ SUMMARY.
(Erase heading not required.)

Army Form C. 2118.

Place	Date	Hour	Summary of Events and Information	Remarks and references to Appendices
IN THE FIELD	26.6.18 (Contd.)		No. 2 Platoon lay in this area but as the following precautions were taken we suffered no casualties 1. No one allowed to sleep on ground affected 2. Box Respirators worn for 2 hrs after Sunrise 3. Shell holes treated with chloride of lime. Number of OR sent to Field Amb. sick with Influenza(?) (P.U.O.E) to day was included in to morrows report (27th).	
"	27.6.18		As reserve Bn, considerable work was done notwithstanding small numbers thro' losses with P.U.O.E. A Coy engaged in the defences of ATHIES MILLS & in shelters construction in CAROLINA TRENCH & at ATHIES the Garrison was employed in salvage work & in disinfecting area gas-shelled. D Coy employed wiring HOLLINS LANE & the reserve Coys B & C in preparing PEPPER TRENCH as a "jumping off" trench the spoil being carefully hidden. They also improved steps & trenches on WEST side of Embankment at STIRLING CAMP. The bath house was repaired & baths could be had. No. 2 Platoon were again subjected to a gas shell bombardment rising to a height at 2.45am & ending at 5.30 am. about 500 fell in all GREEN CROSS & YELLOW CROSS in proportion 1–6. Precautions taken prevented usual casualties. 1 NCO, stretcher bearer & 1 man wounded at 9.30 am, with shell from No. 4 platoon. The work parties of B & C Coys were gas shelled & gas Trench Mortared at 1.30 am. no casualties. Number to Hospital P.U.O.E. for yesterday & to day 7 OR.	
"	28.6.18		Bn. engaged in work much as yesterday. MUSKETRY VALLEY was heavily shelled from 3 am – 4 am	J.B.R.

A6945 Wt. W11422/M1160 35,000 12/16 D. D. & L. Forms/C./2118/14.

Instructions regarding War Diaries and Intelligence Summaries are contained in F. S. Regs., Part II. and the Staff Manual respectively. Title pages will be prepared in manuscript.

WAR DIARY
or
~~INTELLIGENCE SUMMARY.~~
(Erase heading not required.)

Army Form C. 2118.

Place	Date	Hour	Summary of Events and Information	Remarks and references to Appendices
IN THE FIELD	28.6.18 (contd)		with yellow cross gas shells about 100 estimated to have fallen. Weather remains pleasant & warm. H O.R. sent to Hospital for P.U.O.E.	
"	29.6.18		About 2.30 am. MUSKETRY VALLEY was again shelled H.E. & Shrapnel and later at 3.15 am the enemy sent into the same area about 40 light gas shells. The day was quiet until 9.40 pm when the area H19 b including the RAILWAY TRIANGLE where RIGHT BN. HQRS. are was subjected to a furious 15 minutes bombardment with regular but light shelling went on until 10.10 pm. In all 350 — 4.2 & 5.9's must have fallen. The day was warm	
"	30.6.18.		B & C Companies worked on the new FEUCHY RESERVE LINE. B Coy digging a trench under the railway lines at H21 c 10.65. & steps up the side of the cutting while C Coy. worked on the trench to the N of the railway. A & D Companies worked as usual. Operation Orders for the relief of the 8th SEAFORTH HIGHLANDERS in the RIGHT Sector of the Brigade Front to night have been issued see APPENDIX No 6	O.O. No 6 APPENDIX No 16. JSR

D. D. & L., London, E.C. (10340) W1 W5300/P713 ... R 2688 Forms/C2118/16.

Army Form C. 2118.

APPENDIX 17

WAR DIARY
or
INTELLIGENCE SUMMARY.
(Erase heading not required.)

Instructions regarding War Diaries and Intelligence Summaries are contained in F. S. Regs., Part II. and the Staff Manual respectively. Title pages will be prepared in manuscript.

Place	Date	Hour	Summary of Events and Information	Remarks and references to Appendices
			STRENGTH	
			OFFICERS / O.R.	
			STRENGTH OF 1/5TH GORDON HDRS as at 7TH JUNE (AT AMALGAMATION) 40 452	
			Do 8/10TH Do Do Do Do 11 595	
			51 1047	
			SURPLUS PERSONNEL SENT TO BASE	
			1/5TH GORDON HDRS 11 54	
			8/10TH Do Do 104	
			STRENGTH OF 5TH GORDON HDRS 40 889.	
			ON AMALGAMATION.	SEE APPENDIX 17
			NOMINAL ROLL OFFICERS 5TH	APPENDIX
			" " HONOURS + AWARDS	"
			" " BIRTHDAY HONOURS	"
			" " CASUALTIES	"
			ALL MAP REFERENCES FROM J. CORPS T.S. {175 / " / 174 / "} (TAKEN FROM 51b N.W. + S.W.)	APPENDIX / " / " / "

D. D. & L., London, E.C.
(10340) Wt W5300/1713 750,000 3/18 E 2688 Forms/C2118/16.

CONFIDENTIAL

VOL. 38.

APPENDICES.

Army Form C. 2118.

Instructions regarding War Diaries and Intelligence Summaries are contained in F. S. Regs., Part II. and the Staff Manual respectively. Title pages will be prepared in manuscript.

WAR DIARY
or
INTELLIGENCE SUMMARY.

(Erase heading not required.)

Place	Date	Hour	Summary of Events and Information	Remarks and references to Appendices

D. D. & L., London, E.C.
(10340) Wt W5300/P713 750,000 3/18 E 2688 Forms/C2118/16.

SECRET APPENDIX No I Copy No.

Operation Orders No 16A.

By

Lieut: Col. G. A. Smith D.S.O

Cmdg 1/5th Battn. Gordon Highlanders.

PARADE. The Battalion will parade ready to move off at 6.30 am tomorrow morning. "A" Coy will be formed up on the road outside Battalion Headquarters, "B" "C" and "D" Companies will form up near their billets. Companies will move off at intervals of 100 yards.

ORDER OF MARCH. Signallers, Band, "A", "B" "C" and "D" Companies

ROUTE. The Battalion will proceed from La Miquellerie, to La Perriere, thence to Guarbecque, & Berguette thence to Aire.

REPORTS. O.C. Companies will render marching out states to this Office by 6 am tomorrow morning.

DRESS. As shown to Company Commanders today. Uniformity of dress must be observed throughout the Battalion.

BAGGAGE. Officers Valises, Mess Boxes, Dixies, etc, will be stacked at Battalion Headquarters by 6 am.

2nd Lt. Irvine M.C. will proceed to the Station with the Baggage Waggons and ensure that all baggage is loaded on the train.

Lt. R. W. Youngson will report to the R.T.O, Aire at 10 am. He will be responsible for loading and for the taking over of rations at the Railhead

APPX. No [illegible]

TRANSPORT. The Transport will move by road in accordance with Brigade Order S.C. 5459 of 31. 5. 18.

ADDRESS The Battalion proceeds tomorrow to join the 8/10th Battalion of the Gordon Highlanders, and the Commanding Officer desires to say that he feels sure all ranks will endeavour to do their utmost to carry with them the fine reputation the Battalion has earned in the Field and in billets. The esprit de corps stands high in the Battalion, but higher still in the Regiment, and by the splendid combination of Territorial and Service Battalions of the Gordon Highlanders, a new page is about to be opened for even greater service in the history of the Regiment.

A. D. Copland. 2nd Lt. A/Adjt.
1/5th Gordon Highlanders.

31. 5. 18.

APPX. 1.

Addendum to O.O. 20 16a of 31.5.1918.

All operations with the exception of the actual moving of the transport, will be put forward one hour.

A D Copland 2/Lt/Adj.
1/5th Bn. Gordon Hrs.

31.5.1918.

APPENDIX No 2.

Battalion Orders No 22 A.

by

Lieut. Col. J. R. Smith. D.S.O.

Cmdg. 1/5th Battn Gordon Highlanders.

Reveille - 4.45 am.
Breakfast - 5.30 am.
Orderly Officer - Lt. Berwick.

PARADES The Battalion will parade as detailed in Operation Orders No 16 A, ready to march off at 6.30 am.

APPRECIATION. The following letter has been received from Maj. Gen. Colin Mackenzie G.O.C. 61st Division.

"I am sorry to have to say Goodbye "to the Battalion. I am sorry I am "unable to do so personally.
"Since you have been under my "command you have fought splendidly "and have nobly maintained the "reputation of your Regiment and "of Scotland.
"I wish you all good fortune"

(Sd.) C. Mackenzie."
Maj. Gen.

PRISONERS OF WAR - THEFTS FROM General Routine Order No 3723 dated 19th April (as amended by G.R.O. 3984 dated 11.5.18) is republished for information.

"Complaints have been received "alleging cases of theft of personal "property from freshly captured "German prisoners of War. Such "incidents are not only discreditable "in themselves, but they provoke

APPX. 2.

"retaliatory measures on the part of the enemy against British Officers and men who have been captured by them.
All ranks are forbidden to remove from German prisoners any personal belonging, including watches and other jewelry, iron crosses, money, identity discs, pay-books and articles of personal clothing.
Official letters, documents and maps should be collected at the earliest possible opportunity.
Private papers, letters and documents will only be removed under the authorized supervision of a General Staff or an Intelligence Corps Officer, or an Officer of the General branch of the Staff.

APPOINTMENTS AND POSTINGS

The following appointments and postings will take effect as from 1. 6. 18.

POSTINGS

Capt. McHardie J. to 'A' Coy.
Lt. West. W " 'B' "
Lt. Barwick W.T. M.C. " 'B' "
Lt. Ellis J.B " 'C' "
2/Lt Gill J.B. " 'D' "

APPOINTMENTS

Lt. Stewart J.B. will remain in command of 'A' Coy.
Lt West W. will take over command of 'B' Coy.
Lt Currie W.T " remain in " " 'C' "
Lt Russell J.G. " take over " " 'D' "

A. D. Copeland Capt. Adjt.
1/ Batn. Gordon Hdrs.

31. 5. 18.

APPENDIX No 3.

4

SECRET.

15th Division. Q/93/30.

Reference 15th Division G.S.446 dated 14.5.18.

I. The 1/5th Gordon Highlanders
1/8th Argyll and Sutherland Highlanders.
1/9th Royal Scots
will be transferred from 61st Division to 15th Division.
Personnel by Tactical Train on June 1st and Transport by Road on June 2nd.

II. They will arrive rationed for consumption June 2nd. Ration Strength of Battalions is :-

	Rail. All ranks.	Road. All Ranks.	H.D.	L.D.	Cobs.
1/5th Gordon Hrs.	354	69	17	43	7
1/8th A & S. Hrs.	535	95	16	41	6
1/9th Royal Scots.	691	75	17	41	7

III. Personnel will detrain as under :-

1/5th Gordon Hrs.	MAROEUIL.	2 p.m.
1/8th A & S. Hrs.	FREVIN-CAPELLE	2.30 p.m.
1/9th Royal Scots.	MAROEUIL.	2 p.m.

IV. They will be billeted as under :-

1/5th Gordon Hrs.	Y Huts, ETRUN.
1/8th A & S. Hrs.	HAUTE AVESNES.
1/9th Royal Scots.	ARRAS (Petite Place).

V. 3 Lorries, 1 per Battalion, will be detailed to meet these trains and convey the kits, etc. to their respective billets.

VI. The A.P.M. will detail guides to meet these Battalions on arrival and conduct them to their billets.

VII. Brigades, as detailed below, will arrange to send cookers to these billets with hot water ready so that teas can be prepared immediately the Battalions arrive at their billets :-

44th Inf. Brigade	1/5th Gordon Hrs.
45th Inf. Brigade	1/8th A & S. Hrs.
46th Inf. Brigade	1/9th Royal Scots.

VIII. Transport will rest night 1/2nd June at DIVION and will march at 8.30 a.m. June 2nd via HOUDAIN - CHAMBLAIN L'ABBE where Brigades will arrange to send guidesto conduct them to their lines.

1/5th Gordon Hrs.	to	44th Inf. Brigade Transport Lines.
1/8th A & S. Hrs.	to	HAUTE AVESNES.
1/9th Royal Scots	to	45th Inf. Brigade Transport Lines.

C. E. Horsley
Major,
D.A.Q.M.G., 15th Division.

31.5.18.
Distribution -
44th Inf. Bde.
45th Inf. Bde.
46th Inf. Bde.
T.O. 44th Inf. Bde.
T.O.45th Inf.Bde.
T.O.46th Inf.Bde.
15th Div. Train.
A.P.M.
A.D.M.S.
15th Signals.
D.A.D.V.S.
D.A.D.O.S.
"G".
1/5 Gordons.
1/8 A & S.H.
1/9 R.Scots.

WAR DIARY

APPENDIX No 4.

Battalion Orders, No 22A
by
Lt Colonel G A SMITH, D S O,
Commanding 1/5th Batttalion Gordon Highlanders,

2nd June 1918

DETAIL

Orderly Officer : : : 2ND LT W R McINDOE
Reveille :::::::: : : 6 am
Breakfast : : : : :: : 7 am
Sick Parade : : : : : 10 am
Orderly Room : : : : : 9 am

PARADES 9 - 9:30 Insspections, Box Respirators, Rifles, Ammunition, Billets, etc,
9:30 - 10 Saluting Drill, with and without Rifles, also "Eyes Right and Left":
10:10 - 10:30 Gas Drill, to be carried out at the halt and on the move:
10:40 - ~~12~~ 11 o'clock Physical Training:
11:10 - 12 noon Musketry, paying particular attention to Rapid Loading and Bolt drill:

DISCIPLINE The attention of all ranks is directed to fire precautions, which are posted in all huts: Any infringement to these orders will be severely dealt with:

Box Respirators will always be worn, by all ranks, in the vicinity of the Camp: They will be worn at the "Ready" position:

GAS ATTACK: The alarm for Gas Attack will be given at the Area Commandant's Office by sounding the Strombos Horn, that is, 3 blasts, interval, 3 blasts, interval, and so on:

PART 11

No 240308, L/Cpl Gray, F:W to be appointed Battalion Chiropodist as from 12th April, 1918, vice No 240041 Cpl, Neilson, killed in action:

A B Gilsland 2/Lt: A/Adjt:
1/5th Battn Gordon Highlanders:

WAR
DIARY

Battalion Orders
3rd June 1918

War Diary

War Diary
Herewith

APPENDIX No. 5.

5th. Battalion, The Gordon Highlanders.

OPERATION ORDERS No. 1.

By

Lieut-Colonel G. A. Smith, D. S. O., Comdg.

11th June 1918.

1. The 5th Gordon Highlanders will relieve the 4/5th Black Watch in the Left Sector of the Left Brigade to-morrow, night of 12/13th June.
On completion of relief, the Black Watch will become Reserve Battalion.

2. Dispositions :-

"D" Coy. Gordons will relieve "D" Coy. Black Watch in the Right Front.
"B" Coy. " " " "A" Coy. " " " " Left Front.
"A" Coy. " " " "B" Coy. " " " Support (Mac. Trench)
"C" Coy. " " " "C" Coy. " " " Reserve (MISSOURI)
Battn. H. Qrs. " " " Battn. H. Qrs. " " at H. 9. b. 1. 3. (EFFIE)
The relief will be carried out in the above order.

3. Guides :-
For "D" Coy. : 1 per post, 1 per Reserve platoon, and One for Coy. H. Qrs. (nine in all) will be at Junction of EFFIE SWITCH and MISSISSIPPI, H. 10. b. 1. 3. at 10 p.m.
For "B" Coy. : 1 per Post, 1 per Reserve platoon and one for Coy. H. Qrs. (11 in all) will be at Junction of MISSISSIPPI and GAVRELLE Road, H. 3. d. 9. 5. at ~~XXXXX~~ 10. 15. p.m.
For "A" and "C" Coys. : 1 per platoon and 1 for Coy. H. Qrs. will be at Junction of MISSISSIPPI and GAVRELLE Road at 10 p.m.
For Battalion H. Qrs. : No. Guides.

4. ROUTES. :-

"D" Coy.--- EFFIE SWITCH.
"B" Coy.--- GAVRELLE Road --- TOWY ALLEY.
"A" & "C" Coys. --- GAVRELLE ROAD.
Battn. H. Qrs. ------ GAVRELLE ROAD & EFFIE TRENCH.

5. (a) "B" and "D" Coys. willeach send an Advanced Party of 1 Officer and 1 N. C. O. per platoon to-night to take over Stores and thoroughly reconnoitre the Line. Parties will remain in the line. Rations for to-morrow to be carried.
"A" and "C" Coys. will each send an Advanced Party of 1 N. C. O. per platoon at 5 p.m. to-morrow to take over Trench Stores and accomodation.
(b) Advanced Parties from the Black Watch will take over Stores etc. at 5 p.m.

6. All explosive stores. trench stores, tools, Battalion Defence Schemes, Aeroplane photographs and programmes of work will be taken over and receipts given.
"C" Coy. will also take over the stores at the present Battn. H. Qrs. of the Black Watch at H. 4. c. 5. 4.
Lists of full stores taken over will reach Battn. H. Qrs. by 8 a.m., 13th June.

APPX No. 5

OPERATION ORDERS No.1.

7. All six Stragglers Posts at present manned by the Battalion will be taken over by the Black Watch at 6 p.m. to-morrow.
The following Stragglers Posts will be taken over by the Battalion to-morrow at 5 p.m. :-
H.3.d.90.45. (Junction of MISSISSIPPI and GAVRELLE Road)--- "C" Coy.

H.10.a.8.3. (EFFIE SWITCH) -------- "C" Coy.
Each Post consists of 1 N.C.O. and 3 Men.

8. Releif complete to be wired to Battalion H.Qrs. by the Code Word "PEACE"

9. Acknowledge.

G.P. Geddes
Captain & Adjutant,
5th Battn, Gordon Highlanders.

Distribution :-
Copies 1 -- 4. : O.C.Coys.
5. : C.O.
6. : T.O.
7. : Signals.
8. : L.G.O.
9. : M.O.
10. : I.O.
11. : R.S.M.
12. : W.D.
13. : File.
14. : 4/5th Black Watch.

APPENDIX No 6

W.D.

Secret.

8th Battalion, The Gordon Highlanders.

OPERATION ORDER No. 3 by

Lieut-Colonel [illegible], D.S.O., Comdg.

16th June 1916.

1. On the night of the 16/17th June, the 4/5th Black Watch and the 8th Seaforth Highlanders will raid the enemy's trenches as under :-

2. Raids will be simultaneous - Zero Hour will be [illegible] at 1-00 a

3. The object of these raids is :-
(a) To secure prisoners. (b) Damage wire, trenches, etc.
(c) To ascertain the lines of enemy's barrage.

4. RAID "A". :- To be carried out by 4/5th Black Watch.
(1) Locality to be raided :- Enemy's Front Line Trench from [illegible]
:- [illegible]

(2) Strength :- [illegible] Officers and [illegible] Other Ranks.

(3) The raiding party will be assembled in shell holes about [illegible] in front [illegible] of our wire by Zero - 15 minutes.

(4) At Zero the Artillery Barrage opens.

(5) At Zero, plus 15, a GREEN [illegible] LIGHT will be fired across the front as the signal for return. Trench Horns will also be sounded.

(6) The Raiding Party will return via the track leading from the enemy line about [illegible], to our Front Line about the junction of [illegible] and [illegible], and will collect in the dugout at [illegible]. O. C. "[illegible]" Coy. will ensure that this dugout is kept open and cleared of [illegible].

(7) Advanced Battalion H.Q. for the Black Watch will be at [illegible]
(8) Advanced Regimental Aid Post will be established at "[illegible]" Coy's [illegible] in the [illegible] ROAD at [illegible]. Cases will be taken down to the junction of [illegible] TRENCH and the Road, whence they will be evacuated down the road by wheeled stretchers.

(9) "C" Coy Black Watch will detail a Lewis Gun Section to watch the Left Flank of the Raiders. This section will take up a shell hole position at [illegible], by Zero - 30 minutes, and will remain out until Zero plus [illegible].

5. RAID "B". :- To be carried out by the 8th Seaforth Highlanders.
(1) Locality :- Enemy [illegible] at [illegible], 17, [illegible], 67, [illegible]

(2) Strength :- 2 Officers and [illegible] Other Ranks.

6. The Artillery Barrage for both raids will continue for 25 minutes.

7. All men with the exception of the sentries must be kept under cover as far as possible until retaliation has died down.

8. Synchronisation of Watches :- Arrangements to be notified later.

9. Acknowledge.

16th June 1916.

G P Geddes, Captain & Adjutant,
8th Battalion, The Gordon Highlanders.

APPX No 6

7. Arrival in Camp will be reported to Orderly Room.

8. Acknowledge.

16th June 1918.

G.P. Geddes Captain & Adjutant,
5th Gordon Highlanders.

Distribution :-

Copies 1 - 4. O. C. Coys.
5. T. O.
6. L. G. O.
7. Major Wood.
8. R. S. M.
9. 6th Camerons.
10. W. D. ✓

APPENDIX 7

5th Battalion, The Gordon Highlanders.

<u>Secret.</u>

<u>OPERATION ORDER No. 4.</u>

By

Lieut-<u>Colonel G.A. Smith, D.S.O.,</u> Comdg.

16th June, 1918.

1. The 5th Gordon Highlanders will be relieved in the line by the 6th Cameron Highlanders on the night of the 17/18th June.
On relief, the Battalion will withdraw to WAKEFIELD CAMP.

<u>ROUTE:-</u> GAVRELLE ROAD -- PLANK ROAD. (from H.8. central - Artillery Track "A".

2. <u>DISPOSITIONS :-</u>

"D" Coy.	Gordons	will	be	relieved	by	"A" Coy.	Camerons	in	Right Front.
"B" Coy.	"	"	"	"	"	"B" Coy.	"	"	Left Front.
"A" Coy.	"	"	"	"	"	"C" Coy.	"	"	Support.
"C" Coy.	"	"	"	"	"	"D" Coy.	"	"	Reserve.
Battn. H. Qrs.	"	"	"	"	"	Battn. H. Qrs.	"	at	H.9.b.1.3.

The relief will be carried out in the above order.

3. <u>GUIDES :-</u>

(a) <u>For "A" & "B" Coys.</u> Camerons - 1 per Post, 1 for each remaining Platoon, and 1 for Coy. H. Qrs.
(b) <u>For "C" & "D" Coys</u> Camerons - 1 per Platoon and 1 for Coy. H. Qrs.
(c) <u>For Battn. H. Qrs. C</u>amerons - 2 Guides will rendezvous at Battn. H. Qrs. under Lieut. MACDONALD at 10-30 p.m. Guides will then meet the incoming UNIT on the GAVRELLE ROAD, 100 yards West of Road Junction at H.3.d.1.0.

4. <u>ROUTES :-</u>

(a) <u>"A" Coy.</u> Camerons - via Light Railway to NORTHUMBERLAND AVENUE - CABLE.
(b) <u>"B" Coy.</u> Camerons - via GAVRELLE ROAD -- HAEM. TOWN.
(c) <u>"C" Coy.</u> Camerons - via GAVRELLE ROAD -- MACK.

(d) <u>"D" Coy.</u> Camerons - via GAVRELLE ROAD -- MISSOURI.

5. (a) Battn. Defence Schemes, Aeroplane Photographs, Sketch Maps, Explosive Stores, Tools, Tracer & A.P. Ammunition, and programmes of Work will be handed over and receipts taken.
Lists, <u>in duplicate,</u> of articles handed over will reach Battn. H. Qrs. by 9 a.m. 18th June.

(b) Major J. B. WOOD, D.S.O., M.C., will detail 1 Officer per Coy. and 1 for Battn. H. Qrs. to take over stores and accomodation in WAKEFIELD CAMP.

List of Stores taken over will reach Battn. H. Qrs. as in para. 5. (a).

6. Transport Officer will arrange for 1 Limber per Coy. and 1½ for Battalion Headquarters, for Lewis Guns, S.A.A., Dixes, Officers' Mess Kits, and Signalling Gear to be 100 yards West of Road Junction H.3.d.1.0. by 12 midnight. Officers' horses will be at the Junction of PLANK ROAD and the GAVRELLE ROAD at 12-30 a.m.

7. Completion of relief will be reported by wire to Battn. H. Qrs. by Code Words "RATIONS CORRECT".

APPENDIX Nº 8.

R.S.M.

5th Gordon Highlanders

Training Programme for the week ending [illegible] June 1918.

DATE	HOURS.	COYS	NATURE OF TRAINING.	SPECIALISTS.	REMARKS.
19.6.18.	11 A.M. – 12 Noon 12 – 1.20 P.M. 1.20 – 2.40 P.M. 2.40 – 4 P.M. 4 – 5.20 P.M. 5.20 – 6 P.M. 7 – 9 A.M. 9 – 11 A.M. 11 – 1 P.M. 1 – 3 P.M. 3 – 5 P.M.	H.Q. A B C D Specialists H.Q. B C D A	Bathing at [illegible] [illegible] Range.	[illegible]	[illegible]
20.6.18.	7 – 9 A.M. 9 – 11 A.M. 11 – 1 P.M. 1 – 3 P.M. 3 – 5 P.M. 10 – 12 Noon 2 – 3 P.M.	H.Q. C B A D A & D B & C	[illegible] Range [illegible]	[illegible]	[illegible]
21.6.18.	MORNING AFTERNOON	ALL COYS	Battalion Scheme Elementary Training [illegible]	All Specialists [illegible]	[illegible]
22.6.18.	9 – 12 Noon AFTERNOON	ALL COYS	[illegible] Regimental Sports.	[illegible]	[illegible]
23.6.18.	8 – 10 A.M. 10 – 12 Noon 12 – 2 P.M. 2 – 4 P.M. 4 – 6 P.M.	A B C D [illegible]	[illegible] Range		
24.6.18.	ALL DAY. 11 A.M. – 12 Noon 12 – 1.20 P.M. 1.20 – 2.40 P.M. 2.40 – 4 P.M. 4 – 5.20 P.M. 5.20 – 6 P.M.	– H.Q. A B C D Specialists	[illegible] Baths.	[illegible]	

G.P. Geddes
Capt & Adjt.

APPENDIX No 9.

Secret.

The Gordon Highlanders.

OPERATION ORDERS No. 2 by

Lieut-Colonel G. A. Smith, D.S.O. Comdg.

20th June, 1918.

Reference attached Tactical Scheme and Map.

1. The Battalion will attack the trench system outlined on the attached map. Assembly positions, trench marked Blue.
First Objective Trench marked.......... Red.
Second Objective Trench marked.......... Yellow.
Final Objective Trench marked.......... Green.

2. Assaulting Coys:- "B" Coy. - Right. "C" Coy. - Left.
"D" Coy. in Support. "A" Coy. in Reserve.
"B" & "C" Coys will attack on a one platoon frontage in four lines, first two lines capturing first objective, second two lines, the second objective.
"D" (Support Coy.) will attack the final objective.
"A" Coy. will remain in Battalion Reserve and will not move except on the orders of the Commanding Officer.

3. All Coys. will be in position by 6.45 a.m.

4. At ZERO, Trench Mortars will open bombardment on all three objectives, Rifle Grenadiers will bombard first and second objectives.
At ZERO, plus 5 minutes, Infantry will assault.
At ZERO, plus 15, third and fourth waves of "B" & "C" Coys. will attack second objective.
At ZERO, plus 5, T.Ms. on first objective will lift to second objective.
At ZERO, plus 15, all T.Ms. will bombard final objective till ZERO plus 30.
At ZERO, plus 30, "D" will advance from first objective in two lines and pass through "B" & "C" Coys. and capture final objective. After capture, blocks will be made in C.Ts. at points X.

5. O.C. "B" & "C" Coys. will detail parties to clear dugouts in each of 1st and 2nd objectives, also parties to guard C.Ts. leading to final objective.
O.C. "C" Coy. will detail small parties to clear enemy from trenches opposite his front between 1st & 2nd objectives before the attack on 2nd objective is launched, and between 2nd and 3rd objectives before the attack on 3rd objective is launched.

6. Watches will be synchronised at 6 a.m. on the ground.
The following signals will be given by Bugle.
1 G. at ZERO plus 5 when bombardment on 1st objective will lift and assault commence.
2 Gs. when assault on second objective will commence.
3 Gs. when assault on last objective will commence.

20th June 1918.

G. P. Geddes
Captain & Adjutant,
5th Battalion, The Gordon Highlanders.

Distribution:-
O.C. - Coys., S.O.
- B.O., C.O.
- 2nd in Command.

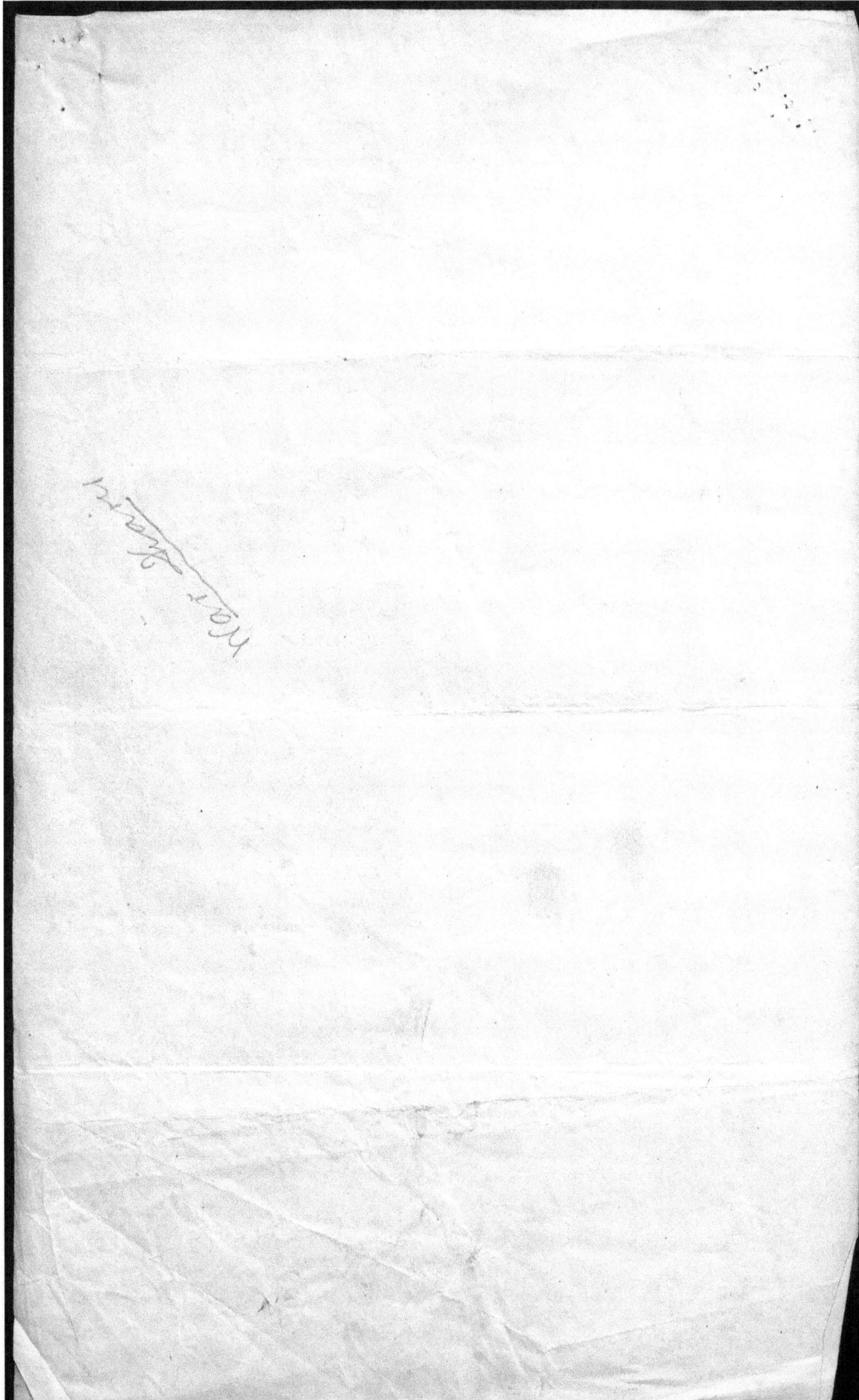

APPENDIX No. 10

G.H./S/21.

Reference Scheme to-morrow:-

Coys. will march off at 7.30.a.m. in the order "D", "C", "B", "A" Coys. and "H.Qrs".

100 yards interval to be maintained between Coys.

DRESS:-

Fighting Order, with Steel Helmets.

Pipers and Drummers to march with their Coys.

20th June, 1918. G.P. Geddes Capt. & Adjt.

5th Battalion, Gordon Highlanders.

Distribution :-

1 - 4 : O.C. Coys.

5 : I.O.

6 : L.G.O.

7 : R.S.M.

8. : Drum Major.

APPENDIX No. 1

FROM

MAROEUIL

1 in 20000

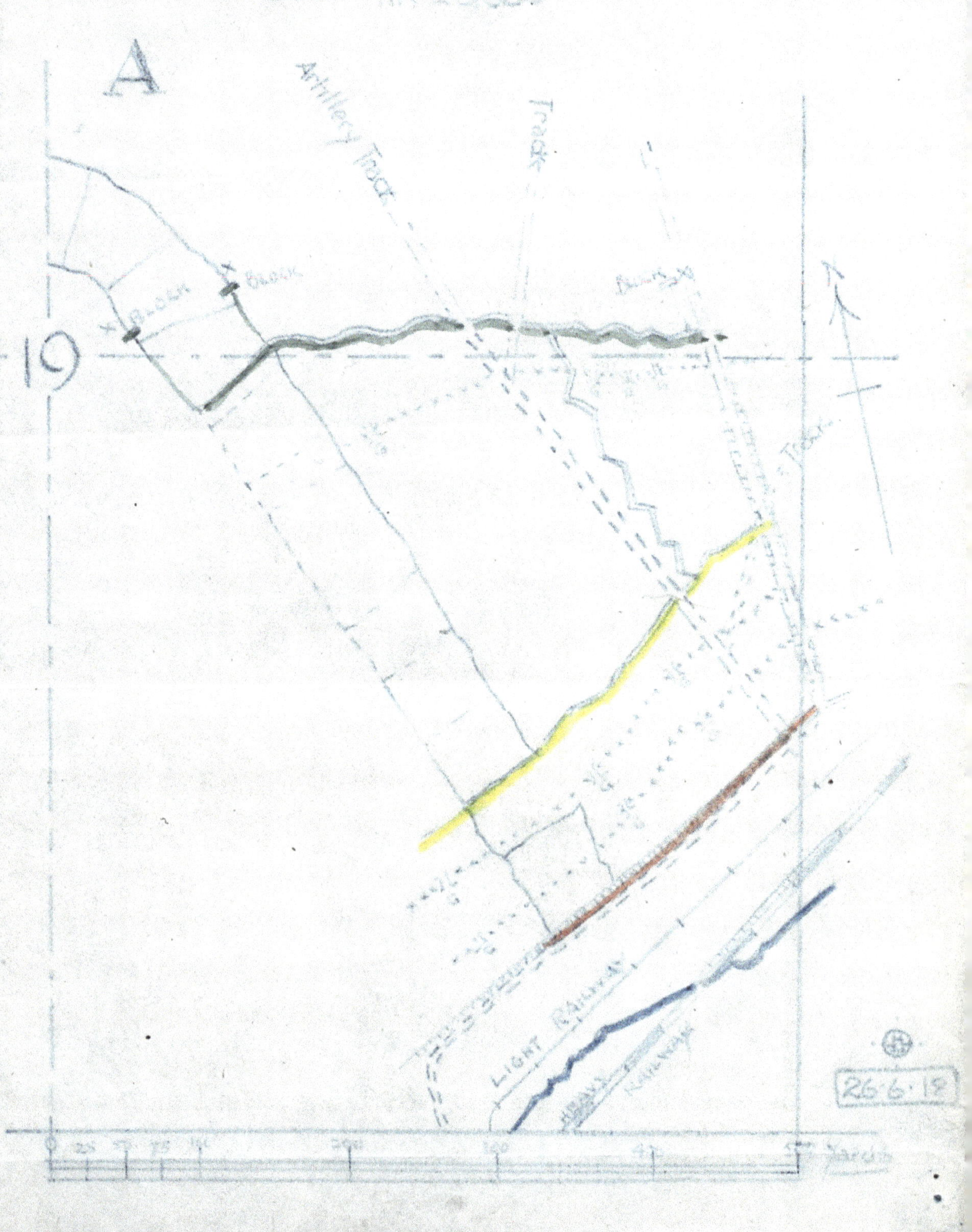

Appendix No 12

The Gordon Highlanders.

BATTALION ORDER No.35.
By
Lieut-Colonel G.A.Smith, D.S.O. Comdg.

23rd June, 1918.

1. Orderly Officer to-morrow - 2/Lieut. A.D.B. Smith.
Next for duty, - 2/Lieut. F.J.T. Bowie.

2. DETAIL FOR TO-MORROW.

Reveille.......... 6. 0.a.m. Dinners... ..... 12.30.p.m.
Breakfast......... 7. 0.a.m. Guard Mounting &
Sick Parade....... 7.15.a.m. Retreat......... 6. 0.p.m.
Orderly Room.......9. 0.a.m. Staff Parade.... 9.30.p.m.
Lights Out.....9.45.p.m.

3. TRAINING:-

Muskatry:- Battalion Musketry Competition.
1. Individual Marksmanship:- 5 rounds Application.
1 Minute Rapid Fire (unlimited No. of rounds).
Not more than 1 man per section to enter or 16 men per Company.
Prizes:- 1st - 25 frcs. 2nd - 20 frcs. 3rd - 15 frcs.
4th - 10 frcs. 5th - 5 frcs.

2. THE Elusive Hun". - Section Competition.
Sections not to be less than 1 N.C.O. & 6 Men. If Sections in Companies are too small owing to illness, two small Sections can be combined.
If two sections of unequal strength are firing against each other, the result will be judged by the average number of hits per man in each section.
Prizes:- 50 Francs for best section per Company &
50 Francs for best section in Battalion.

Only S.M.L.E. Rifles to be used.
Battalion Headquarters will fire with their Companies.

3. Revolver Competition for Nos. 1 & 2 of Lewis Gun Sections and for Pipers will take place 25/6/18.
Time to be notified later.
Prizes:- 1st. - 10 Francs. 2nd. - 5 Francs.

4. Competition for Best Lewis Gun Section will take place 25/6/18. Time and particulars to be notified later.

5. Prize for Brigade Competition for Snipers - 20 Francs.

Coys. will fire as under:-

"D" Coy. - 9. 0.a.m. - 11. 0.a.m.
"B" Coy. - 11. 0.a.m. - 1. 0.p.m.
"A" Coy. - 2.30.p.m. - 4.30.p.m.
"C" Coy. - 4.30.p.m. - 6.30.p.m.

APX 1.2

Second Sheet. No. 35. 23rd June, 1918.

5. **MUSKETRY.**

O. C. "C" Coy. will detail 1 N. C. O. and 10 Markers,
2 Fatiguemen for Sentries,
2 Buglers with bugles,
2 Signallers with D3s.

Party will parade at Orderly Room at 8. 30. a. m.

O. C. "B" Coy. will detail the above party for the after-noon. Parade at Orderly Room at 2. p. m.

The N. C. O. in charge of the above parties will march them off and report to Lieut. MacHardie at the Butts.

6. **LEWIS GUN PARADE.**

2 Lewis Gun Sections per Coy. will report to L. G. O. for Gun Drill at times stated as under:-

"B" Coy............. 8. 45. a. m.
"A" Coy............. 9. 45. a. m.
"C" Coy............. 10. 45. a. m.
"D" Coy............. 11. 45. a. m.

Sections who paraded on the 21st instant will not parade if possible.

Each Section will take 1 Lewis Gun and Bucket with magazines

7. **BATHS.**

As per Training Programme issued.

23rd June, 1918.

(Signed) G. P. Geddes, Captain & Adjutant,
5th Battalion, Gordon Highlanders.

APPENDIX 13

G.H.M./12.

<u>To O.C. - Coys. & R.S.M.</u>

1. O.C. Coys. will detail the following Party tonight for burying cable:-
"A" Coy...... 1 Officer & 2 Platoons.
"B" Coy...... .... 1 Platoon.
"C" Coy...... 1 Officer & 2 Platoons.
"D" Coy...... 1 Officer & 1 Platoon.
Each Platoon to be of a working strength of 21 exclusive of N.C.Os.

2. Party will parade on the road, ready to march off at 7.30. p.m., when guides from the Divisional Signal Coy. will report

3. <u>MOVEMENT</u> to be by platoons at 100 yards interval.

4. Shovels (1 per man) to be drawn from the R.S.M. at 6.p.m.

24/6/18. (Signed) C.P. Geddes, Captain & Adjutant.
5th Battalion, Gordon Highlanders.

'WAR DIARY'
24·6·18

Appendix No. 14

The Gordon Highlanders.

BATTALION ORDER No. 36.
By
Lieut-Colonel G. A. Smith, D.S.O. Comdg.

24th June, 1918.

1. Orderly Officer to-morrow, - 2/Lieut. F.J.T. Bowie.
Next for duty, - 2/Lieut. A. Brown.

2. DETAIL FOR TO-MORROW.

Reveille.......... 6. 0.a.m. - Dinners.............. 12.30.p.m.
Breakfast......... 7. 0.a.m. - Sick Parade........... 7.15.a.m.
Orderly Room.........9.a.m.

3. LEWIS GUN TEAM COMPETITION.

A Team of 4 men to be selected from each section and commanded by Section Leader.
Each team will fire 8 magazines of 25 rounds (2 magazines per man) 4 loaded, 4 unloaded (latter to be filled during contest).
Time $3\frac{1}{2}$ minutes. Time to include Orders given by N.C.O. etc.
"Load". Fire order. Unload, Change Round.
Team scoring greatest number of hits (2.1). to be winner.
Teams may be disqualified for bad drill etc.
Teams will parade as under, 200 yards South of No.1 Range Firing Point

"C" Coy. - 9. 0.a.m.) 1 N.C.O. and 8 men and 2 Buglers to parade
"D" Coy. - 9.30.a.m.) at 8.30. under Cpl. Williamson.
"A" Coy. - 10. 0.a.m.) 2 Picks and 2 shovels required.
"B" Coy. - 10.30.a.m.)

Prizes:- 1st - 50 Francs. 2nd - 25 Francs.

4. RESULT OF BATTN. INDIVIDUAL MARKSMANSHIP. COMPETITION

1st	"A" Coy.	S/17153	Pte.	Hislop,	55.
2nd.	"A" Coy.	292233	Pte.	Jeffrey,	54.
3rd.	"B" Coy.	22334	Pte.	Sutherland,	53.
4th.	"D" Coy.	S/17518	Pte.	Gibb,	50.
5th.	"B" Coy.	S/43296	Pte.	Dalrymple,	46.
6th.	"C" Coy.	290165	L/c.	Wright,	46.
7th.	"C" Coy.	S/7949	L/c.	Grice,	46.

RESULT OF BATTN. SECTION COMPETITION.

1st. Corporal Gilletts & 7 men, "D" Coy. 10 Hits.

RESULT OF COY. SECTIONS COMPETITION.

"A" Coy. Cpl. McLean & 6 men, 8 hits)
"A" Coy. L/c. McRae, & 6 men, 8 hits) Average 1.14.

"B" Coy. Cpl. Dale & 7 men, 9 hits. Average 1.12.

"C" Coy. Cpl. Stuart & 7 men 9 hits. Average 1.12.

"D" Coy. Cpl. Gillett & 7 men, 10 hits. Average 1.25.

All the above will parade at Orderly Room to-morrow at 9.a.m. to receive prises.

APX 14

Second Sheet. No. 36. 24th June, 1918.

5. **BOX RESPIRATORS.**

Several cases have recently occurred where small box respirators on being condemned, have been found to have the elastic bands torn off, thus rendering them useless.
This practice must cease.

6. **CARE OF SMALL BOX RESPIRATORS.**

Attention is drawn to the following points :-

1. In some cases S.B.R. haversacks are still being washed, especially by troops in reserve. This is contrary to G.R.O. 3981. Besides diminishing the water-resisting power of the fabric this tends to rust the container. Haversacks should be dried when opportunity offers and the mud brushed off.

2. In one or two cases recently the elastic bands of respirators otherwise defective have been, evidently, deliberately removed.

3. Every S.B.R. should have a record card attached and an entry made of the number of hours actually worn in gas, together with date of issue. When a respirator is found defective the defect should be entered on the record card by a Gas N.C.O.

7. **REVOLVER COMPETITION.**

The Revolver Competition will be held to-morrow at 11 a.m. Competitors will report at the Range.

24th June, 1918. (Signed) G.P. Geddes, Captain & Adjutant,

9th Battalion, The Gordon Highlanders.

N O T I C E.

Noted (initials)

It is notified for information that money can be drawn by men proceeding on leave at the office of the Divisional Disbursing Officer (Divisional Claims Officer), No. 3 Billet, ETRUN, between the hours of 9 a.m. and 10 a.m. and 6 p.m. and 7 p.m.

APPENDIX No 15.

Secret.

5th Battalion, The Gordon Highlanders.

O P E R A T I O N   O R D E R   No. 4.
By
Lieut-Colonel G. A. Smith, D.S.O. Comdg.

25th June, 1918.

1. The 5th Battn., Gordon Highlanders will relieve the 10th Battalion, Scottish Rifles as Reserve Battalion of the Right Brigade, to-night 25/26th June.

ROUTE :- "B" Track - BLANGY Road.

2. The Battalion will parade on the road, ready to march off at 9.30.P.M. in the following order :- "A", "D", "C", "B", Coys & Battn. H. Qrs. All movement to be by platoons at 100 yards interval.

3. Dispositions :-

A. Coy. Gordons will relieve D. Coy. Scottish Rifles; Coy. H. Q. at H. 14. d. 8. 7.
D. Coy. " " " B. Coy. " " ; Coy. H. Qrs, H. 13. b. 00. 25.
C. Coy. " " " C. Coy. " " ; Coy. H. Qrs, H. 13. d. 8. 6.
B. Coy. " " " A. Coy. " " ; Coy. H. Qrs, H. 13. d. 9. 9.
Battn. H. Qrs. " " Battn. H. Qrs. " ; B. H. Qrs, at H. 13. d. 8. 8.

4. Guides :- As follows, to be on BLANGY - FAMPOUX Road, 150 yards west of Road Junction, H. 13. b. 6. 5. at 10. 15. P. M.
~~For A & D Coys. : 1 Officer per Coy. Gas N.C.O. & 1 N.C.O. per platoon.~~
~~For~~ A & D. Coys. : 1 per platoon & 1 for Coy. H. Qrs.
For B. & C. Coys. : 1 per Company.
For Battn. H. qrs. : One.

5. Advanced parties as follows will parade at Orderly Room at 5.P.M. and proceed to take over Stores and accommodation :-

A & D. Coys. : 1 Officer per Coy. Gas N. C. O. & 1 N. C. O. per platoon.

B & C. Coys. : 1 Officer per Coy. Gas N. C. O. & 1 other N. C. O. per Coy.

Battn. H. Qrs. : 2/Lieutenant Barron & 1 N. C. O.

6. 1 Limber per Coy., for Lewis Guns, S. A. A., Signalling Gear, Mess Kit, etc., and Mess Cart for Canteen Stores will be at Camp at 8. 30. P. M. All limbers must be loaded by 8. 45. P. M.
Officers' valises, tailors and shoemakers gear, and all other stores to go back to Q.Ms. Stores, will be loaded on G. S. Wagons at 5. P. M.

7. Relief complete to be wired at once to Battn. H. Qrs. by the Code Word "RAIN"

8. Acknowledge.

25th June, 1918.

G P Geddes Captain & Adjutant,
5th Battn., Gordon Highlanders.

Distribution :-

Copies 1 - 4 : O. C. Coys.
5 : L. G. O.
6 : Signals.
7. : Q.M.
8. : R. S. M.
9. : Scottish Rifles.
10. : W. D.
11. : File.

APPENDIX No. 16.

Secret. 5th Battalion, The Gordon Highlanders.

OPERATION ORDER No. 6.
By
Lieut-Colonel G. A. [illegible], D.S.O. Comdg.

29th June, 1918.

1. The 5th Gordon Highlanders will relieve the 6th Seaforth Highlanders in the Right Sector of the Brigade Front, to-morrow night, 30th June/1st July.

2. Dispositions.
(C Coy. and 1 Platoon Coy. H. Qrs.
(A Coy. Gordons will relieve D Coy. Seaforths in the front line H. 21. c. 6. 5.
A Coy. less 1 platoon, " C Coy. " in immediate support, Coy. H. Qrs. H.20. d.0.9.
B Coy. Gordons will " B Coy. " in Support, Coy. HQ H. 20. d. 7. 7.
D Coy. " " " A Coy. " in Reserve, Coy. HQ H. 19. centre
Battn. H. Qrs. " " Battn. H. Qrs. at H. 20. b. 4. 5.
Relief to be carried out in above order.

3. GUIDES:-
For C & A Coys:- 1 per post, 1 for each remaining platoon and 1 for Coy. H. Qrs. will be at Road Junction, - SPIDER CORNER H. 21. a. 00. 25. at 10. 30. P. M.

For B & D Coys:- 1 per platoon and 1 for Coy. H. Qrs. will be at the RAILWAY BRIDGE H. 19. b. 35. 65. at 10. 30. P. M.

For Battn. H. Qrs.:- No Guides.

4. (i) Advanced parties will proceed as follows:-
"A" Coy. :- 1 Officer and 1 N.C.O. per platoon to meet guide from Seaforths at SPIDER CORNER at 10. 30. P. M. to-night.

"C" Coy. :- 1 Officer and 1 N.C.O. per platoon to meet guide from Seaforths at BRIDGE, H. 19. b. 35. 65. at 10. 30. P. M. to-night.

"B" & "D" Coys. :- 1 Officer and 2 N.C.Os. per Coy. to parade Battn. H. Qrs. at 5. 30. P. M., 30th June.

"Battn. H. Qrs". :- 2/Lieut. [illegible] and 2 N.C.Os. to parade Battn. H. Qrs. as above.

4. (ii) Advanced parties from the Seaforths will report at their respective Coys. to take over stores etc. to-morrow afternoon.

5. All Trench Stores, Defence Schemes, Aeroplane Photographs, Anti-Gas appliances, etc. will be taken over and handed over and receipts forwarded to Orderly Room by 9. A.M., 1st July.

6. STRAGGLERS' POSTS. (Each of 1 N.C.O. & 3 men) will be taken over as follows:-
"B" Coy. :- At Junction of [illegible] TRENCH & The ROAD, H. 20. a. 2. 3.
"D" Coy. :- At Railway BRIDGE, H. 19. b. 35. 65.

7. Completion of relief will be wired to Battn. H. Qrs. by the Code Word "BON[illegible]"

8. ACKNOWLEDGE.

29th June, 1918.

G P Geddes
Captain & Adjutant,
5th Battalion, The Gordon Highlanders.

Distribution :-

Copies 1 - 4 : O.C. Coys.
5 : I.O.
6 : Signals.
7 : Details.
8 : R.S.M.
9. : 8th Seaforths.
10 : W.D.
11 : File.

Instructions regarding War Diaries and Intelligence Summaries are contained in F. S. Regs., Part II. and the Staff Manual respectively. Title pages will be prepared in manuscript.

WAR DIARY
or
INTELLIGENCE SUMMARY.
(Erase heading not required.)

Army Form C. 2118.

APPENDIX 17A

Place	Date	Hour	Summary of Events and Information	Remarks and references to Appendices

5th Bn. Gordon Highlanders

Statement showing Strength of Battalion at various dates during the month of June 1918 as detailed overleaf

Date		O	OR	Date				O	ORs
1918 31st May	Strength of 5th Gordon Hrs as at 1/6/18 →	40	452	14th June	Increase during week			40	889
	Increase during week				From Divisional Wing	+ 2	28		
	Joined from 6th Gordon Hrs on amalgamation	+ O 11, OR 591			Taken on strength from 6th GH employed at Div Depot	+ 1			
	Reinforcements from Div Wing	4			Reinforcements from Div Wing		13		
		11 · 595			Men returned from surplus personnel dispatched to base 14/6/18		4		
	Decrease during week				Taken on strength from 21st Employ Coy 12/6/18		1		
	Surplus off strength on amalgn.	+ 8				3	18		
	Sick do	+ 2			Decrease during week				
	Detached do	1			Evacuated sick		15		
	Over 7 days in F Amb	4			Over 7 days in F Amb		4		
	Evacuated	1			Wounded		1		
	Surplus off strength on amalgn. 5th GH	11				–	20		
	do do 8/10th GH	34		21st June	Increase during week			42	887
	do do 15th Bn Wing	39			From Division Wing		39		
7th June	Strength of Combined Battn after dispatch of surplus personnel	40	958		Decrease during week				
	Increase during week				Evacuated sick		32		
	Rejoined from Hospital	2			Over 7 days in F Amb		4		
	Decrease during week				Wounded		2		
	Sick 7 days in F Amb	13					38		
	Wounded	3		28th June				42	888
	To Base Unfit	1							
	Surplus off strength	54							
		71							

Place column (marginal list of officers):
+ A/Major Wood, Brosame.
A/Capt. Adj. Gordon [illegible] DSO
T/Capt Moffat [illegible] DSO
T/Lt Scott [illegible]
do Black R.A.M.
T/2/Lt. Lowe J.W.
do Morrison A.
do Keir John
do Smith A.D.B.
do Keir John
do Insch [illegible]
do Bowie [illegible]
do Cruickshank [illegible]
[illegible]
[illegible]
[illegible] W.R.
do Wardrop H.S.
do Smith [illegible]
do Kellan [illegible]
do Wood W.
do Manson R.
do Murray [illegible]
do Stephen R.
do Harding [illegible]

(A7092). Wt W12839/M1293 75 ,o,o 1/17. D. D. & L., Ltd. Forms/C.2118/14.

WAR DIARY or ~~INTELLIGENCE SUMMARY.~~ (Erase heading not required.)

Army Form C. 2118.

Instructions regarding War Diaries and Intelligence Summaries are contained in F. S. Regs., Part II. and the Staff Manual respectively. Title pages will be prepared in manuscript.

Place	Date	Hour	Summary of Events and Information	Remarks and references to Appendices

EXTRACT FROM B.O. No 27A.

BY LT COL. G.A. SMITH D.S.O.

COMMANDING 5TH BN. GORDON HDRS.

THE FOLLOWING IS A LIST OF OFFICERS NOW ON THE STRENGTH OF THE AMALGAMATED BATTALION.

HEADQUARTERS.

	LT. COLONEL	SMITH, G.A: D.S.O.	COMMANDING OFFR.
X	MAJOR	J.B. WOOD, DSO MC.	2ND IN COMMAND.
X	CAPTAIN	G.P. GEDDES, DSO.	ADJUTANT.
	2/LIEUT.	COPELAND A.D.	ASST. ADJUTANT.
	LIEUT.	REID, J.T.	LEWIS GUN OFFICER.
	2/LIEUT.	BARRON, J.U.E.	SIGNALLING OFFR.
	"	MACDONALD, D.S.	INTELLIGENCE OFFR.
	CAPTAIN.	MARR, J. MC.	QUARTER MASTER.
	LIEUT.	YOUNGSON, R.W.	TRANSPORT OFFR.
	2/LIEUT.	SCOTT, W.J.	ASST. TRANSPORT.

A. Coy.

	LIEUT.	STEWART. J.M.	COMMDG.
	"	McHARDIE J.	2ND IN COMMAND.
	2/LT.	CURRIE, J.	
	"	MIDDLETON, G.A.	
	"	BROWN, A.	
X	"	KEIR, JOHN.	
X	"	BOWIE F.J.T.	

B. Coy.

X	CAPTAIN.	KEMP. W.S.	COMMDG. (ALDERSHOT)
	LIEUT.	WEST. W.	ACTING IN COMMD.
	"	BERRY C.M.	
X	"	KEIR. JAMES.	
	"	WARRACK, D.L. M.C.	
	2/LT.	IRVIN. M.H: M.C.	
	"	FRAZER. D.A.D.	
	"	HADDEN. W.J.	

THIS OFFICER NOT SHEWN ON "STRENGTH" APPENDICES 17.17A.

C. Coy.

X	CAPTAIN	MOFFAT. F.J.C: D.S.O.	COMMDG.
	LIEUT.	CURRIE W.T.	2ND IN COMMD.
	"	ELLIOTT L.B.	
X	2/LT.	SMITH A.D.E.	
	"	BUCHANAN. A.H.	
	"	STRATHDEE R.B.	

D. Coy.

X	LIEUT.	BLACK. R.A.M.	COMMDG.
	"	RUSSELL. J.C.	2ND IN COMMD.
	2/LT.	CRANNA A.P.	
	"	GILL. I.M.	
	"	ANDERSON D.K.	
	"	CAMERON. R.A:	
X	"	LOVIE. F.W.	
X	"	MORRISON. A.	
X	"	INSCH J.G: M.M.	
	LIEUT.	KAY. J.W.	

NOTE. THE TWELVE OFFICERS WITH MARK X WERE 8/10TH GORDON OFFICERS. REMAINDER CAME WITH 1/5TH GORDONS.

NOTE. 2/LT. CRUICKSHANK. X
LIEUT. DOULL. J. X
ABOVE 2 8/10TH OFFRS TAKEN ON STRENGTH AFTER AMALGAMATION

APPENDIX. 18

J.S.R.

(10340) Wt.W5900/P713 750,000 5/18 D. D. & L., London, E.C. E 2688 Forms/C2118/16.

APPENDIX 19

Army Form C. 2118.

Instructions regarding War Diaries and Intelligence Summaries are contained in F. S. Regs., Part II. and the Staff Manual respectively. Title pages will be prepared in manuscript.

WAR DIARY
or
INTELLIGENCE SUMMARY.
(*Erase heading not required.*)

Place	Date	Hour	Summary of Events and Information	Remarks and references to Appendices
	For gallantry in the Field during operations from 21st March - 2nd April 1918.		Honours and awards.	
			Bar to Military Cross	
			Capt Thomas Macnaughton Sawe M.C.	
			Military Cross	
			2nd Lieut Magnus H Irvine	
			Distinguished Conduct Medal	
			No 241468 Sgt Thomas Annand.	
			Bar to Military Medal	
			No 9838 Sgt William Gordon M.M	
			Military Medal	
			No 242381 Sgt Robert McAllister No 14360 Pte W Thornley	
			240444 Cpl James Johnston 242077 " WW Duffus	
			241284 " Charles Dunn	
			242465 L/C John Smith	
			240964 " William Milne	
			241311 Pte John Watson	

A6945 Wt. W11422/M1160 35,000 12/16 D. D. & L. Forms/C./2118/14.

APPENDIX 20.

Army Form C. 2118.

Instructions regarding War Diaries and Intelligence Summaries are contained in F. S. Regs., Part II. and the Staff Manual respectively. Title pages will be prepared in manuscript.

WAR DIARY
or
INTELLIGENCE SUMMARY.
(Erase heading not required.)

June 1918

Place	Date	Hour	Summary of Events and Information	Remarks and references to Appendices
		Birthday Honours	Military Cross	
			Capt + QM J Marr	
			Meritorious Service Medal	
			RQMS James Chalmers	
			CQMS James Taylor.	
			Cpl Rolland M Neilson	

D. D. & L., London, E.C.
(10340) Wt W5500/1713 750,000 3/18 E 2688 Forms/C2118/16.

APX.21

APPENDIX 21.

Army Form C. 2118.

WAR DIARY
or
INTELLIGENCE SUMMARY.

Instructions regarding War Diaries and Intelligence Summaries are contained in F. S. Regs., Par. II. and the Staff Manual respectively. Title pages will be prepared in manuscript. Casualties

(Erase heading not required.) June 1918

Place	Date	Hour	Reg N°	Rank & Name		Summary of Events	Nature. of. Casualty & Date		Remarks and references to Appendices
			S/15924	Pte	Calder	a	Wounded	10-6-18	
			S/12009	"	Bookless	b	do	do	
			S/9838	Sgt	Gordon	W.A. MM+Bar	do	do	
			S/3037	Pte	Brown	b	do	15. 6 18	
			235415	L/C	Milne	J	do	27 6 18	
			240541		Watson	H.Q.	do	do	

A6945 Wt W11422/M1160 35,000 12/16 D. D. & L. Forms/C./2118/14.

APPENDIX 22
№175
CORRECTED TO 10.5.18.
H
I
POINT DU JOUR REDOUBT
EFFIE
EFFIE TRENCH
TRENCH
MISSISSIPPI
MISSOURI
TOWY ALLEY
THAMES
TRENT
TRENCH
TRIPOLI
CABLE
CABLE AVE
CASTLE
LANE
ELBA ALLEY
CAM
CAM AVENUE
AVENUE
CAROLINA
PERU TR
STONEWALL
PUDDING TR
PORT TRENCH
LEMON
STOKE
CAMEL
CAMEL AVENUE
Fampoux
Fouchy
Athies
Roeux
Pelves
Plouvain
Greenland Hill
Hausa Wood
Delbar Wood
CALEDONIAN AVENUE
CHICKEN RES
CHALK RES
CHILI
CUBA
CONRAD
CIVIL AVENUE
HUMID
HOARY
HUSSAR
BAZAROOF
TRENCH
JUTLAND
ZION ALLEY
HAVANA TR
CLYDE
CADIZ RES
CLARKE
CALABAR
CALF RES
CRETE
CRUMB
CRASH TR
CEYLON AVE
CORAL
CORDITE
CHINA TRENCH
CORONA
CORONA ALLEY
CYCLE
CHEMICAL
CORFU AVE
COLOMBO
CHURCH
CORN
CHAPEL
CARROT
CARAVAN
CANDY
CYRIL
CLOD
CAPSTAN
CHIN
CRIB
WURZEL
WALNUT
WILLOW
WALK
WALLACE
WHISPER
WEASEL
WOOL
WAVY
WASTE
WEE
MORAY TR
JUNKER TR
LANCER TR
TRENCH
BELT

APPENDIX 23
TRENCHES CO
SCAPA TR
BATTERY TRENCH
DUNBLANE
ABERDEEN TR
HALIFAX TRENCH
CALIFORNIA
VIPER
GIN TR
INVERGORDON TRENCH
JERICHO
JERUSALEM TR
JUNKER
JAMAICA TRENCH
JOHNSON AVE
LONE
ORANGE AVENUE
LIME AVE
OHIO TR
WELLFORD
BANCHET
RIFLE TR
MUSKET TR
HOUGHY TR
DEVILS TR
FRICTION
STOKES
CARTRIDGE
FUEL TR
TUSK
TRUNK TR
PUG
POODLE TR
FOX
LONG TR
IN USE
SPOON TR
BUCKLE TR
BADGER
BEETLE TR
FROG
SPRING TR
SUPPORT AVE
TROWEL
VINE
AVENUE
PICK AVENUE
SHIRT TR
FORK TR
SHRAPNEL
CONCO
COLUMBUS
PILE TR
SPADE TR
HOE TR
GORDON AVE
SOUTH
MORROCCO
MERCHISTON TR
CORSICA
CARLISLE
CROMARTY TR
CHAPEL ALLEY
SPORRAN TR
KILT TR
NEW TR
BOB
JIN TR
MALTA
MINORCA
SCOTIA
ROSE
MIDLAND TR
EDINBURGH TR
ROME TR
SHAMROCK TR
GLASGOW TR
DALKEITH
51B N.W.
51B S.W.
Monchy le Preux
Guémappe

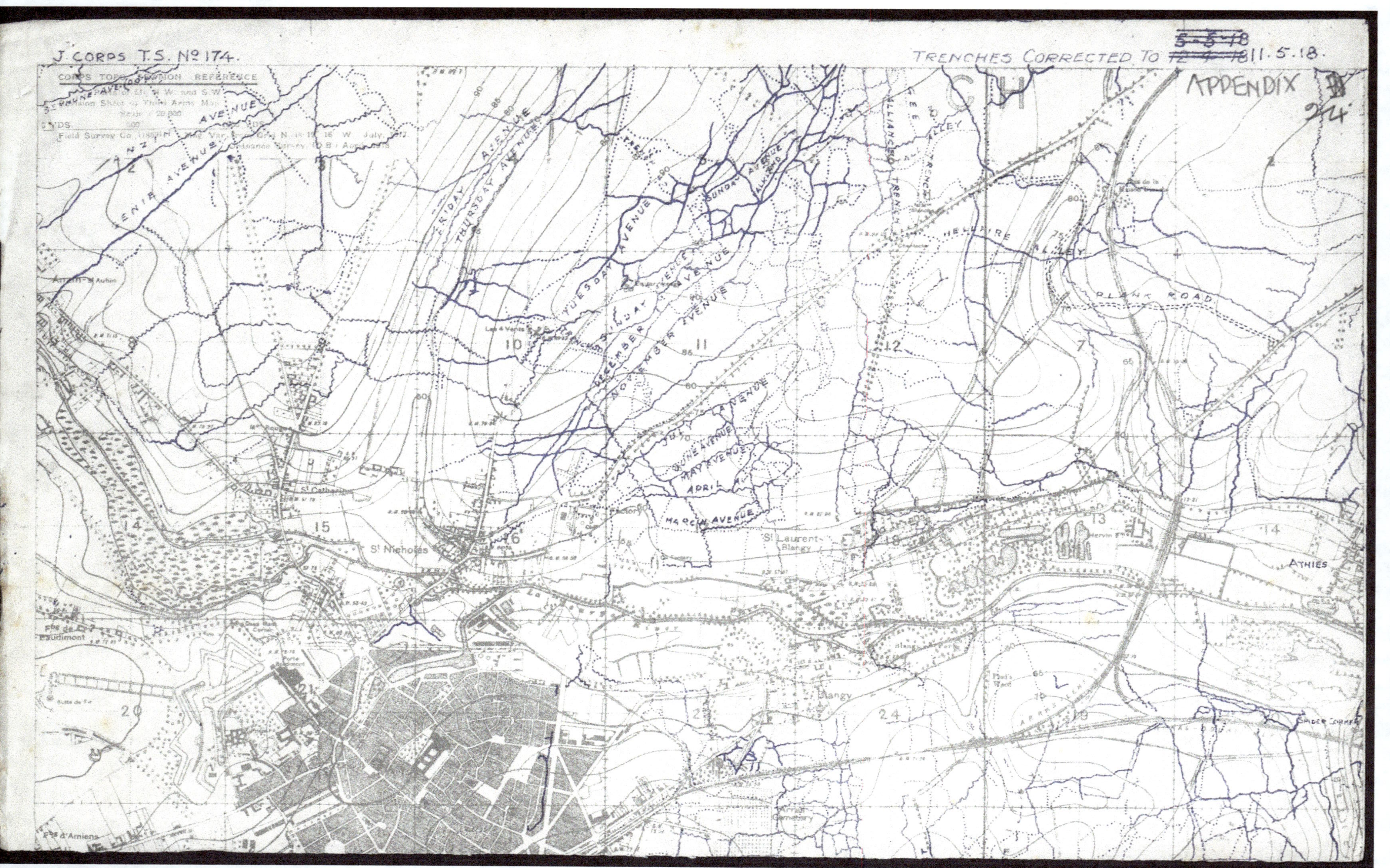

J. CORPS T.S. No 174.
TRENCHES CORRECTED TO 11.5.18.
APPENDIX
FRIDAY AVENUE
THURSDAY AVENUE
TUESDAY AVENUE
SUNDAY AVENUE
DECEMBER AVENUE
NOVEMBER AVENUE
JULY AVENUE
JUNE AVENUE
MAY AVENUE
APRIL AV.
MARCH AVENUE
ALLIANCE TRENCH
HELLFIRE ALLEY
PLANK ROAD
St Nicholas
St Laurent-Blangy
Blangy
Athies
Fbs d'Amiens
10
11
12
13
14
15
20
24

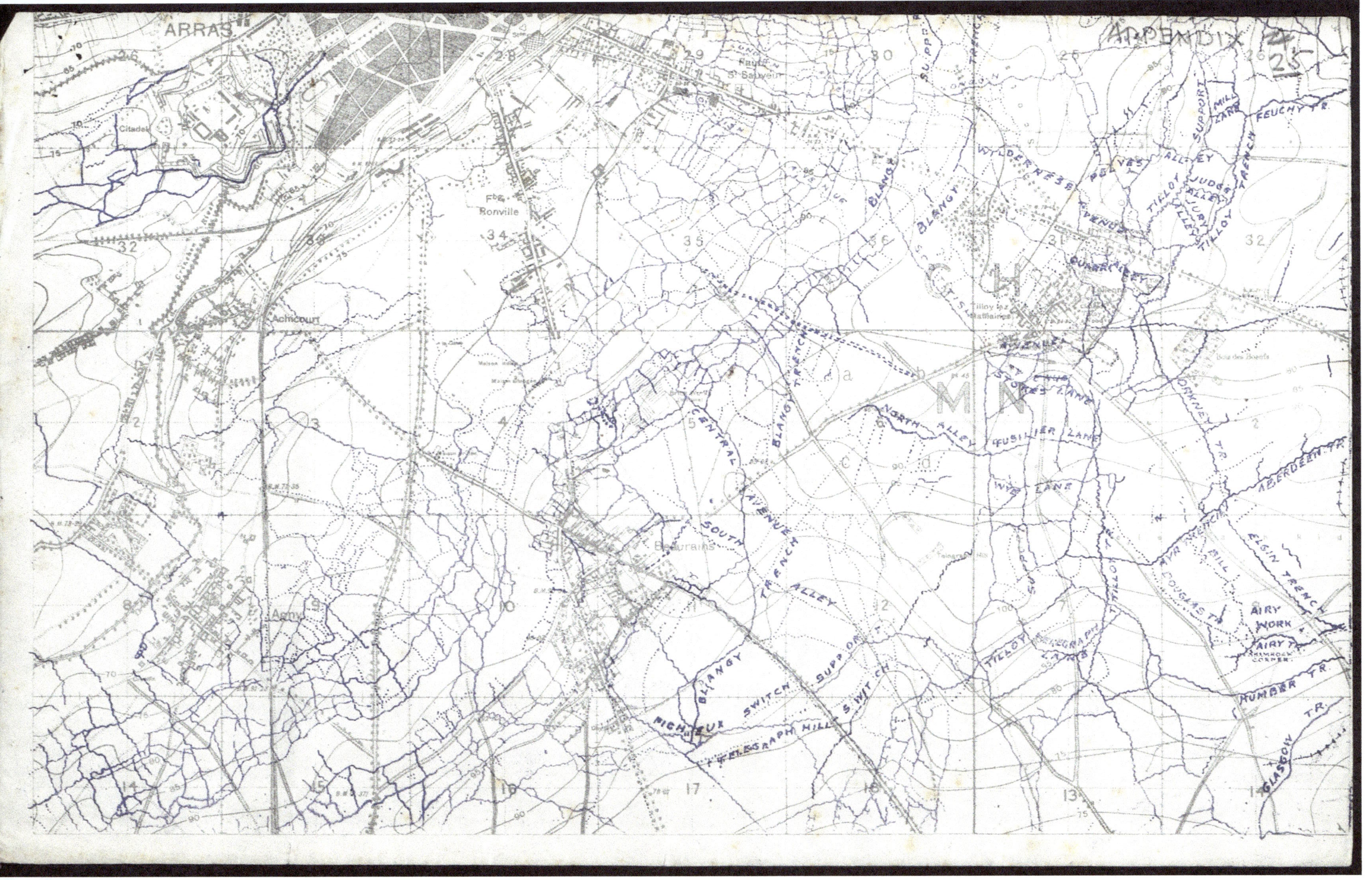
APPENDIX 25
ARRAS
Citadel
Fbg. Ronville
Achicourt
Agny
Beaurains
Tilloy les Mofflaines
WILDERNESS AVENUE
BLANGY
SUPPORT
MILL LANE
FEUCHY TR.
TILLOY ALLEY
JUDGE ALLEY
JURY ALLEY
NORTH ALLEY
FUSILIER LANE
CENTRAL AVENUE
SOUTH TRENCH ALLEY
BLANGY TRENCH
ORKNEY TR.
ABERDEEN TR.
ELGIN TRENCH
DOUGLAS TR.
AYR TRENCH
AIRY WORK
HUMBER TR.
GLASGOW TR.
TELEGRAPH HILL SWITCH
BLANGY SWITCH SUPPORT
NEUVILLE VITASSE

TRENCH MAP

51B N.W. & S.W.

1: 20,000

OFFICE COPY.

Base.

44/15

Confidential

5TH. BAT. GORDON HDRS.

Vol 39

WAR DIARY

FROM 1ST. JULY TO 31ST. JULY

1918

VOLUME 39

Major

Instructions regarding War Diaries and Intelligence Summaries are contained in F. S. Regs., Part II. and the Staff Manual respectively. Title pages will be prepared in manuscript.

WAR DIARY
or
~~INTELLIGENCE SUMMARY.~~
(Erase heading not required.)

Army Form C. 2118.

Place	Date	Hour	Summary of Events and Information	Remarks and references to Appendices
IN THE FIELD R. Bn R. BDE (FROM SCARPE S TO BROKEN MILL)	1st JULY		The relief of the 8th SEAFORTH HDRS was reported complete shortly after MIDNIGHT, & immediately the Bn settled down to normal trench activity, work being started immediately. A difficult piece of work was undertaken in cutting across RAILWAY in FRONT LINE (BROKEN LANE). Owing to the hard nature of the soil a considerable amount of noise was inevitable & its flinty ~~content~~ caused sparks to fly from picks. The enemy molested the party on this work with Trench Mortars & Rifle grenades. With the exception of the intense bombardment of FEUCHY, where we have few men, the remainder of the area was quiet. The weather continues to be excellent & the victims of P.U.O.E. [illegible] now rare owing to the out door life led in the Trenches. The platoon of A Coy which were gassed slightly in front of ATHIES still suffer considerably when any ~~[illegible]~~ exertion is demanded of them.	
	2ND "		The Bn front falls naturally into 2 sectns; from the SCARPE to the ARRAS–DOUAI RAILWAY where at present isolated posts form the out post line & where movement is impossible during the day & from the RAILWAY to BROKEN MILL where a new grid trench (BROKEN LANE) allows of free movement. The sector during the day was quiet. Enemy artillery activity being below normal very slight & scattered. A patrol sent out near BROKEN MILL found evidences of Enemy occupation in 2 shell holes connected by a trench. At 3 AM a Bosch raiding party consisting of 1 officer & about 12 O.R. attempted to lift our Lewis Gun post ~~at~~ BROKEN MILL. The succeeded to creep up quite close to the post but threw bombs before they got within range. The Lewis Gun was brought to bear upon them when they retired in disorder leaving a rifle & soft grey cap.	
	3RD		Again to day the sector was shelled slightly only 56 77 mm & 16 4.2 shells of which 6 were dud being counted. But our own corps artillery kept sending over salvos during the whole afternoon at stated intervals with excellent results. 2 or 3 Trench Mortar positions were set on fire one of which blew up about 10 pm (H23 c 15.55). A Lewis gun course was started to train a team for each of the 2 Rear most Companies. 2 hours in the afternoon & 2 in the evening were spent in training the men doing their usual share of work during the night. Our patrols were as active as usual one along S. edge of RAILWAY had a duel with a M.G. firing Rifle Grenades [illegible].	[illegible initials]

D. D. & L., London, E.C. (10340) Wt W5300/P713 750,000 3/18 E 2688 Forms/C2118/16.

Instructions regarding War Diaries and Intelligence Summaries are contained in F. S. Regs., Part II. and the Staff Manual respectively. Title pages will be prepared in manuscript.

WAR DIARY
or
INTELLIGENCE SUMMARY.
(Erase heading not required.)

Army Form C. 2118.

Place	Date	Hour	Summary of Events and Information	Remarks and references to Appendices
IN THE FIELD	4th July		The day passed as usual the weather remaining fine & at night the normal routine of work & patrols was interrupted by an inter company relief (SEE O.O. 7) a fair amount of work was done and 3 small patrols examined the front.	APPENDIX I O.O. 7
	5th July		Nothing marked today specially. An enemy aeroplane more daring than usual flew over our area & attempted to destroy our observation balloon behind but the Anti Aircraft shells turned him before he could do so. 2 of our observers leaving the SNIPERS POST held by us at H22 d 40.95 pushed out as far as the ROAD running from SCARPE between two lagoons & observed an enemy track in the grass about 3 days old.	
	6th July		Work and a little training of Lewis Gun sections went on undisturbed by enemy activity and at night a fairly strong patrol was sent out from Left Outpost Platoon under the guidance of one of the Snipers who had discovered the tracks. No 9 post supplied this patrol & being a Lewis Gun Section took their gun with them. Unfortunately no enemy appeared altho. they waited all night on the road between the lagoons.	
	7th July		From an early hour this morning Bn Hqrs & the Road especially & indeed all the Bn area behind Outpost Coy Hqrs were subjected to heavy shelling from guns of 77mm 4·2 + 5·9 calibres. This shelling was kept up all night. There is every reason to think with good reason that this is due to the enormous movement along the FEUCHY Road which is under observation from the Double Railway Bridges at Bn Hqrs & beyond almost to SPIDER CORNER. Steps have been taken to divert traffic to RIVER Bank & to RAILWAY. Our patrols were active on the left near South end of CAUSEWAY & again between lagoons where they lay last night but with no result. On the Right no patrolling was possible owing to preparations on our front for a raid by a Bn in the Right Division (Queens Westminster Rifles) which is to take place tomorrow.	[illegible initials]

(10340). Wt W5300/P713 750,000 3/18 E 2688 Forms/C2118/16. D. D. & L., London, E.C.

Instructions regarding War Diaries and Intelligence Summaries are contained in F. S. Regs., Part II. and the Staff Manual respectively. Title pages will be prepared in manuscript.

WAR DIARY
or
~~INTELLIGENCE SUMMARY.~~
(Erase heading not required.)

Army Form C. 2118.

Place	Date	Hour	Summary of Events and Information	Remarks and references to Appendices
IN THE FIELD.	7th July	(contd)	The rather extensive operation of cutting our wire necessitated parties amounting to 70 of Q.W.R + LRB (Bn holding line on our R) attracted the attention of the Hun who sent over some trench mortar bombs. 2 of our men were hit one killed + 1 severely wounded. (died of wounds 8th) Several of the LRB's were hit & the officer in charge Q.W.R was badly wounded.	
	8th July		The new division in front of us which had taken over the sector on the night of the 5/6th kept up its offensive artillery programme to-day + the shelling increased toward night growing heavier especially in the area between the SCARPE + the ARRAS–DOUAI Railway + WATERY WOOD + Bn Hqrs. Two men were killed in TILLOY TRENCH near ROAD. The proposed inter company relief was postponed on account of the Raid by the Brigade on our Right ~~See APPENDIX 2~~. A patrol went out on the left to reconnoitre enemy post but got no information.	~~APPENDIX 2~~
	9th July		The weather continues to be pleasant allowing of normal trench activity. Result of the Raid of last night is now forthcoming See APPENDIX 2. To-night the inter-company relief was effected A Coy changing over with B. See APPENDIX #3 O.O. 8.	APPENDIX 2 XVII CORPS. SUMMARY. No 541 APPENDIX 3 O.O. 8. INTER COY. RELIEF
	10th July		A considerable amount of rain fell in the night drenching our working parties patrols etc. During the forenoon the several indications of a coming relief materialised in the shape of Canadian officers of the 5th + 8th Bns come to reconnoitre ground. Most of the day was spent in assisting this reconnaissance explanation of the situation etc. The Canadians were familiar with the sector having held it until they went out for Corps Training 3 months ago. Preparations for our relief on the night of the 13th/14th were commenced. Patrols were very active on our front during the day. SEE APPENDIX 4.	APPENDIX 4 PATROLS for 10th + 11th
	11th July		Again to-day a good deal of time was spent in showing round the officers of the incoming Battns. Their dispositions are to be totally different to ours (1) They will hold the line with a much larger force (2) They will not have battalions organised in depth. Parts of 2 Bns may relieve us so that careful preparations are necessary to avoid delay + confusion. For Patrols, see APPENDIX 4. A thunderstorm put a period to the fine weather of the last few months wetting men on working parties	J.S.R.
	12th July		To-day dull + cloudy but with only a few showers of rain. The forward (A) Coy were subjected to	

Instructions regarding War Diaries and Intelligence Summaries are contained in F. S. Regs., Part II. and the Staff Manual respectively. Title pages will be prepared in manuscript.

WAR DIARY
or
INTELLIGENCE SUMMARY.
(Erase heading not required.)

Army Form C. 2118.

Place	Date	Hour	Summary of Events and Information	Remarks and references to Appendices
IN THE FIELD	12th July		5 minutes intense bombardment about 1.45 am when it is estimated that about 1000 shells fell in the company area. Owing however to the good trenches and the lightness with which the front is held no casualties resulted. The remainder of the day passed quietly with the exception of the ~~[illegible]~~ steady shelling of HERMES TRENCH at 11.45 pm towards 100 4.2 + 5.9s falling. No special patrol was sent out but each post examined its own front for damage done by the morning bombardment. Administrative Orders SEE APPENDIX 5 were issued with regard to the relief.	APPENDIX 5 A.O. issued in conjunction with.
	13th July		The weather to-day cooler but quite good. This morning O.O. No 9 was issued with regard to the relief by the 5th + 8 Bn. CANADIANS. The Bn then moved into billets in Arras.	APPENDIX 6. O.O. 9
	14th July		Bn spent the night forenoon in ARRAS. The Bn then moved to SAVY by light Rly. and all arrived in by 8 P.M. A. B. + C Coys proceeded to BERTHONSART D Coy with HQRS to MINGOVAL to their billets. Instructions were received for the Bn to undergo vigorous training.	
	15th July		The forenoon was devoted to a general cleaning up of the men, equipment, etc, training grounds were reconnoitred by various officers. A sudden warning order was received from BDE at 11. A.M. to the effect that the Bn must be prepared to move by 2. A.M. the following morning, speculation rife as to the destination. Remainder of day devoted to making preparations accordingly. Operation orders received about midnight, though fortunately some important instructions had	Operation orders attached No. 7.

K. [illegible]

Instructions regarding War Diaries and Intelligence Summaries are contained in F. S. Regs., Part II, and the Staff Manual respectively. Title pages will be prepared in manuscript.

WAR DIARY
or
INTELLIGENCE SUMMARY.
(*Erase heading not required.*)

Army Form C. 2118.

Place	Date	Hour	Summary of Events and Information	Remarks and references to Appendices
In the field	15th July (contd.)		been received by telephone from Bde HQRS. All surplus kit was dumped & conveyed to Aubigny. "B" Coy furnished a loading party for the bus at TINCQUES.	
	16th July		Breakfast was served early & the bus was ready to move off at scheduled time to TINCQUES. The time of leaving was postponed from 7 to 9. A.M., then again, until finally the train did not steam off until 5.30. P.M. This was due to congestion on the lines as very often the case in France. There was still no knowledge of the destination but as 4 days rations were issued in advance, prophets began to get busy. The weather was ideal.	Operation Order No 74. attached.
	17th July.		As rumours were heavy about another push down South by the unspeakable Hun the train was moving through an entirely new stretch of country it was generally deduced that there was to be some fighting. The route lay through ST OMER-EN-CHAUSSEE, BEAUVAIS, & HERMES, the line for a long way running along the banks of the RIVER DE THERAIN. The OISE was passed & finally detrainment was carried out at LAIGNEVILLE. Here the bus rested for a short time	[illegible]

Instructions regarding War Diaries and Intelligence Summaries are contained in F. S. Regs., Par. II. and the Staff Manual respectively. Title pages will be prepared in manuscript.

WAR DIARY
or
INTELLIGENCE SUMMARY.
(Erase heading not required.)

Army Form C. 2118.

Place	Date	Hour	Summary of Events and Information	Remarks and references to Appendices
In the field	17th July (Contd.)		& then marched to billets at MOGNEVILLE near LIANCOURT. After arrival the bn almost en masse proceeded to an adjoining stream for a bathe. Our people had the distinction to be the first British troops ever to visit that region, & created quite a flutter amongst the inhabitants.	
	18th July.		Bde sent instructions to the bn to be prepared at a moment's notice to move. Later the bn was informed they would likely be in this region for some time. A route march was therefore planned for the following day.	
	19th July		Verbal orders followed a little later by definite instructions were received at 1. A.M. for the bn to move at 5. A.M.; later this was postponed to 7. A.M. An advance party was sent on to fix up billets & at 8 A.M. French lorries arrived to take the bn to their destination. The route lay through gorgeous country ~~past~~ LAIGNEVILLE, CLAREMONT, thence east through ARSY, skirting over the river OISE the western edge of the COMPEIGNE FOREST. From here the route lay east past the grand CHATEAU of PIERREFONDS	Operation Orders No 8. attached. [illegible]

A6945 Wt. W11422/M1160 35,000 12/16 D. D. & L. Forms/C./2118/14.

WAR DIARY
or
INTELLIGENCE SUMMARY.
(Erase heading not required.)

Army Form C. 2118.

Instructions regarding War Diaries and Intelligence Summaries are contained in F. S. Regs., Part II and the Staff Manual respectively. Title pages will be prepared in manuscript.

Place	Date	Hour	Summary of Events and Information	Remarks and references to Appendices
In the field.	19th July (Contd.)		where a number of French & American wounded were lying. The Bn then detrained at LAMOTTE from there marched to billets at TROSLY-BREUIL, which was very beautifully situated. French troops were also billeted in that village before the Bn could move into them much cleaning up was necessary. The inhabitants had vacated the village when the Boche advanced in March. No movement was permitted in the street owing to enemy aircraft no lights were allowed.	
	20th July.		TROSLY-BREUIL was bombed in the early hours of the morning rather heavily, but the Bn escaped with no casualties. Warning orders were received for the Bn to prepare to move in fighting order, but later the time was changed the Bn settled down to rest in their billets for the night. Previous to this all surplus kit had been collected including greatcoats.	
	21st July.		The Bn moved off at 6.30 A.M. less details to CHELLES, a distance of 10 kms, the transport accompanying them. Details proceeded to BREUIL under orders to be prepared to move again at a moment's notice. Bn billetted at BERONGE. Later on fresh orders for a move were received.	Bde O.O. No: 9. attached. BN OO. No10. attached.
	22nd July.		Bn moved to ST PIERRE-AIGLE at 12 mn, where they were allotted fresh billets. The division then became a reserve for the 2nd U.S. DIV:	

Instructions regarding War Diaries and Intelligence Summaries are contained in F. S. Regs., Part II. and the Staff Manual respectively. Title pages will be prepared in manuscript.

WAR DIARY
or
INTELLIGENCE SUMMARY.
(Erase heading not required.)

Army Form C. 2118.

Place	Date	Hour	Summary of Events and Information	Remarks and references to Appendices
In the field.	22ND JULY (contd)		The ~~transport~~ details moved to BREVILLE, where the pipes delighted the French Poilus located in the village, their bands in turn played to our men. This mutual exchange overcame all language difficulties & a great fraternal spirit was awakened in the breasts of both Scotch & French. Fresh orders were again issued the Bn: were to be prepared to move at 11.15. P.M, as the division were taking over the line from the 1st U.S. DIV: As the 44th Inf: Bde were placed in reserve the Bn did not see the front line that night.	Operation Orders No 11. attached.
	23RD JULY.		Orders were received from Bde that the relief must be completed by 3. A.M. The 15th DIV: was now a unit in the 10th French Army & the whole were to attack on the morrow as per O.O. attached. 44th BDE detailed as DIV: Reserve.	BDE. O.O. No 12. attached.
	24th JULY.		BDE was not used & the attack proved abortive. 3 men were wounded & 2 killed. LT. J. McHARDY was killed & the doctor Capt BAXTER wounded by a stray shell.	
	25th July.		The Bn relieved the 9th Royal Scots on the right sector of the bivouac front, "C" Coy relieving "B" Coy R.S. & "B" Coy relieving "D" Coy R.S. on the right & left fronts respectively. "D" Coy moved into close support & "A" Coy of the Bn relieved "C" Coy of the R.S. in reserve. Relief completed by midnight. 6 men wounded during day.	Bn O.O. No 13. attached.
	26-27th JULY.		The Bn lay in their improvised shelters during this period. These consisted of trenches, pits, etc the line lay on the edge of a wood	[illegible signature]

Instructions regarding War Diaries and Intelligence Summaries are contained in F. S. Regs., Part II. and the Staff Manual respectively. Title pages will be prepared in manuscript.

WAR DIARY
or
INTELLIGENCE SUMMARY.
(Erase heading not required.)

Army Form C. 2118.

Place	Date	Hour	Summary of Events and Information	Remarks and references to Appendices
In the field.	26-27th July.		to the edge of BUZANCY CHATEAU. On the 27th orders were received for an attack on the morrow on the CHATEAU & BUZANCY village. The Bn was allocated the high ground lying to the north of the village as their objective. The scheme of operations can best be followed by the annexed map of the ground studied in conjunction with the operation orders.	O.O. No. 14. attached.
	28th JULY.		Full account of the operation is attached. The attack commenced at 12.28. P.M & 2 mins later the Bn moved forward towards its objective. 300' further on a strong point was encountered but after a sharp bombing fight the resistance was overcome & the advance passed on. On the right a MG. in the walls of the CHATEAU proved troublesome & LIEUT F.W. LOVIE with a platoon from the support coy worked round a flank & rushed the gun capturing both gun & crews. Thereafter the advance met with no further obstacle & the objective was carried by 1.20. P.M. Consolidation was much hindered by MG fire from the direction of NOYANT & BUZANCY. The enemy counter attacked at 4. P.M. against the French, who were forced to withdraw, at 4.20. P.M. the Seaforths fell back from its front of BUZANCY. This left the Bn right flank exposed at 5. P.M. they were obliged to fall back so as to conform. The enemy	Narrative of fight attached No. 15. [illegible]

D. D. & L., London, E.C. (10340) W1 W5300/1721 750,000 3/18 E 2688 Forms/C2118/16.

Instructions regarding War Diaries and Intelligence Summaries are contained in F. S. Regs., Part II. and the Staff Manual respectively. Title pages will be prepared in manuscript.

WAR DIARY
or
INTELLIGENCE SUMMARY.
(*Erase heading not required.*)

Army Form C. 2118.

Place	Date	Hour	Summary of Events and Information	Remarks and references to Appendices
In the field.	28th July.		were quick to follow ~~to follow~~ up pushing forward his light M.G's very skilfully. Considerable damage was inflicted on him from rifles & Lewis guns, at 5.45 P.M. the Bn arrived back at the starting point. The total casualties suffered by the Bn amounted to 225 of which 14% were killed. Lt Col Smith D.S.O. who was dearly loved and worshipped by the Bn, one and all, was alas! one of those who lost his life during this operation. A great thrill of sorrow went through the Bn on the news of his death as also for those other officers — Capt Currie W.T., Lt Moore F.W., 2.Lt. BROWN A. who were wounded. Capt. Currie fell mortally wounded, died later on the 31st in hospital. Major G.H. Wood D.S.O. M.C. assumed command of the Bn. Annexed are copies of a telegram congratulating the Bn on their performance from the G.O.C.	Copy of congratulations received from the G.O.C. enclosed No. 16.
	29th July.		The lines were heavily shelled during the day and orders for a relief had been received & Bn prepared to move. A portion of the 136th French regiment took over from the Bn, the relief being completed by 11.30 P.M. The enemy put down a heavy barrage during the relief using an abundance of gas shells, though the Bn suffered no casualties from this detestable form of warfare. They were obliged to march [illegible] for about 3 miles in respirators to billets. Billets reached by 1 A.M.	Operation Order No 17. attached. [signature illegible]

(10540) W1 W5300/P713 750,000 3/18 E 2688 Forms/C2118/16.

Army Form C. 2118.

Instructions regarding War Diaries and Intelligence Summaries are contained in F. S. Regs., Part II. and the Staff Manual respectively. Title pages will be prepared in manuscript.

WAR DIARY

or

INTELLIGENCE SUMMARY.

(Erase heading not required.)

Place	Date	Hour	Summary of Events and Information	Remarks and references to Appendices
In the field.	30-31st JULY.		The Bn arrived at CRAVANCON TRENCH at 1 A.M. on the 30th & were placed in Div: reserve with the remainder of the Bde. These two days were spent by the Bn in refitting & cleaning. Enemy shelled vicinity of trenches during these 2 days. 7 men were wounded & 8 gassed. Weather good.	
			APPENDIX	
			1.) A casualty return for the period 24-31st JULY (incl) is appended No. 18.	
			2.) A strength return for month of July is appended. No. 19.	
			J. W. Wood Major Comdg 5th Gordon Highrs.	
			13/8/18	

D. D. & L., London, E.C. (10340) Wt W5300/P713 750,000 3/18 E 2688 Forms/C2118/16.

APPENDICES

JULY '18

Copy 2

5th Battalion, The Gordon Highlanders
Operation Order No. 7
By
Lieut-Colonel H. A. Smith, D.S.O. Comdg.

4th July 1918.

1. The following inter-company reliefs will be carried out tonight, 4/5th July:–
(1) B. Coy. will relieve C. Coy and the forward platoon of A Coy.
(2) D. Coy. " " A. Coy. less one platoon.
On relief, C and A Coys will occupy positions vacated by B. and D. Coys respectively.

2 <u>Guides</u>:–
For (1) – 1 per post to be at Road junction SPIDER CORNER, H.21.a.00.25 at 10.20 p.m.
For (2) – 1 per platoon to be at junction of Railway and TILLOY TRENCH, H.20.c.40.95 at 10.30 p.m.
There will be no movement forward of Battn. H. Qrs before 10. p.m.

3. Advanced parties of 1 Officer per Coy and 1. N.C.O. per platoon from each of B & D. Coys and of 2 N.C.Os per Coy from each of C. and A. Coys will proceed in advance to take over stores, accomodation, etc from their respective Coys.

4. All trench stores, explosive stores, tools etc will be handed over and taken over. Lists will be handed in to Orderly Room by 9 a.m. 5th July.

5. Completion of relief will be wired to Bn. H. Qrs. by Code Words "GH/102 NOTED"

6. Acknowledge.

(Sgd.) G. P. Geddes, Capt & Adjt.
5th Bn. Gordon Highlanders

<u>Distribution</u>
Copies No. 1–4 : O. C. Coys. 8 : W. D.
5 : I.O. 9 : File.
6 : Signals
7 : R.S.M.

APPENDIX A.1

APPENDIX 2

Not to be taken beyond Art. or Inf. Brigade H.Q. No. 541.

XVII Corps Intelligence Summary.

From 8 p.m. 8th to 8 p.m. 9th July, 1918.

OPERATIONS.

A successful raid was carried out by right division on old gunpits at H.27.d.45.90. Three prisoners and one M.G. were captured affording a normal identification of the 358 I.R., 214th Division. The entrances to the dugout were bombed and successfully blown in by means of R.E. mobile charges. According to prisoners' statements, the Coy. Commander and the remainder of the company were in the above-mentioned dugout at the time.

Raid by left division in B.11.b. failed to secure identifications.

Patrols were out on the remainder of the Corps front, but no enemy were encountered.

ARTILLERY.

Our Activity.

Field Artillery: At 9.50 p.m. batteries put down a barrage in support of raid by right division; AIRY WORK was bombarded at the same time, and a smoke screen was placed on ICELAND Trench. Harassing fire was carried out during the night at irregular intervals. Enemy movement was successfully engaged.

Heavy Artillery: 8-7-18. 11 effective counter-battery shoots were carried out and 2 Corps and 4 brigade salvoes fired during the day. BREBIERES Station and dump S. of SAILLY were harassed. Enemy movement was successfully engaged and casualties inflicted. Between 9.50 and 10.30 p.m. 6" hows. of right group fired in support of raid by right division. 25 hostile batteries were also engaged for 30 minutes. During the night harassing fire was carried out on enemy communications and centres of activity, and three hostile batteries were subjected to a 3-minute burst of lethal gas shell.

9-7-18. 6" hows. of left group bombarded trenches in B.5.c. during raid by left division.

Hostile Activity.

Right Sector. Between 9.55 and 10.40 p.m. yesterday 7.7 cm. were active on N.7.a. and b. This morning 15 cm. hows. fired 15 rounds in G.29. and 30 rounds on AGNY. A 21 cm. battery carried out a destructive shoot on battery position in M.9.d. between 10.40 am. and 2.30 p.m. ST. SAUVEUR, TELEGRAPH HILL and BEAURAINS received slight attention at intervals. Retaliation for raid was practically nil.

Centre Sector. Yesterday evening 7.7 cm. fired about 80 rounds on H.13. a. and b., and 10.5 cm. hows. about 100 rounds on G.17.a.& b. H.9.a. was intermittently shelled during the morning by 10.5 cm.hows.

Left Sector. Yesterday afternoon WILLERVAL, THELUS and FARBUS were intermittently shelled by 10.5 cm. hows. Enemy retaliation for our raid was practically nil. During the forenoon to-day, hostile artillery was active on areas TOWY ALLEY, TOWY Track, B.27.b. and vicinity of GAUL POST. A destructive shoot was carried out by 15 cm. hows. on B.19.

INTELLIGENCE.

MOVEMENT.

Right Sector. Between 7 p.m. and dusk yesterday continuous movement was observed at AIRY WORK.

At dusk yesterday and between 5 a.m. and 8 a.m. this morning, there has been abnormal individual movement in N.8., 9. and 10.

/ 16 men .....

APPENDIX 2

16 men in full marching order left trench at N.9.d.70.45 and moved S. 20 men seen at N.9.b.35.10 disappeared into SHAMROCK Trench in N.9.a.

Between 8.30 and 11.30 a.m. there was considerable individual movement in N.9.b.

A party of 50 men was seen at 11.5 a.m. and another of 30 men at 12.20 p.m., proceeding towards SAILLY on CORBEHEM - SAILLY Road.

Centre Sector. No abnormal movement has been reported.

Left Sector. A good deal of individual movement was observed about Red Cross station in C.21.b. at 6 p.m. yesterday.

At 9.35 a.m. this morning, a carriage with a party apparently officers proceeded along IZEL - ROUVROY Road and halted in U.29.a. where they appeared to be inspecting battery positions (artillery informed; 1 effective and 1 O.R. observed.).

Transport. No abnormal transport movement has been observed. 26 M.T. have been observed during the day moving towards NOYELLES on SAILLY - NOYELLES Road.

Trains.

8-7-18. DOUAI - CANTIN Line 1 going N.

9-7-18. DOUAI - CANTIN Line 1 " N. and 2 going S.
DOUAI - LILLE Line. 2 " N.

WORK.

I.13.a.80.15. Loophole about 2 feet long is visible in CUTE Trench.
I.13.a.4.3. Camouflage has been erected across road at this point.

FIRES AND EXPLOSIONS.

H.34.a.85.85. A fire was caused at Coy. H.Q. here by our artillery fire, and burned for 6 hours.
N.9.b.6.5. Dump blown up here at 7.15 p.m. and burned till 8 p.m.

IDENTIFICATIONS.

214th Division.

358 I.R. 9th Coy. H.27.d. 8/9th July. 3 pris. (Normal).

AIRCRAFT. At 7.15 a.m. this morning an E.A. over our lines in H.16. was apparently hit by M.G. or A.A. fire and landed behind NEUVILLE VITASSE. At 11 a.m. an E.A. was brought down by one of our machines in the WILLERVAL area.

7 two-seaters and 21 single-seaters were observed; 8 were engaged by A.A. fire. 1 E.A. carried out back area reconnaissance.

MISCELLANEOUS.

At 7.35 a.m. an engine and 3 wagons flying red cross flag were seen on light railway in C.4.b. moving towards QUIERY.

H.Q., XVII Corps.
9th July, 1918.

[signature]
Major, G.S.
for B. G. G. S.

NEW TRENCH NAMES.

The following new names have been approved :-
H.3.c.50.15 -- H.4.c.00.85. CHANTECLER SWITCH.
B.27.b.50.05 -- B.28.c.15.85 FRED ALLEY.

ALBANIAN FRONT.

Offensive operations undertaken by French and Italian troops is progressing satisfactorily; over 1,000 prisoners have already passed through collecting station.

FRENCH FRONT.

S. of the AISNE French troops attacked the enemy's positions at the edge of the FORET de RETZ. In the area N.E. of LONGPONT, on a front of 3 kilometres, they have advanced to a depth of 1,200 metres and captured the farm of CHAVIGNY. In this operation 347 prisoners, including 4 officers, were captured.

ITALIAN FRONT.

During the fighting on the 7th the Italians completed their occupation of the right bank of the NEW PIAVE. From June 15th to July 6th the captures made by the Italians amount to 523 officers, 23,911 other ranks, 63 guns and 1,234 machine guns. In addition, the Italians have completely recovered their lost artillery.

Extract from G.H.Q. Summary:-

Discipline in the German Army.

The following is an extract from an order, dated the 7th June, 1918, signed by General der Kavallerie von der MARWITZ, commanding the Second German Army. -

"Discipline, which is the keystone of our army, is
"seriously shaken.
"I cannot permit that commanders should take upon themselves
"to shield, by an excess of indulgence, officers, non-
"commissioned officers and men guilty of breaches of
"discipline and military regulations, and should inflict
"upon them disciplinary penalties of too mild a nature, or
"even not punish them at all."

On the 12th June, von der MARWITZ issued a further order, from which the following is extracted :-

"Cases of soldiers openly refusing to obey orders are
"increasing to an alarming extent."

The above should be read in connection with the order showing the want of discipline in the back areas of the Eighteenth German Army (von HUTIER), extracts from which were published in Corps Summary No. 536, of the 4th July, 1918.

H.Q., XVII Corps.

9th July, 1918.

~~Secret.~~

The Gordon Highlanders.

OPERATION ORDER No.8.

By

Lieut-Colonel C. A. Smith, D.S.O. Comdg.

9th July, 1916.

1. The following inter-company relief will be carried out to-night:- "A" Company will relieve "D" Company in the Front Line.

   On relief "D" Company will become reserve Company.

2. GUIDES, (1 per post) from "D" Company will be at the Junction of BULLY ALLEY and SPIDER CORNER, M.[illegible].d.8.8. at 10.30.P.M.

3. Advanced parties from each Company will proceed in daylight to take over stores and accommodation.
   Cooks and Mess Orderlies must not leave their Company areas before 9.0.P.M.

4. There will be no movement on the [illegible] ROAD East of the RAILWAY before 10.0.P.M.

5. Rations for "A" and "D" Companies will be at [illegible] HILL SIDING and BROKEN BRIDGE SIDING ([illegible] CAMP) respectively at 10.0.P.M.
   Officers Commanding Companies concerned will detail a guard to unload the rations and remain with them till completion of relief.

6. Completion of relief to be wired to Battalion Headquarters by the Code Words "[illegible]".

7. ACKNOWLEDGE.

9th July, 1916.

G. Geddes Captain & Adjutant,
9th Battalion, The Gordon Highlanders.

Distribution.

Copies 1 - 4 : O. C. Coys.
5 : R. S.M.
6 : Sig. Officer.
7 : I. O.
8 : [illegible]
9 : File.
10 : ----

APPENDIX 4/3

IV

Gordon Highlanders

44th 'Highland' Brigade Intelligence Summary,
For period from 7 A.M. 10th to 7 A.M., 11th July, 1918.

---

1. OPERATIONS. O U R S.

Infantry. P A T R O L S.

5th Gordon Highrs. Right Front Battalion.

8th Seaforth Highrs. Left Front Battalion.

A T T A C H E D.

Stokes Mortars.

At 2.30 P.M. the RAILWAY and NEW WORK at IONIAN Trench were fired on. 20 rounds were expended in retaliation to Light T.M.fire. 41 rounds expended during period.

E N E M Y'S.

Infantry. N I L.

Artillery.

Enemy artillery was fairly active during the period.

T I M E.	AREA SHELLED.	NO. OF ROUNDS.	CALIBRE.
7 a.m.	RAILWAY, H.20.c. & d.	12.	4.1. H.V.
7.30 a.m.	ATHIES.	20	77mm. shrapnel.
7.40 a.m.	H.20.c.	6.	4.1. H.V.
10.40 A.M.	WATERY WOOD.	20.	" "
11 a.m.	H.19.a.	14.	" "
10 a.m.	PORT Trench.	10.	10.5.
12.55 P.M.	H.16.d.	20.	4.2.
1 P.M.	H.14.a. & b.	16.	5.9. shrapnel.
2.30 P.M.	H.14.c.	Salvoes.	77mm.
3.40 P.M.	H.14.a. & c.	6.	5.9. shrapnel.
4.45 P.M.	H.13.c. & d.	12.	4.1. H.V.
5 P.M.	ROAD, H.19.a. & c.	Heavy.	77mm.
6.30 P.M.	H.15.d.	10.	5.9. shrapnel.
6 - 8.30pm.	CAM VALLEY.	30.	4.2.
7.30 P.M.	H.15.d.	8.	5.9.
6.30 a.m.	ATHIES.	20.	77mm.

From 7.15 a.m. to 4.50 p.m. area H.20.d. was shelled at intervals varying from 15 minutes to 75 minutes, by 77mm. guns. 180 shells are reported to have landed of which 13 failed to explode.

Trench Mortars.

At H.22.a.75.20., near our BROKEN BRIDGE Post medium bombs dropped during the day. At 1 a.m. FEUCHY was heavily bombarded with heavy bombs. 3 heavy bombs fell in vicinity of STOKES SUPPORT. 1 failed to explode. From 6 - 6.30 P.M. aerial darts were fired on this area. from house at H.23.a. 8.6.

Machine Guns.

Stokes Trench and STOKES SUPPORT were subjected to bursts during the night from a M.G. reported to be firing from H.23.a. 52.60.

2. G E N E R A L.

Information from Patrols. See Patrol Reports.

Enemy Aircraft.

5 planes were seen during period. 2 of these crossed our lines and the others patrolled our front. These were all engaged by A.A. and ~~....~~ M. guns.

Other Observations.

The smoke of a gun firing was observed from H.16.d.10.65. 133° from this point.

Smoke of guns ~~were~~ also seen 121° from H.16.d.10.65., location about I.25.d.

M.G. reported to fire from H.23.a.52.60.

30 aerial darts were fired from (suspected) house at H.23.a.8.6.

2.......................

-0-0-0-0-0-0-0-0-0-0-0-0-0-0-0-

Other Observations. contd...

Enemy New Work observed at H.28.a.30.75. sap running out from ICELAND camouflaged. Also a narrow slit trench has been dug from junction of IONIAN Trench and ROAD at H.28.a.55.85. to about H.28.a.70.85. at this latter point 'T' Head has been dug, the whole new work has been very carefully camouflaged.

2 H.T. were seen at 9 P.M. on PELVES LANE with 3 men behind each. These wagons disappeared in HAPPY VALLEY. At 9.15 P.M. these wagons re-appeared and went off in PELVES direction.

H.T. were seen on ARTILLERY LANE during the day.

HARNESS LANE was much used by individuals going to MONCHY.

Individuals were seen going from H.30.d.5.8. to H.30.b.7.3. at intervals durinh the day.

At 7.50 P.M. 2 men were seen about I.31.c. They disappeared behind TANK.

A RED CROSS Flag was seen at N.4.c.7.9.

Geo J Lumsden Capt.
for Brigadier General,
11th July, 1918. Commanding, '44th 'Highland' Brigade.

PATROL REPORTS. 5th Gordon Hdrs

Right Front.

At 3.20 A.M., 10th inst a patrol left from PILL BOX at H.22.c.10.97. Their objective was H.22.c.6.2. Patrol was out until 5. 15 A.M. without seeing any movement. Voices were heard about H.22.d.7.3. Patrol entered our lines at H.22.c.10.97. The ROUTE followed was Light Railway running South from H.22.c.6.2., crossed edge of pool at H.22.c.3.6. over planks and Southwards towards H.22.c.4.1. They returned by same route.

At 1.45 P.M. another patrol left our lines from H.22.c.10.97. with the same objective as the above patrol. Stokes fired 4 rounds to stir the enemy at 2.30 P.M. in the vicinity of H.28.a.3.8. and 6 rounds on H.28.a.45.70. No movement was seen and patrol returned at 4.20 P.M. to H.22.c.10.97.

At 1.30 a.m. a patrol left from H.21.d.9.1. with the above mentioned objective. Again Stokes fired but no movement was seen. New work, apparently sap, seen at H.28.a.25.75. running from ICELAND Trench and seems to be camouflaged slightly by duckboards. Patrol returned at 4 A.M. to H.21.d.9.1.

The Post around BROKEN MILL about H.27.b.25.35. was patrolled from 11 P.M. to 2 A.M. Patrol left and returned to our lines by H.27.b.50.25. No movement was seen. Very Lights were fired from Railway at H.28.a. 6.9. A M.G. was firing but was not located.

A Patrol left from H.22.c.70.75. at 12.30 A.M. They patrolled the BROKEN MILL area but saw nothing of the enemy. They returned to our lines at 1.30 a.m. at H.22.c.70.75.

8th Seaforth Highrs. Left Front.

A Patrol left from H.17.b.3.2. at 11.30 P.M. They proceeded South for 120 yards and listened. No movement was heard or seen. They then proceeded N.E. until the SUNKEN Road was reached, where they halted and listened. Wiring and talking was heard at about H.17.b.5.0. Transport was also heard about this point. Patrol returned to our lines and L.G. fire was directed on the enemy. Patrol entered our lines by H.17.b.3.2. at 1.15 A.M.

-o-o-o-o-o-o-o-o-o-o-o-o-o-o-o-o-o-o-

APPENDIX 4

Secret. V.

The Gordon Highlanders.

A D M I N I S T R A T I V E   I N S T R U C T I O N S
(Issued in conjunction with O.O. No.6.)

12th July, 1918.

1. On completion of relief the Battalion will proceed to billets in ARRAS as follows :-

A Coy. - - - - - - - -	5, PLACE ST. CROIX.	All Officers to
B Coy. & Bn. H. Qrs. -	13, RUE de TRENOY.	
C Coy. - - - - - - - -	2, RUE de M. MONSIGNOR.	31, RUE de FOUR -
D Coy. - - - - - - - -	GRANDE PLACE (cellars)	ST. ADRIEN.

Billeting party, consisting of Lt. BARRON, 1 N.C.O. and 1 Runner per Coy. 1 from Battn. H. Qrs. and 2 Runners, will parade at Bn. H. Qrs at 10 A.M. 13th., and report to Major WOOD at Town Commandant's Office, "D" AREA, at 11 A.M.
Billeting parties will meet their Companies at the junction of the RUE ST. MICHAEL and the DOUAI Railway Bridge, H. 28. b. 90. 75. at 12.30. A.M., 14th July.

2. **TRANSPORT.**

(1) 1 limber for Bn. H. Qrs. Lewis Guns, S.A.A., Signalling Gear, Dixies Officers' Mess Kits, etc. will be at Battn. H. Qrs. at 10. P.M.
(2) 1 limber for each Coy. will be at Battn. H. Qrs. at 11 P.M.
R.S.M. will detail an Orderly to take forward A, & B. Coys. limbers to SPIDER CORNER.

3. Cooking utensils, dixies and L.Gs. will be taken to ARRAS and afterward afterwards be carried to the entraining Station, at BEAUMONT GATE on afternoon of the 14th.

4. Breakfasts and dinners will be served in ARRAS. Teas on arrival in new area.

5. The following trench stores will be handed over to relieving units:- A.A. Poles and mountings, Hot food containers, Emergency Rations, S.A.A. and Bombs etc. Tools, Gas stores, A.A.L.G. forward area sights will NOT be handed over.
The handing over of stores must be done with the greatest care. Stores must be in good order and carefully collected in dumps.

6. O.C. Coys. must ensure that trenches, dugouts, cubby holes, and latrines are left scrupulously clean, and the certificates counter-signed by the relieving Officer, forwarded to that effect.

7. **PRECAUTIONS against LOOTING, STRAGGLERS, etc.**

No men will be allowed out of billets in ARRAS, except to enable men to proceed to latrines or on special duty. This order must be strict strictly enforced.
On arrival in billets, O.C. Coys. and R.S.M. will post sentries on main exits from billets to prevent a possibility of looting and straggling. All men must be warned of serious consequences entailed in the infringement of the above order.

G.P. Geddes
Captain & Adjutant,
5th Battalion, The Gordon Highlanders.

Distribution :-

Copies 1 - 4 : O.C. Coys.	7 - Details.
5 : I.O.	8 - R.S.M.
6 : Signals.	9 - File.

APPENDIX 5

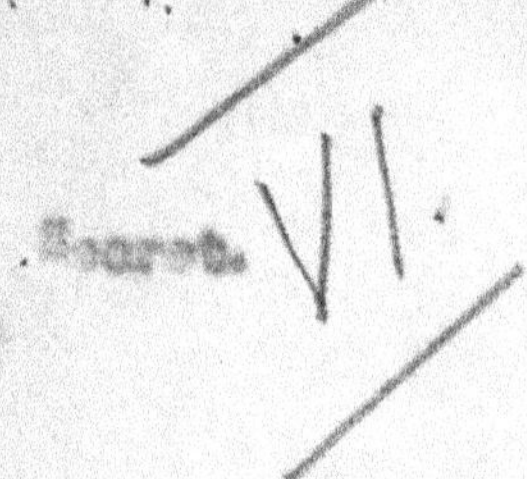

Secret.

The Gordon Highlanders.

O P E R A T I O N O R D E R No. 9.

By

Lieut.- Colonel G. A. Smith, D.S.O. Comdg.

13th July, 1918.

1. The 5th Gordon Highlanders will be relieved in the Line to-night, 13/14th July, as follows :-
A Coy. Gordons will be relieved by A Coy. 5th Canadian Regiment.
B Coy. " " " " " B Coy. 8th Canadian Regiment.
C Coy. " " " " " C Coy. " " "
D Coy. " " " " " D Coy. " " "
Battn. H. Qrs. " " " " Battn. H. Qrs. " "
Relief will be carried out in above order.
On relief the Battalion will proceed to Billets in ARRAS as laid down in para 1. Administrative Instructions.

2. GUIDES.

A Coy. – – – – – – 1 per post and 1 for Coy. H. Qrs. }
B, C, D, Coys. – – 1 per Platoon and 1 for Coy. H. Qrs. } will report to Lieut. REID at Battalion Headquarters at 9.30 P.M. Guides will meet incoming Companies at the Double Arches at Battalion Headquarters.

3. All Defence Schemes, Trench Maps, Aeroplane Photographs, Programmes of Work, Tools, Explosive Stores and Dumps will be handed over and receipts obtained.
Duplicate receipts to reach Battn. H. Qrs. by 12 NOON, 14th JULY.

4. The following Officers and N.C.Os. will be left with relieving Coys. till 10 A.M. 14th July.
Battn. H. Qrs. – Lieut. REID Each Coy. – 1 Officer, and 1 N.C.O. per Platoon.

5. Every effort will be made to keep the relief concealed from the Enemy. There will be no movement of advanced parties by day, over the open. Particular attention is to be paid to this matter.

6. Completion of relief will be wired to Battalion Headquarters by the Code Words " C.51, [illegible]".
Arrival in BILLETS will also be [illegible] reported.

7. ACKNOWLEDGE.

G.P. Geddes Captain & Adjutant,
5th Battalion, The Gordon Highlanders.

Distribution :-

Copies 1 – 4 : O.C. Coys.   8 : 5th Canadian Regiment.
5 : I.O.   9 : 8th Canadian Regiment.
6 : Signals.   10 : W.D.
7 : R.S.M.   11 : File.

Issued through Signals at 9 A.M., 14th July, 1918.

APPENDIX 6.

<u>Secret</u>

O C – Signals

(94)

O.O. No. 9.

"A" Form.

Army Form C. 2121.
(In pads of 100.)

MESSAGES AND SIGNALS.

No. of Message...............

...Code......m.	Words.	Charge.	This message is on a/c of:	Recd. at ....m.
...gin and Service Instructions.	Sent		.... Service.	Date................
VII	At..............m.			From................
	To..................			
	By..................		(Signature of "Franking Officer.")	By..................

TO { Black Watch — 44 Inf Bde; Seaforth Highrs — 9th Field Coy RE; Gordon Highrs

Sender's Number.	Day of Month.	In reply to Number.	AAA
*BM 58	15		

WARNING	ORDER	AAA	The
Division	will	be	prepared
to	move	by	train
AAA	Entraining	will	commence
at	2 AM	16th	AAA
Acknowledge		AAA	wire
Entraining strength			

From 44 IB
Place
Time

[Signature], Capt. for BM

The above may be forwarded as now corrected. (Z)

.... *Censor.*

Signature of Addressor or person authorised to telegraph in his name.

* This line should be erased if not required.

(3796.) Wt. W 492/M1647. 650,000 Pads. 5/17. H. W. & V., Ld. (E. 1187.)

Secret   5th Gordon Highrs
Operation Order No. 11

VIIA

16th July, 1918.

1. The 5th Gordon Highrs (less D Coy with cooker & team) will move by train today, 16th July to a destination to be notified later.

2. The train leaves TINQUES Station at 11.38am.
The battalion will parade ready to march off at 8.30am. from the Starting Point at the BETHONSART-SAVY, — MINGOVAL-VILLERS BRULIN Cross Roads (V.21.d.9,7). Column facing South.
Order of March – Band, H.Qrs, A, B & C Coys. Dress: Full marching order with steel helmets.

3. Transport will move off at 6.30am and report to R.T.O. at 8.30am.

4. Each train will consist of 1 Coach, 30 covered trucks, 17 flats.

5. MAJOR J.B. WOOD, DSO, MC will act as Entraining Officer. He will report to an Officer of Brigade Staff at 10am.

6. Acknowledge

G.F. Geddes
Capt & Adjt.

Secret

War Diary Copy

5th Gordon Highlanders
Operation Order No 12.
By
Lieut Colonel G.H. Smith DSO Comdg
19th July 1918.

1. The 5th Gordon Highrs will move by bus today to an area to be notified later

2. Embussing will take place on MONDEVILLE - MANCHY - ST ELOI Road facing South with head of column at [illegible]NEVILLE

3. Battalion will parade ready to march off at 7.15 PM in the order B. C Bn HQ. D & A Coy. Head of column at the Church.

4. Companies will be told off in loads of 1 Officer or senior NCO & 20 ORs

5. Major R.L. Wood DSO MC will superintend the Embussing

6. Acknowledge

Copies to OC Coys
Major Wood
Lt Reid
R.Q.M. W.D. [illegible]

Captain & Adjt

SECRET. 44th Brigade G.34.- 19.7.18.

1. The Division is to be at one hour's notice from 4 A.M. to 9 A.M. daily.

2. Units will nightly turn in with their fighting kit made up, and be ready to immediately move on receipt of orders.

3. Haversacks, and all kit surplus to battle order will be nightly stacked in one store in each unit's area. In the event of a move 1 N.C.O. and 1 man per unit will be left in charge of these stores.

4. O.C.Units will select Battalion or Company assembly points, as is most suitable in their area, where, on receipt of orders the units will at once assemble and march off to any starting point which may be ordered from this office. All officers will forthwith reconnoitre all routes from these assembly points to the main roads.

5. The area occupied by the Division has been heavily bombed every night. A.A.Lewis Guns or Machine Guns are to be mounted; and the greatest care taken that no lights are exposed after dark.

6. As far as possible each man will be told off to a cellar to which he will at once proceed in the event of hostile shelling or bombing.

7. The water in the area is not fit for consumption unless it is either chlorinated or boiled.

8. For the present all troops are confined to their respective billeting area.

9. Assembly points to be reported to this office.

Geo K Lumsden Captain,
A/Brigade Major,
44th Infantry Brigade.

Black Watch.
Seaforth Highrs.
Gordon Highrs.
44 T.M.Battery.
Bde. Signals.

'A' Coy., 15th Bn., M.G.C.
91st Field Coy., R.E.
No.2 Coy., Train.
45th Field Ambulance.

Secret

5th Gordon Highrs

Operation Order No. 13

IX

2-7-18

1. The 5th Gordon Highrs less [illegible] Personnel will march to the [illegible] ST NICHOLAS [illegible] Road Junction, just South of Railway [illegible] North West of the [illegible]

Time – 5.50 AM

Order of March: Bn HQ, A, B, C, D Coys & Transport

Route GUISE LAMOTTE – ROYELAYE – MARTIMONT

2. The Fighting Personnel & [illegible] will collect in the [illegible] area at [illegible] occupied by the 5th Seaforths. Separate orders for this move will be issued by Major J B Wood, DSO MC. Motor lorries will report at QM Stores at 5am

3. Distances of 100 yds. to be maintained between Coys. & between D Coy & Transport. Distances of

Secret

5th Gordon Highrs

Operation Order No. 14.

21st July 1918.

1. The 5th Gordon Highrs will continue the move by march route tonight 21st/22nd July to the ST PIERRE AIGLE Area.
Route: MORTEFONTAINE – RAPERIE – COEUVRES – ST PIERRE AIGLE.

2. Starting Point: Road junction 200 yds South of the B in [illegible].
Time: 12 midnight.
Order of march: Btn HQ, D, C, A, B Coys, Transport.

3. Distances 100 yds between Coys.
300 " " Btns.

4. On arrival in new area the Division will be in support to the 2nd American Division.

5. Advance parties will meet the battalion at GOEUVRES.

6. OC Coys & RSM will take every precaution that men keep under cover in the forward area and that every measure

400 yards between battalions.

4. Advanced party consisting of 2/Lt.
A.D. COPELAND, C.Q.M.S. Sergt.
Wilson & Drummer from Bn.
H.Q. will report at O.R.
with bicycles at 5 a.m. They
will report to the Staff Captain
at the Church [illegible] at
6 a.m.

5. Reveille — 4 A.M.
Breakfast 4.30 A.M.
Lewis Guns, S.A.A., Signalling gear,
& mess kits to be loaded on
limbers at the square by 5.15 A.M.

6 Acknowledge.

G.P. Vedder
Capt & Adjt

Distribution

O.C. Coys
Major Wood
2/Lt Copeland
QM & T.O
I.O
RSM
File
W.D.

~~Secret~~ 5th Gordon Highrs.
Operation Order No 15.
by
Lt. Col. G.A. Smith, D.S.O. Cmdg.

XI.

22nd July 1918.

1. The 20th French Corps and 69th French Division have driven back the enemy to the approximate line PARCY TIGNY – W. of BUZANCY – E. of BERZY-le-SEC – VAUXBUIN.

2. The 15th Division will relieve the 1st. U.S. Division in the line on night 22nd/23rd July.
The 44th Inf. Bde will be in Reserve.

3. The 5th Gordon Highrs will take over the area astride the PARIS – SOISSONS Road between CRAVANCON Fm and Road Junction 300 yds N.E. of the S in PARIS.
Dispositions will be as follows.
D Coy will relieve 1 Coy. U.S. Engineers.
C " " " 180 M.M.Ps. & Stragglers.
B " " " 1 Coy U.S. Engineers.
A " " " 1 Coy Reinforcements & Ammunition Train.

Bn. H.Q. will be established at the ~~Road Junction~~, PARIS – SOISSONS and MISSY – PLOISY Cross Roads.

4. The battalion will parade, ready to march off at 11.15 pm. in the order Bn HQ, D, C, B + A Coys. Head of column to be at junction of the track + road, 300 yards N. of the last E of MONTEVOURE.
Intervals of 100 yards will be maintained between platoons.

5. Guides. The advance parties will meet the battalion at CRAVANÇON FARM.

6. One limber per Coy + 1 for Bn HQ, will carry Lewis Guns, S.A.A., dixies, signalling gear + men's kits. Limbers will be unloaded at the Bn + Coys will move on passing.
Limbers to proceed behind in rear of first platoon of each Company.
Bn Reserve of tools will be taken into the line. Limber to proceed with Bn HQ. RSM will detail 1 NCO + 2 men to unload the tools + issue them equally between Coys on completion of relief.

7. All stores, SOS signals etc will be taken over + lists forwarded to OR by 8 am 23rd.
Sketch shewing dispositions + Coy. HQ

SECRET Copy No.

XII

44th Highland Brigade Operation Order No. 287

23.7.18

1. Relief of the 1st U.S. Division (less Artillery) by 15th Division (less Artillery) is to be completed by 3 AM 23rd July. Command of the Divisional Sector will pass to G.O.C. 15th Division at 12 midnight 22/23rd July.

2 The Tenth French Army is to attack tomorrow.

3 The 15th Division (Left Division 20th Corps) will attack with the 87th Division on the Right.

4 The 46th Inf Bde will attack on the right and the 45th Inf Bde on the left. The 44th Inf Bde will be located S of PLOISY. 8th Seaforth Hghrs is placed ~~at the disposal~~ in 20th Corps Reserve and will not be engaged without orders from DIV. H.Q.

(2)

5. The 46th Inf Bde will capture the line CHIVRY - Pl. 148.6 and at the same time keep close touch with the 87th Division who are to capture BUZANCY and the high ground East of it. On reaching the above line the 46th Inf Bdy will capture the village of ROZIERLES

6. The 45th Inf Bde will conform to the movements of the 46th Inf Bde and will form a strong defensive flank to connect the left of the 46th Inf Bde to the Right of the 69th Division at LA TURBINE - (800 yards East of BERZY le Sec)

7. All ground gained will be consolidated and held by specially detailed Units.

8. Infantry will attack at 5 AM

9. Artillery preparation will be arranged by CRA 1st U.S. DIV. as follows —

will be forwarded by the same hour.

8. All movement will be reduced to a minimum during the hours of daylight as most parts of the area are under observation.

The utmost precautions will be taken to prevent smoke from fires. Lights at night will be carefully shaded.

9. Completion of relief will be reported by runner to Bn HQ.

10. Acknowledge.

C.P. Geddes,
Capt & Adjt
5th Gordon Highrs

Copies to:

OC Coys
Sig. Offr
QM & TO
RSM
WD
File

(3)

Bombardments 4.15 AM to 4.45 AM

At 4.55 AM barrage will drop in advance of the first line when the infantry will assemble as close as possible in rear of barrage.

At 5 AM barrage will move forward at 100 yards in three minutes to a distance of 400 yards beyond the objective. Here it will search for 1 hour at which time it will roll across the river CRISE then fighting patrols will push forward and keep touch with the enemy and exploit to the utmost any ~~[illegible]~~ weakening of hostile resistance.

10 The 15th Bn M.G.C. will be disposed to support the attack as follows:–

1 Machine Gun Coy is allotted to 46th Inf Bde (H.G. CHAUDIN.

(4)

2 M.G. Coys are allotted to the 45th Inf Bde (HQ MAISSY au Bois)

Portions of these companies must be responsible for the protection of the left flank of the Division about PLOISY VALLEY

1 M.G. Coy will be in Div reserve with 44th Inf Bde (H.Q. just N of CRAVENCON)

M.G. Company Commanders will report to the G.O.C. Inf Bdes to which they are allotted for detailed orders as regards the attack

11 The 9th Gordons (Pioneers) will move to the area S.E. of MISSY AUX BOIS near the VAUXBAIN - CRAVANCON Farm road

Field Coys R.E. will be held at the disposal of C.R.E. and will be moved forward to assist infantry Brigades as necessary

12. French aeroplanes will make contacts at the following hours:-
6 AM.
6-45 AM
Signal from contact planes calling for infantry positions will be 6 white stars.
Infantry to respond by waving helmets on their rifles.

13 ~~[illegible]~~ In the event of the transport being ordered forward, the M.G. limbers, SAA & Grenade limbers and officers' riding horses will move in the first instance to a place to be selected by the BTO 1 Km E. of DOMMIERS.

14 / 15 – SEE PAGE 6

Issued thro
Signal –
4.40 AM

Capt
A/Bde Major
44th Inf Bde

1 4/6th Black Watch
2 8th Seaforth
3 5th Gordons
4 44th Battery.

(6)

14. The Divisional Advanced Dressing Station will be situated in CHAUDUN

15. Reports to Bde HQ which is situated in CRAVANCON Ranch 400 yards East of main SOISSONS - PARIS Road

Geo[illegible] Lumsden
Capt
[illegible]/Bn

XIII

5th Gordon Highrs.

Operation Order No 15
by
Lieut-Col. G A Smith, DSO

Ref Sheets – SOISSONS & OULCHY, 1/20000.

25-7-18

1. The 5th Gordon Highrs will relieve the 9th Royal Scots in the Right Sector of the 15th Div Front tonight, 25/26th July

2 Dispositions:

C Coy Gordons will relieve B Coy Royal Scots in the Rt. Front.

B Coy Gordons will relieve D Coy Royal Scots in the Left front.

D Coy Gordons will be in Support & move into a position at present unoccupied.

A Coy Gordons will relieve C Coy Royal Scots in Reserve.

Bn HQ will relieve Bn HQ Royal Scots in the bank at 69.91 – 500 yards almost due East of Railway Crossing

3 Guides as follows:-

B & C Coys : 1 per platoon & 1 for Coy HQ

D Coy : 1 per platoon. Coy HQ to be established

A Coy : 1 guide

will be at Advanced Brigade HQ at Cave ⅓ kilo. N of C of CHAZELLE at 10 pm.

4. Companies will move off by platoons at 100 yards interval by the order C, B, D, A Coys & HQ. First platoon of C Coy to move off at 9.30 pm.

5. All Reserve SAA will be taken over.

6. OC Coys will forward by 6 am a sketch shewing their dispositions & location of Coy HQ.

7. Completion of relief to be reported at once to Bn. HQ by runner. Signalling Officer will arrange to send back Bn runners with the Coy runners to their respective Coy HQ.

8. Acknowledge.

G P Geddes.
Capt & Adjt
5th Gordon Highrs

Copies to:
OC Coys.
Sigs
RSM
[illegible] [illegible]
File W.D.

6. Dispositions of Battalion:-

C Coy on Right front.

B Coy on Left front.

A Coy on Close Support.

D Coy in Reserve in Bois de GERRARD.

Advanced Bn HQ. in Bois de GERRARD at a point about 200 Yds South of Bois GERRARD. Rear Bn HQ at present location.

7. Method of Attack:-

By lines of Platoons and sections as shown in Appendix 'B' attached. At Zero the remaining companies will advance. When these companies are clear of the assembly positions the positions will at once be occupied by 'D' Coy.

One platoon of 'D' Coy will be prepared to reinforce the front companies in the event of their being held up and 2 platoons will be held in reserve for local counter attack.

Reinforcements will be used sparingly in localities and only in case of urgent necessity.

'A' Coy will not move without orders from Bn HQ.

8. Consolidation

On reaching the objectives one double Lewis Gun Section and 5 one

Rifle sections per company will be pushed out at least 50 yards to cover the work of consolidation. These sections will occupy shell holes, or dig in, and be prepared to deal with any immediate local counter attack.

The remainder of the assaulting companies will consolidate in depth, by making section posts covering their front. The work must be carried out with all possible speed after carefully selecting positions with good field of fire.

9. The closest touch must be maintained with 8th Seaforth Highlanders on the Right.

One platoon 8th Argylls will follow on the left flank of D Coy and protect the left flank of the battalion.

10. Aircraft:– 20 flares will be issued to each of B & C Coys and 10 to D Coy.

At Zero +1 hour and Zero +3 hours, contact aeroplanes will fly over the objectives. Flares will be shown by garrison of outpost and front lines.

At Zero +15 minutes, fighting planes will probably fly over the ground being attacked.

11. Communication.

All reports to Advanced Bn HQ

5

A Relay Post for runners will be establish-
-ed at C Coys H.Q. in old front line.

12. Synchronisation of Watches.

A runner from Bn. HQ will take round a watch to Companies commencing with A Coy at 9 P.M.

13. Medical

The R.A.P. will be established at present Bn HQ. All wounded will be sent back as quickly as possible but Stretcher cases will not be lifted until consolidation is well in hand.

Route for wounded:- Across Country to Advanced Bn HQ — thence down track along southern edge of BOIS de GERRARD.

14. Zero hour will be 12-30 pm. 28th July.

15. Acknowledge

G.P. Geddes
Captain & Adjutant
6th Gordon Highlanders

Distribution.
Copies 1-4 O.C. Coys
5. I.O
6. Sigs
7. [illegible]
8. [illegible]
9. M.O.
10. R.S.M.
11. W.D.
12. File

Secret. 5th Gordon Highlanders
Operation Orders No 16.
By 27.7.18
Lieut Colonel J.G. Smith. D.S.O. Comdg.

XIV

Reference Sheets:
SOISSONS – GOUNCHY 1/20,000.

1. General:– The 152nd Highland Brigade and the 91st French Regiment will attack to-morrow 28th July and capture the CHATEAU and village of BUZANCY, and the high ground on either flank.

2. Objectives:–
The 91st French Regt will attack on the right South of BUZANCY.
The 8th Seaforth Highrs will capture the Chateau & Village of BUZANCY.
The 5th Gordon Highrs will attack on the left and capture the high ground North of the Chateau (See Appendix "A", attached.)

3. Artillery:–
Preliminary bombardment was carried out to-day, and the following bombardment will take place to-morrow:–
4.30 – 5.30 AM. BUZANCY
7.30 – 8.30 AM. NOYANT
9.30 – 10.– AM. CHIVRY FM. & ROZIERES
11.30 AM. 12.30 PM. BUZANCY.
If the wind is favourable a smoke screen will be placed round NOYANT and

2

BUSANCY.

At ZERO – 2 minutes the creeping barrage, consisting of field guns and howitzers supported by French '75s and heavy guns will commence in front of the assembly positions.

At ZERO the infantry will advance and the barrage will creep forward at the rate of 100 yards in 3 minutes.

On the capture of the objectives the barrage will form a protective barrage 300 yards in front to permit of immediate reorganisation and consolidation.

4 Trench Mortars –:

4 Stokes Mortars will be attached to the battalion. Programme of firing to be notified later.

5 Machine Guns.

16 M.G's to fire from ZERO – ZERO + 14 minutes on the direct front of BUSANCY sweeping South of the Chateau wall. These guns will then jump to an S.O.S. line where they will remain until ZERO + 74 minutes (i.e. for one hour as a protective barrage barrage.)

Other 16 guns have been detailed to deal with BERCY-LE-SEC – ROYANT and TURBINE

G.97.

Headquarters
44th Infantry Brigade

XV

Account of the Operations on the 28th July 1918 –

At Zero Hour the 5th Gordon Highrs were disposed as follows:–

B & C Coys in the front line along the East edge of the wood.

D Coy in Close Support 100 yards in rear

A Coy in Reserve in BOIS de GERARD.

Advanced Bn HQ at 98.92.

At 12.25pm the barrage opened and at 12.30pm it continued to lift, and the assaulting troops advanced 50 yards behind it.

For the first 300 yards the advance met with no opposition. About Point 16.92, however, at the edge of the cornfield, a strong point was encountered which gave considerable trouble. After a sharp bombing fight the resistance was overcome & the advance continued.

On the right the advance was

2

held up for a few minutes by a M.G. in the Chateau Wall at about 12.50. A platoon of the support company under 2/Lt. F.W. LOVIE, worked round the left flank, rushed the gun, and captured both gun and team. The platoon suffered heavy losses at this point. Practically no further opposition was met with and the objective was reached at 1.30 pm with slight casualties.

The right company at once got into touch with the 8th Seaforth Hghrs, and the left company with the 1/8 Argylls who had established posts to protect our left flank.

Carrying parties were at once thrown out and consolidation commenced. This proved very difficult as at least 2 M.Gs were holding out in BUZANCY and firing from the rear. M.Gs were also firing from the direction of NOYANT.

At 6pm, the enemy counterattacked the French, who were forced

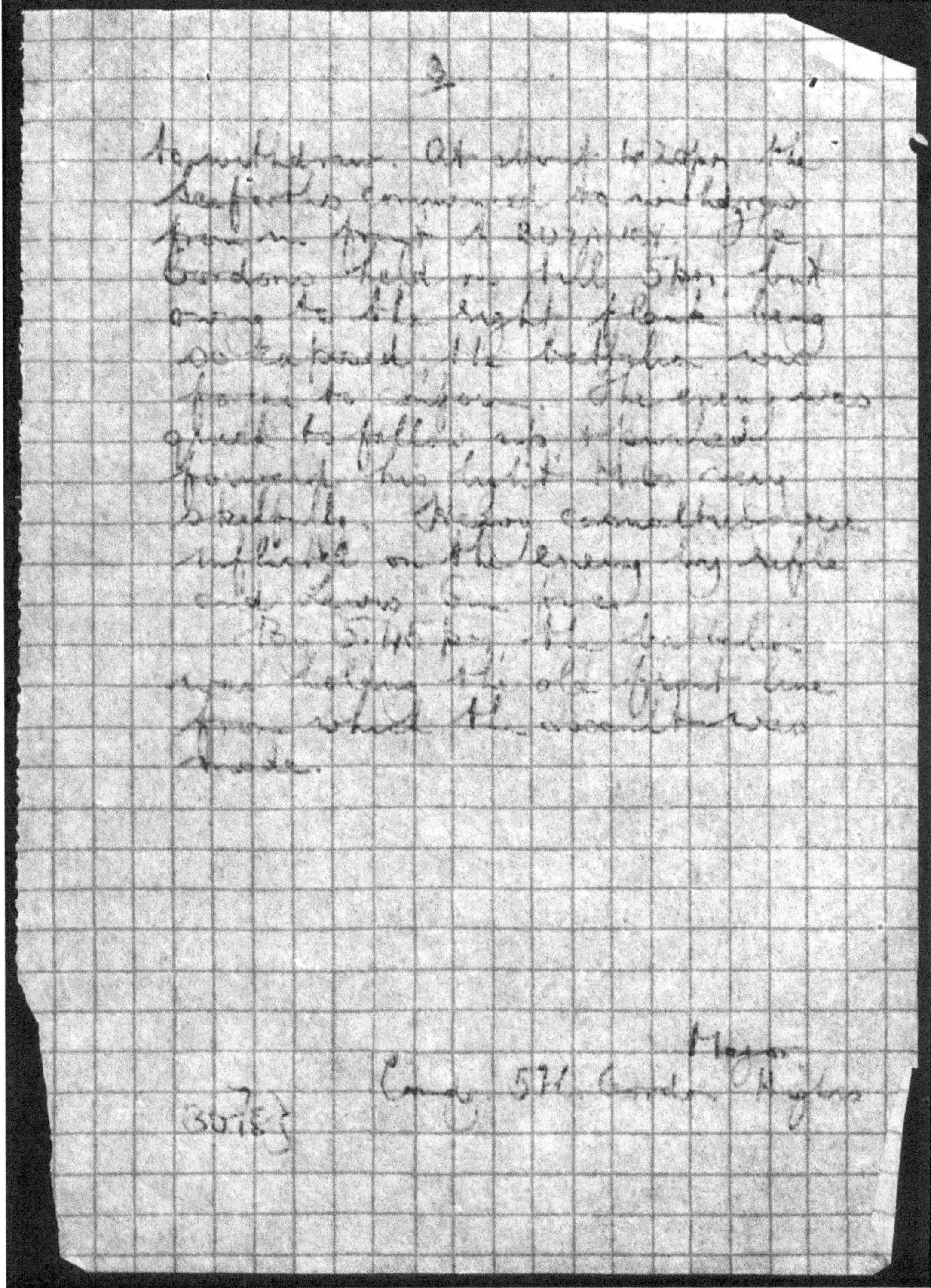

3

to withdraw. At about [illegible] the Seaforths commenced to withdraw from [illegible] Buzancy. The Gordons held on till 5 pm, but owing to the right flank being exposed, the battalion was forced to retire. The enemy was afraid to follow up & [illegible] forward. This fight was carried out steadily. Heavy casualties were inflicted on the enemy by rifle and Lewis Gun fire.

By 5.45 pm the battalion was holding its old front line from which the assault had been made.

Major
Comdg 5th Gordon Highlanders

30.7.18

COPY OF TELEGRAM RECEIVED FROM G.O.C. 15th DIVISION.

29th July, 1918.

I would like to express to all ranks 5th Gordon Highlanders, my deep sympathy in the loss of Lt. Colonel Smith. The behaviour of the Battalion yesterday was beyond all praise and in keeping with the great traditions of the Gordon Highlanders.

SECRET. 5TH GORDON HDRS. COPY No.

OPERATION ORDER No 17

by.

XVII.

MAJOR J.B. WOOD. D.S.O., M.C.

COMDG.

29TH JULY 1918

1. The 5th GORDON HDRS will be relieved in the line to-night 29/30th July by part of the 136th FRENCH REGT.

On relief the battalion will withdraw to a part of CRAVANCON TRENCH, between the X of AMOUREUX (S.E. of CHAUDIN) and X ROADS, 1500 yards SOUTH of the last E in LECHELLE on the CHARANTIGNY — VIERZY. Road.

Advanced party will meet companies at these X Roads.

2 GUIDES: O.C. Coys will each detail 5 guides (1 per PLATOON +1 for COY H.Q.) to report to Bn Hqs at 8.30 p.m.

Guides must come down in small parties.

3. All tools + petrol tins will be carried out.

4. Completion of relief to be reported to Bn Hqs by wire by Code words "WATER RECIEVED" + by runner.

ACKNOWLEDGE.

DISTRIBUTION. 1–4 OC Coys. capt + adj.

5. W.D.

6 R.S.M.

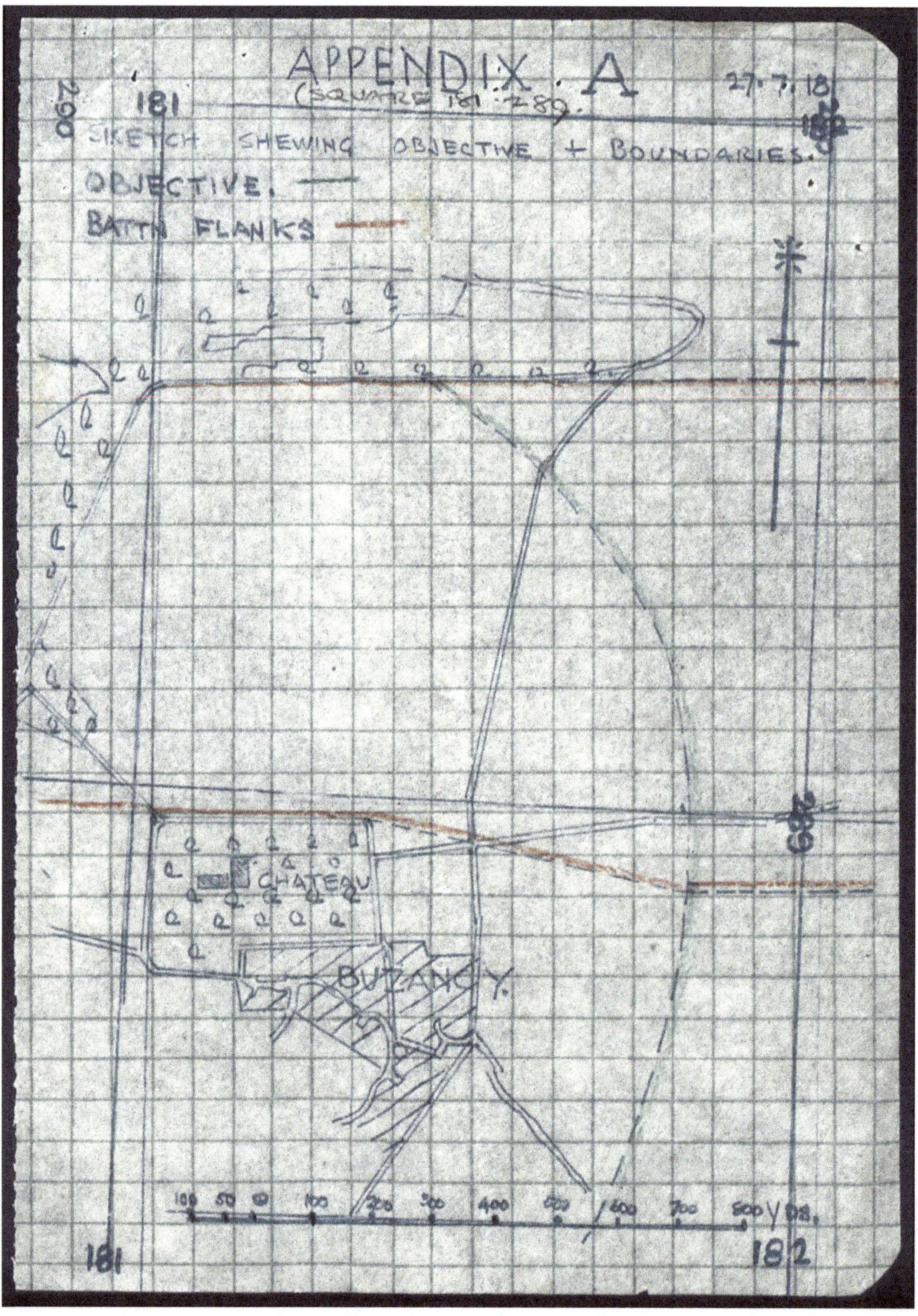
APPENDIX A
(SQUARE 181 289.
27.7.18
290
181
SKETCH SHEWING OBJECTIVE + BOUNDARIES.
OBJECTIVE.
BATTN FLANKS
CHATEAU
BUZANCY.
100 50 0 100 200 300 400 500 600 700 800 YDS.
181
182

Army Form C. 2118.

Instructions regarding War Diaries and Intelligence Summaries are contained in F. S. Regs., Par. II. and the Staff Manual respectively. Title pages will be prepared in manuscript.

WAR DIARY
or
~~INTELLIGENCE SUMMARY.~~
(Erase heading not required.)

Place	Date	Hour	Summary of Events and Information										Remarks and references to Appendices
XVIII			CASUALTIES from 24th to 31st July.										
			OTHER RANKS.								OFFICERS.		
	1918		Wded.	Gassed	Missg.	Wded Missg	Killed.	Wded (S.I.W)	Wded at duty.	Total	Killed.	Date.	
	24th		3				2		1	6	Lieut Col G.A. Smith D.S.O	28th	
	25th		6							6	Capt R.A.M. Black	27th	
	26th		-							-	Lieut. J. McHardy	24th	
	27th		18					2	2	22	Wounded.		
	28th		154	2	19	12	33		1	221	Capt. W. J. Currie	28th	
	29th						4			4	Lieut. J.B. Elliott	27th	
	30th		5						1	6	" J.W. Lovie	28th	
	31st		1	3						4	" J.L. Warrack M.C	29th	
											2/Lieut. A. Brown	28th	
											Gassed.		
											2/Lieut. R.A. Cameron	30th	
											Killed Wded Gassed	Total	
			187	5	19	12	39	2	5	269	3 5 1	9	

A6945 Wt. W11422/M1160 350,000 12/16 D. D. & L. Forms/C./2118/14.

XIX

Strength during Month of July 1918

Army Form C. 2118.

WAR DIARY

or

INTELLIGENCE SUMMARY.

(Erase heading not required.)

Instructions regarding War Diaries and Intelligence Summaries are contained in F. S. Regs., Part II, and the Staff Manual respectively. Title pages will be prepared in manuscript.

Place / Increase	O	OR	Decrease	O	OR	Total O	Total OR
28.6.18						42	888
Increase	O	OR	Decrease	O	OR		
Reinf from Div! Wing	-	28	Wounded	-	2		
Lieut (A/Capt) W. S. Kemp MC taken on strength on return from CO's Course Aldershot	1						
Reinf at Div! Wing taken on strength Lieut T M Muir & 2 OR	1	2					
5.7.18	2	30		-	2	44	916
Joined from Div! Wing	-	42	Killed	-	3		
Taken on Strength from Div! HQ formerly Div! Burial Officer, 8/10 G.H. Lieut J E Adam	1		Died of wounds	-	2		
			Wounded	-	7		
			Evacuated sick	-	6		
			To Base unfit	-	1		
			Over 7 days in FA sick	-	10		
12.7.18	1	42		-	29	45	929
2/Lt J F Martin (B.I.O.) taken on strength from 8/10 Gordon Highrs, not previously shown	1		Wounded	-	2		
			To U.K. for commission	-	1		
Joined from Div! Wing	-	11					
Evac (Rejoined from Hospital)	-	16					
Classified "P" & returned to duty from APM, 15th Division	-	1					
19.7.18	1	28		-	3	46	954

Increase	O	OR	Decrease	O	OR	Remarks O	Remarks O.R.
19.7.18	1	28		-	3	46	954
Nil			Struck off strength (errata in 130 of 8/10 GH)	-	1		
			To UK for commission		1		
			Killed - Lieut J McHardy	1	-		
			Killed - O.Rs.	-	2		
			Wounded	-	3		
26.7.18	-	-		1	7	45	947

XIX.

Army Form C. 2118.

WAR DIARY
or
INTELLIGENCE SUMMARY.
(Erase heading not required.)

Instructions regarding War Diaries and Intelligence Summaries are contained in F. S. Regs., Part II. and the Staff Manual respectively. Title pages will be prepared in manuscript.

Casualties — July 1918.

Place	Date	Hour	Summary of Events and Information	Remarks and references to Appendices
No 265520	Pte		Fraser R G Wounded 3. 7. 18	
14402	"		Wilson J B " 1. 7. 18	
17791	"		Gregory A " 4 7 18	
310012	"		Wood W " 3. 7. 18	
10099	"		Tunnach J " 4 7 18	
10244	Cpl		Robertson J " 3 7 18	
18094	Pte		Brewster H Killed 7. 7 18	
S/4384	"		Cook J " 8. 7. 18	
S/7598	"		Gentleman J " 8. 7. 18	
260106	"		Mitchell J Died of Wounds 7. 7. 18	
516976	"		Newman R Wounded 8 7 18	
S/17789	"		McDonald W " 8 7 18	
41263	"		Woodcock G " 7 7 18	
12884	"		Milne R " 8. 7. 18	
291174	"		Lockwood J " 8 7 18	
S/18944	"		Lawrie J " 8 7 18	
266891	"		McKay J " 8 7. 18	
516976	"		Newson R Died of wounds 8 7. 18	
S/14707	"		Collier L Wounded 11 7 18	
S/6498	"		McGiver H " 11. 7. 18	
S/10743	Cpl		Smith J S.I.W. 12 7 18	
S/17061	Pte		Cooper W " 11. 7 18	

(A7092). Wt. W12839/M1293. 750,000. 1/17. D. D. & L., Ltd. Forms/C.2118/14.

44th Bde
15th Div

5th Gordon Hrs.

August 1918

CONFIDENTIAL

5th BATTN. THE GORDON HIGHLANDERS.

VR 40

WAR DIARY

**** FOR THE MONTH OF ****

AUGUST.

------ VOLUME 40 ------

J O S Nord

Lieut-Colonel,

Cmdg., 5th Battalion, The Gordon Highlanders.

Instructions regarding War Diaries and Intelligence Summaries are contained in F. S. Regs., Part II. and the Staff Manual respectively. Title pages will be prepared in manuscript.

WAR DIARY
or
INTELLIGENCE SUMMARY.
(Erase heading not required.)

Army Form C. 2118.

Place	Date	Hour	Summary of Events and Information	Remarks and references to Appendices
In the field.	1.9.18		The bn. was placed under orders to attack the G.M.P. trench between TAUX and BOIS DE TAAST & capture the latter place. This objective was to serve as a flank defence, the attack was to take place provided the French succeeded in an attack they were making further south. The 7th Brigade & 46th Bde were to make the first attack & the 44th Bde was to leap frog them. The bn moved into their assembly position in some corn fields between VIERCY and LA RAPERIE by 3 A.M. & awaited the signal to attack, which was to be given by an aeroplane firing a rocket. The signal was received at 8.10 A.M. the guns opened, the attack commenced at 9am. 45th & 46th Bdes were unable to advance owing to heavy M.G. fire from some derelict French tanks & BOIS HARTENNES, the bn had to stop its advance at the front line. At 12 noon another attempt was made to advance but again the front brigades were unable to advance. The 44th Bde relieved the 46th in the evening, the bn was placed in brigade reserve. They took up their position in G.M.P. trench between VIERCY and CHAUDUN, [illegible] the right was [illegible]. Contrary to the experience of the BUZANCY attack	Bn. O.O. No. 20 attached. App. No. I.

(10540) W1 W5300/P713 750,000 3/18 E 1888 Forms/C2118/16.

Instructions regarding War Diaries and Intelligence Summaries are contained in F. S. Regs., Part II. and the Staff Manual respectively. Title pages will be prepared in manuscript.

WAR DIARY
or
INTELLIGENCE SUMMARY.
(Erase heading not required.)

Army Form C. 2118.

Place	Date	Hour	Summary of Events and Information	Remarks and references to Appendices
In the field.	1.8.18.		very little shell fire was experienced. The total Bn casualties during this operation were 75 of which 12 were killed.	
	2.8.18.		At 11. A.M. information was received that the enemy were falling back & orders were received for the Bn to move forward to its objective of the previous day. This was reached without opposition by 2. P.M. The Bn then pushed forward in a N.E. direction to VILLEBLAIN then AMBRIEF, both of which ~~arrived~~ were reached without opposition. The enemy were shelling AMBRIEF heavily when our advance parties were approaching it, thus showing that they had evacuated the place. An outpost line was thrown out between Ambrief & Chacrise with the Seaforths on our right and the 9th Gordons on our left. Bn HQrs was installed in the distillery at AMBRIEF & "A" "D" Coys were retained as Bn reserve, in an adjoining cave.	These orders were all verbally given.
	3.8.18.		68. ranks of "A" & "D" Coys were gassed in the cave they were living in. The reason for this appears to have been that when the men entered the cave they lit fires, this brought out the gas which the enemy must have left before retiring. At 5. A.M. the 68th Regiment of the French relieved the Bn, who marched back to RAPERIE where they had breakfast & buried the dead. The march	[illegible]

Army Form C. 2118.

WAR DIARY
or
INTELLIGENCE SUMMARY.
(Erase heading not required.)

Instructions regarding War Diaries and Intelligence Summaries are contained in F. S. Regs., Part II. and the Staff Manual respectively. Title pages will be prepared in manuscript.

Place	Date	Hour	Summary of Events and Information	Remarks and references to Appendices
In the field	3.8.18.		was then continued, in the afternoon, on to DOMIERES, where the night was spent.	
	4.8.18.		The Bn proceeded by march route to SOUCY where they entrained for RIEUX in the LAIGNEVILLE — MOGNEVILLE area. A billeting party had been sent on earlier & when the Bn arrived at RIEUX at 6 P.M. everything was in order for them. Night was spent there.	O.O. No 21 attached Appx. No. II. Casualties 1-4.8th attached No. III.
	5.8.18. [illegible]		The day was spent quietly at RIEUX. General Mangin's order of the day showing appreciation for the 15th Div's part gave great pleasure & satisfaction to all ranks.	French 10th army order attached. No. IV.
	6.8.18.		The Bn received orders to prepare to move back to the First Army area the entraining point being POINT ST. MAXENCE. The move to commence at 2.40 A.M. the following day.	O.O. No. 22 attached Appx. No: V.
	7.8.18.		Train steamed out at 9 A.M. the whole day was spent in the train.	
	8.8.18.		Bn detrained at TINQUES then marched up to IZEL-LE-HAMEAU arriving at 8 A.M. After a wash & brush up the Bn lined the streets pending the arrival of H.M. The King who was motoring through. [illegible] & Bde were all present & cheered him heartily as he passed.	1.5 hrs.

Army Form C. 2118.

Instructions regarding War Diaries and Intelligence Summaries are contained in F. S. Regs., Part II. and the Staff Manual respectively. Title pages will be prepared in manuscript.

WAR DIARY
or
INTELLIGENCE SUMMARY.

(Erase heading not required.)

Place	Date	Hour	Summary of Events and Information	Remarks and references to Appendices
In the field	8.8.18.		The day was spent in resting.	
	9.8.18 – 11.8.18.		The period was spent in short parades recording deficiencies, which were indented for. The men were bathed on the 10th and on the 11th the Bn attended divine service.	
	12.8.18.		The great event of the day was a presentation of French decorations by Gen: Reid, the divisional commander. In his address he paid a very high compliment to the work of the Bde. His words were listened to very thoughtfully by all ranks of the Bde. Appended are a list of decorations bestowed on the Bn.	List of decorations bestowed on the Bn by the French staff. Appx No: VI.
	13.8.18		Coy parades were held in the forenoon. In the afternoon rumour had it that the Div: was under orders to move into the line. This caused great depression amongst all ranks, as everybody felt that they had earned a rest, especially after a programme of training had been arranged & the Bn expected to be out for at least a fortnight. There was bombing activity at night in the vicinity of the village.	
	14.8.18		Definite orders had now been received concerning the relief, which was to take place on the morrow. NEUVILLE VITASSE believed to be the Bn sector. More bombing activity at night.	[illegible]

D. D. & L., London, E.C.
(10340) Wt W5300/P713 750,000 3/18 E 2688 Forms/C2118/16.

Instructions regarding War Diaries and Intelligence Summaries are contained in F. S. Regs., Part II. and the Staff Manual respectively. Title pages will be prepared in manuscript.

WAR DIARY
or
INTELLIGENCE SUMMARY.
(Erase heading not required.)

Army Form C. 2118.

Place	Date	Hour	Summary of Events and Information	Remarks and references to Appendices
In the field.	15.8.18		The Bn left IZEL-LE-HAMEAU at 5 P.M. by light rly for WAILLY where they detrained. From here they marched up into the NEUVILLE VITASSE sector where they relieved the 7th Middlesex Regt, in support to the right brigade. The Black Watch took over the front line the Seaforths were in reserve. The 44th Bde was now on the extreme right of the First Army sector & was in a position of great importance. This sector was reported very quiet by the outgoing people.	O.O. No 24 attached. Appx. No. VI A
	16.8.18		The day passed very quietly on the Bn front the air was very warm. 5 of our Sopwith Camel Scouts attracted the attention of all ranks by chasing an enemy machine down behind their lines until it crashed, & then moving away. They were within 500′ of the ground and fire was opened on them by the enemy. A portion of the Bn carried wire to the front line by night & the remainder were employed in salving materials of which there was a great deal lying about. Curiously enough the sector now held by the Bn was where the Bn transport was before the CAMBRAI show, the wired camps were to be seen all over the countryside some being in [illegible].	W. [illegible]

D. D. & L., London, E.C. (10340) Wt W5500/P713 750,000 3/18. E 2688 Forms/C2118/16.

Instructions regarding War Diaries and Intelligence Summaries are contained in F. S. Regs., Part II. and the Staff Manual respectively. Title pages will be prepared in manuscript.

Army Form C. 2118.

WAR DIARY
or
INTELLIGENCE SUMMARY.
(Erase heading not required.)

Place	Date	Hour	Summary of Events and Information	Remarks and references to Appendices
In the field.	17.8.18.		The enemy sent about 20 gas shells into the sunken road just behind Bn HQRs before stand to in the morning; for the remainder of the day there was absolute quietude. Working parties at night were engaged in repairing trenches, carrying materials, & general salving.	
	18.8.18.		The front line trenches were heavily bombarded by T.M's about 4. A.M. signifying a raid was in progress. The day was otherwise quiet. There were the usual working parties at night.	
	19.8.18		Another very quiet day in the Bn sector. Working parties were supplied at night for work with the Black Watch in the front line.	
	20.8.18.		Fire from enemy artillery was slightly increased during the day. Our machines were in great prominence throughout the day holding full sway of the upper world. There were the usual working parties at night. Rumours of an impending relief were circulated.	
	21.8.18.		The day passed quietly on the whole, at night the Bn relieved the 4/5 Black Watch in the front line being relieved in turn by the 8th Seaforths, as per Operation Orders attached. Definite instructions for a relief the following night were received & a reconnoitring party was despatched to investigate the new area (LOOS.) E.A. bombed WARLY [illegible] killing 5 horses. Presumably they were trying for tanks of which a number were passing through. 1 E.A. brought down in flames.	O.O. Nos 25 + 26 attached Appx No.S. VII + VIII. 15 Th[illegible]

Instructions regarding War Diaries and Intelligence Summaries are contained in F. S. Regs., Part II. and the Staff Manual respectively. Title pages will be prepared in manuscript.

WAR DIARY
or
INTELLIGENCE SUMMARY.
(Erase heading not required.)

Army Form C. 2118.

Place	Date	Hour	Summary of Events and Information	Remarks and references to Appendices
In the field.	22.8.18		The day passed quietly on the Bn front. At night the 31st Canadian Bn relieved our people, as per O.O. order attached. There was great bombing activity behind the lines, the enemy seemed to have got scent of our approaching attack. Our artillery had come up during the night behind the Ry embankment, camouflaged aeroplanes were also in position. Everything was ready for our attack the following morning. The Bn. moved back to [illegible], where the night was spent.	O.O. No 27 attached. Appx No. IX.
	23.8.18.		At 7 A.M. the Bn entrained for Fosse 10. near Cupigny where they arrived by 12 noon, spent the remainder of the day. There were no huts but bivouacs were provided. A list of Honours and Awards was published.	List of Hon. attached. Appx No. X.
	24.8.18.		The forenoon was spent in the camp. At 2.30. P.M. the Bn entrained at CUPIGNY for LA BREBIS en route for the HULLUCH sector of the line. This was reached [illegible] the relief of the 11th [illegible] completed by 8.30. P.M. The entraining pleased all ranks as no time was lost, the worst part of the relief was the distance the Bn had to march before arriving at their destination. The outgoing Bn cheered all ranks up by informing us that this was a quiet sector, the trenches were certainly fine specimens though a trifle wide. Every platoon had a dug out! The strange part about the line was the fact that it constituted the reserve line & main line of	O.O. No. 28 attached. Appx No. XI.

15th [illegible]

Army Form C. 2118.

Instructions regarding War Diaries and Intelligence Summaries are contained in F. S. Regs., Part II. and the Staff Manual respectively. Title pages will be prepared in manuscript.

WAR DIARY
or
INTELLIGENCE SUMMARY.
(Erase heading not required.)

Place	Date	Hour	Summary of Events and Information	Remarks and references to Appendices
In the field.	24.8.18.		resistance was held in this sector as the front line, the front line being merely patrolled.	
	25.8.18		As far as the enemy were concerned the day passed quietly but our artillery made three 2 hour concentrated shoots on the enemy to assist, as explained officially, another operation i.e. the attack on [illegible]. At 2. P.M. the fire increased to practically drum fire, shells of every calibre were sent over. The weather became stormy, though no rain fell.	
	26.8.18		Cloudy weather continued & little rain fell. The enemy retaliated a little for the previous days shelling & 3 men of "A" Coy were killed & 1 wounded by a direct hit on a trench near Quarry [illegible] where they had gone for rations. Work parties were busy at night in generally [illegible] repairing the trenches.	
	27.8.18		The weather became worse. Activity of all kinds was reduced. There was some more enemy retaliation for the bombardment on the 26th. A patrol reconnoitred the enemy front line at night & found no signs of the Boche. The trenches were very badly battered.	
	28.8.18		Another drizzly day little activity. 3 men of "B" Coy were wounded by a 4.2 direct hit in the early morning. In the afternoon the bn	[illegible]

Instructions regarding War Diaries and Intelligence Summaries are contained in F. S. Regs., Part II. and the Staff Manual respectively. Title pages will be prepared in manuscript.

WAR DIARY
or
INTELLIGENCE SUMMARY.
(Erase heading not required.)

Army Form C. 2118.

Place	Date	Hour	Summary of Events and Information	Remarks and references to Appendices
In the field	28.8.18		was relieved by the 4/5th Black Watch. "B", "C" & "D" Coys returned to MAZINGARBE & "A" Coy remained behind in Lone Locality. This Coy was joined by a Coy of the Seaforths who were holding the left sector of the line; the whole were placed under the command of Major Moffat D.S.O. The billets proved very comfortable & the village in extraordinary good condition considering the proximity of the line for the past 4 years.	O.O. No. attached 29/ Appx No: XI
	29.8.18		There were Coy inspections during the forenoon & general cleaning up, & in the afternoon the Bn were all bathed.	Awards No 55 attached Appx No XII.
[illegible]			Some more honours awards were announced, as per appendix.	
	30.8.18		There were the usual parades during the day & "C" Coy were suddenly warned to proceed up the line to reinforce the Lone Locality re-inforcement. This was because the G.O.C. had been up the line & considered the Bde reserve i.e. garrison of Lone Locality, not strong enough. In the evening the men amused themselves playing football. The weather turned colder & the heavens very cloudy.	Orders concerning "C" Coy attd. Appx No. XIII.
	31.8.18		Platoon parades or fine working parties was the order of the day. Dugouts were commenced round the huts where the Bn was billeted for refuge in case of bombing or shelling. All ranks were very elated with [illegible] news; the prophets becoming busy ending the war.	[signature]

Instructions regarding War Diaries and Intelligence Summaries are contained in F. S. Regs., Part II. and the Staff Manual respectively. Title pages will be prepared in manuscript.

WAR DIARY
or
INTELLIGENCE SUMMARY.
(Erase heading not required.)

Army Form C. 2118.

Place	Date	Hour	Summary of Events and Information	Remarks and references to Appendices
			Casualties from 1st to 31st August 1918.	
			2nd Lieut. Currie f Wounded gassed 18-8-18	
			No 201024 Pte Ironside J Wounded 22-8-18	
			3/6518 " McKenzie G Killed 21-8-18	
			5/13135 " Paton J do do	
			242108 " Taylor JP do do	
			42734 " Stevenson J Wounded do	
			42724 L/c Highland WJ do 27-8-18	
			22731 Pte Fyfe G do do	
			260250 " Youngs J do do	
			23091 McDonald J do 29-8-18	

D. D. & L., London, E.C.
(10340). Wt W5300/P713 750,000 3/18 E 2688 Forms/C2118/16.

Instructions regarding War Diaries and Intelligence Summaries are contained in F. S. Regs., Part II. and the Staff Manual respectively. Title pages will be prepared in manuscript.

WAR DIARY

or

~~INTELLIGENCE SUMMARY.~~

(Erase heading not required.)

Army Form C. 2118.

Place	Date	Hour	Summary of Events and Information	Remarks and references to Appendices

Strength during August 1918

Date	Increase	O	OR	Decrease	O	OR	O	OR
26/7/18	NIL			Wounded - Officers	9	-	45	947
				" - OR		245		
				Killed - Officers	2			
				" - OR		61		
				Missing - OR	-	44		
				Died of wounds	-	3		
				To Calais for postg to 1st Gordons	1			
2/8/18		-	-		12	353	33	594
	Taken on Strgth transferred from 9th Gordon High	-	1	Over 7 days in FA	-	22		
	Overestimated casualties -			Struck off strength classified B1. 2/Lt John Keir	1	-		
	Missing		7	Wounded -	1	-		
	Wounded		8	Wounded - Gassed	5	67		
	Killed		12					
	Reinf from Base		16					
9/8/18		-	44		7	89	26	549
	Reinf from Base	1	57	Over 7 days in FA	-	20		
	Taken on Str on being classified A (from 9th Scottish Churches)	-	2	Wounded	-	1		
				Taken on list of 44th Inf Bde	-	1		
16/8/18		1	59		-	22	27	586

Date	Increase	O	OR	Decrease	O	OR	O	OR
16/8/18							27	586
	Reinf from Base	7	226	Over 7 days in FA	-	5		
	Crossposted from 9th Gordon Highrs	4	-					
23/8/18		11	226		-	5	38	807
	Reinf from Base	2	8	Evacuated	1	21		
30/8/18		2	8		1	21	40	794

D. D. & L., London, E.C. (10340) Wt W3300/P713 750,000 3/18 E 2688 Forms/C2118/16.

[Not for publication or communication to the Press.]

Care must be taken that the information contained herein does not fall into the hands of the enemy.

General Headquarters,
British Armies in France,
11th. August, 1918.

No. ....

My dear Plumer,

The situation with regard to man-power has rendered it impossible to maintain all the units now in the field, and in consequence the Army Council have issued orders that a large number of battalions must be broken up. I wish, through you, to convey to the Commanders and all ranks of the battalions about to be disbanded my great regret that this step should have been found necessary.

I know how deeply officers and men will feel the severance of the ties binding them to the units in which they have served and fought with such splendid gallantry and success and with which they had hoped eventually to return home after the great struggle had been won and their task achieved. But I know also that since this reorganization has to be it will be accepted with the loyalty and devotion with which every trial has been met by British officers and men throughout the war.

Please convey to the officers and other ranks concerned, with my deep appreciation of their services in the past, my confidence that they will accept this disappointment in the right spirit and will give to their new units to which they are transferred the same devotion and esprit-de-corps that they gave to those they have been with until now.

Yours very truly
D. Haig.

Gen. Sir H. C. O. PLUMER,
G.C.B., G.C.M.G., G.C.V.O., A.D.C.,
Commanding Second Army.

8/10th. Battalion, Gordon Highlanders.

The Gordon Highrs
Operation Order No 20
By
Major J B Wood DSO MC Comdg
1st August 1918

1. The 44th Inf Bde will relieve the 46th Inf Bde in the line tonight

2. Dispositions
8th Seaforth Highrs on Left
4/5th Black Watch on Right
5th Gordon Highrs in Reserve

3 As soon as it is dusk Coys will withdraw to GMP Trench West of CROSS ROADS at D.6.0.2 (VIERZY CHARANTIGNY–CHAUDUN TIGNY CROSS ROADS) Battn H Qrs will be at Junction of Tract and Trench at point D. 3. 0. 2.
A Coy will be in Trench West of Bn H Qrs
B & D Coys in Trench East of Btt Qrs

4 Guides will meet Coys at the Cross Roads

5. Motor Ambulances are being sent up to LA RARER; tonight - All wounded not yet evacuated will be sent down by these Cars.

6 O.C. Coys. will report arrival in New Area to Bn. H. Qrs.

7 Acknowledge

G.P. Geddes Capt & Adjt
5th Battn, Gordon Hghrs

Secret

5 Gordon Highrs

Operation Order No 21

by

Major J.B. Wood DSO. Comdg.

4/8/18

1. The Bn will proceed by march route and bus today to the LAIGNEVILLE – MOGNEVILLE area.
Embussing point: W exit of SOUCY on the SOUCY-VIVIERES Road.
Time 12.20 pm.

2. The Bn will proceed ready to march off at 8.20 am. in the order Bn. HQ, D, A, B & C Coys.
Head of Column to be at Bn HQ facing West.
Route:- ST. PIERRE AIGLE – COEUVRES – SOUCY.

3. Intervals of 100 yds to be maintained between Coys and between units

4. Before marching off the Bn will be told off in parties of

2

in parties of 1 Officer or NCO and 20 ors.

5. Capt. F J C MOFFAT, DSO, will act as embussing Officer

6. Billeting party, at present at PIUSEUX, will embus at S. exit of SOUCY at 10 am.

7. Transport will move by march route in accordance with instructions issued to TO.

8 ACKNOWLEDGE

(Sgd) G P GEDDES
Capt & adj
5 Gordon Highrs

Copies to:-
Coys
Capt Moffat
QM & TO
RSM
WD & File

Instructions regarding War Diaries and Intelligence Summaries are contained in F. S. Regs., Part II. and the Staff Manual respectively. Title pages will be prepared in manuscript.

WAR DIARY
or
INTELLIGENCE SUMMARY.

(*Erase heading not required.*)

III.

Army Form C. 2118.

Place	Date	Hour	Summary of Events and Information	Remarks and references to Appendices

CASUALTIES from 1st to 4th AUGUST 1918

OTHER RANKS

August 1918.	Wded.	Gassed	Missg.	Wded Missg.	Killed	Wded (S.I.W)	Wded at duty	Total.
1st.	56	1	6		12			75
2nd.	-		-		-			-
3rd.	-	68.						68.
4th.		3						3
	56	72	6		12			146

OFFICERS.

		Date.
Killed.	NIL	
Wounded.		
Lieut.	J. T. Reid	1st.
"	G. M. Berry	1st.
"	J. E. Adam	1st.
2/Lieut.	G. A. Middleton	1st.
Gassed.		
Captain	W. S. Kemp M.C.	3rd.
Lieut.	D. A. D. Fraser	3rd.
2/Lieut.	J. M. Gill	3rd.
2/Lieut.	J. G. Insch M.M.	3rd.
2/Lieut.	J. T. Martin	3rd.

Killed.	Wded.	Gassed.	Total.
0	4.	5	9

A6945 Wt. W11422/M1160 350,000 12/16 D. D. & L. Forms/C./2118/14.

Army Form C. 2118.

Instructions regarding War Diaries and Intelligence Summaries are contained in F. S. Regs., Part II. and the Staff Manual respectively. Title pages will be prepared in manuscript.

WAR DIARY
or
INTELLIGENCE SUMMARY.
(*Erase heading not required.*)

Place	Date	Hour	Summary of Events and Information	Remarks and references to Appendices

CASUALTIES from 1st to 4th AUGUST 1918.

OTHER RANKS

August 1918.	Wded.	Gassed	Missg.	Wded Missg.	Killed	Wded (S.I.W.)	Wded at duty	Total.
1st.	56	1	6		12			75
2nd								
3rd		68.						68.
4th		3						3
	56	72	6		12			146

OFFICERS.

		Date.
Killed.	NIL	
Wounded.		
Lieut	J. T. Reid	1st.
"	G. M. Berry	1st.
"	J. E. Adams	1st.
2/Lieut	G. A. Middleton	1st.
Gassed.		
Captain	W. J. Kemp M.C.	3rd.
Lieut.	D. A. D. Fraser	3rd.
2/Lieut.	J. McGill	3rd.
2/Lieut	J. G. Inch M.M.	3rd.
2/Lieut	J. T. Martin	3rd.

Killed.	Wded.	Gassed	Total.
0	4.	5	9

D. D. & L., London, E.C. (10340) Wt W5300/P713 750,000 3/18 E 2688 Forms/C2118/16.

Instructions regarding War Diaries and Intelligence Summaries are contained in F. S. Regs., Part II. and the Staff Manual respectively. Title pages will be prepared in manuscript.

WAR DIARY
or
INTELLIGENCE SUMMARY.
(*Erase heading not required.*)

Army Form C. 2118.

Place	Date	Hour	Summary of Events and Information	Remarks and references to Appendices

CASUALTIES from 1st to 4th AUGUST 1918

OTHER RANKS

August 1918	Wdd	Gassed	Missg	Wded Missg	Killed	Wded [illegible]	Wded [illegible]	Total
1st	56	1	6		12			75
2nd								
3rd		68						68
4th		3						3
	56	72	6		12			146.

OFFICERS

		Date
Killed	Nil	
Wounded		
Lieut	J. J. Reid	1st
"	[illegible] M. Berry	1st
"	[illegible] Adams	1st
2/Lieut	C. G. [illegible]	1st
Gassed		
Captain	R. [illegible] M.C.	3rd
Lieut	[illegible]	3rd
2/Lieut	J. M. [illegible]	3rd
2/Lieut	[illegible] M.M.	3rd
2/Lieut	J. [illegible] Martin	3rd

Killed	Wded	Gassed	Total
0	4	5	9

D. D. & L., London, E.C. (10340) Wt W5300/P713 750,000 3/18 E 2688 Forms/C2118/16.

Xe ARMÉE

ETAT-MAJOR

3e BUREAU

—:—

Au Q. G. A., le 5 Août 1918.

III.

Au Q. G. A., 5th August 1918.

ORDRE GÉNÉRAL N° 343

OFFICIERS, SOUS-OFFICIERS ET SOLDATS DES 15e ET 34e DIVISIONS BRITANNIQUES.

Vous êtes entrés dans la bataille à son moment le plus rude. L'ennemi vaincu une première fois, ramenait contre nous ses meilleures divisions, en nombre plus considérable que les nôtres.

Vous avez continué à avancer pied à pied, malgré sa résistance acharnée, et vous avez gardé le terrain conquis, malgré ses violentes contre-attaques.

Puis dans la journée du 1er Août, vous avez enlevé, côte à côte avec vos camarades Français, la crête qui domine toute la contrée entre l'AISNE et l'OURCQ, et que ses défenseurs avaient l'ordre de tenir coûte que coûte.

Ayant échoué dans sa tentative pour la reprendre avec ses dernières réserves, l'ennemi dut battre en retraite, poursuivi, bousculé, pendant 12 kilomètres.

Tous, Anglais et Ecossais, jeunes soldats et vétérans des FLANDRES ou de PALESTINE, vous avez montré les magnifiques qualités de votre race, le courage et l'impertubable ténacité.

Vous avez fait l'admiration de vos compagnons d'armes. Votre pays sera fier de vous, car vos chefs et vous avez eu une large part dans la victoire que nous venons de remporter sur les barbares ennemis des peuples libres.

Je suis heureux d'avoir combattu à votre tête et je vous remercie.

ORDRE GENERAL N° 343

OFFICERS, NON COMMISSIONNED OFFICERS AND MEN OF THE 15th AND 34th BRITISH DIVISIONS.

You entered the battle at its fiercest moment. The enemy, already once vanquished, again brought up against us his best divisions, considerably outnumbering our own.

You continued to advance step by step, in spite of his desperate resistance, and you held the ground won in spite of his violent counter-attacks.

Then, during the whole day of the 1st of August, side by side with your French comrades, you stormed the ridge dominating the whole country between the AISNE and the OURCQ, wich the defenders had received orders to hold at all cost.

Having failed in his attempt to retake the ridge with his last reserves, the enemy had to beat a retreat pursued and harassed for 12 kilometers.

All of you, English and Scottish, young soldiers and veterans of FLANDERS and PALESTINE, you have shown the magnificent qualities of your race : courage and imperturbable tenacity.

You have won the admiration of your companions in arms. Your country will be proud of you for to your chiefs and to you is due a large share in the victory that we have gained over the barbarous enemies of the free.

I am happy to have fought at your head and I thank you.

MANGIN.

V

Secret.

The Gordon Highlanders.

OPERATION ORDER No.22.
By
Major J.B.Wood,D.S.O.,M.C. Comdg.
6th August,1918.

1. The 5th Gordon Highlanders will move by train from present area to First Army Area to-morrow, August 7th.
   Entraining Station :- POINT ST. MAXENCE.
   Time of Entrainment:- 5.30.A.M. 7th August.
   Time of Journey :- 8 - 10 Hours.

2. The Battalion will parade, ready to march off, at 2.40.A.M. in the order :-
   Battalion Headquarters,
   Pipers and Drummers,
   D,C,B,A, Companies,
   Transport.
   Head of Column to be at Church, facing North East.

3. DRESS : Full marching order. Tam O'Shanters will be worn.

4. BILLETING PARTY. - As per Billeting Order issued to-day.

5. The unexpended portion of the day's rations will be carried on the man.
   Dixies will be taken on the train.
   Rations for the 7th instant will be issued at the Station.

6. ACKNOWLEDGE.

Captain & Adjutant,

5th Battalion, The Gordon Highlanders.

Distribution :-
Copies 1 - 4 : O.C.Coys.
5 : 2nd in Command.
6 : Qr.Mr.
7 : T.O.
8 : I.O.
9 : R.S.M.
10 : W.D.
11 : File.
12 : 2/Lt. Irvine,M.C.

6th August
1918.

<u>Secret.</u>

Arrangements for MOVE (issued in
Conjunction with Operation Order No.22.)

---

1. Officers' valises will be ready for loading and dumped at Officers' Messes by 6. P.M.
T.O. will send round G.S.Wagons to collect.

2. Officers' Mess Kits will be collected by the Mess cart at 9.30.P.M.

3. Lewis Guns and Drums etc., will be loaded by 6.P.M.

4. <u>Reveille</u> : 1.30.A.M.
<u>Breakfasts</u> will be served at the Station.

6th August, 1918. (Signed) G.P.Geddes, Captain & Adjutant,
5th Battalion, The Gordon Highlanders.

<u>Distribution</u> :-
Copies 1 - 4 : O.C.Coys.
5 : H.Qrs.Mess.
6 : Qr.Mr.
7 : T.O.
8 : R.S.M.

VI

The Gordon Highlanders.
BATTALION ORDER No. 51.
By
Major J.B.Wood,D.S.O.,M.C. Cmdg.
12th August, 1918.

1. Orderly Officer to-morrow - 2/Lieut. J.T.Currie.
Next for Duty " " James Keir.

2. DETAIL FOR TO-MORROW

Reveille	7.00 am.	Dinners	12.30 pm.
Breakfast	7.30 am.	Guard-mounting & Retreat ..	6.00 pm.
Sick Parade	8.00 am.	Staff Parade	9.30 pm.
Orderly Room.	12 noon	Lights Out	9.45 pm.

3. Parades.

8.30 am. - 9.00 am.	Platoon Inspections.
9.00 am. - 9.45 am.	Section and Platoon Drill.
10.00 am. - 11.0 am.	Lecture to Battalion by Divisional Gas Officer, followed by inspection of Box Respirators, and Gas Drill. Companies will parade for this lecture in same field as Church Parade was held. Any available time up till 12 noon will be devoted to Physical Training.
2.00 pm	Demonstration of Inspection of Platoon by 2nd in Command, on "C" Coys parade ground. O.C. "C" Coy will provide a platoon 20 strong. All Officers will attend.

All Battalion and Company Signallers and Battalion Runners will parade under the Signalling Officer at Orderly Room at 9 am until 10 am when they will parade with their Companies to attend Gas Lecture.

4. Honours and Awards.

The C.O., is pleased to announce the following awards:-

Legion of Honour and Croix de Guerre with Palms.

Captain & Adjutant G.P.Geddes, D S.O.

Medaille Militaire and Croix de Guerre with Palms.
S/13186 Sgt. J.Iveson. "D" Coy.
2021 " W.Raphel. "D" "

Croix de Guerre with Palms.
Major J.B.Wood, D.S.O., M.C.
2/Lieut. I.M.Gill.
3/6583 Sgt. J.Urquhart. "C" Coy.
S/13308 L/C J.Mercer. "C" "

Croix de Guerre with Star.
3/6678 Sgt. H.Leith. "B" Coy.
242305 Cpl. A.Easton. "C" "
267172 Pte. W.Inkster. "C" "
240341 L/C. C.Greig. "D" " (Tpt.)

WAR DIARY.

SECRET

5th BATTN. THE GORDON HIGHLANDERS.

OPERATION ORDER No. 24.

By

Lt. Col. J. B. WOOD, D.S.O., M.C. Cmdg.

15th August, 1918.

1. The 44th Highland Brigade will relieve the 167th Infy, Bde, in the line to-night, August, 15th/16th.
   5th Gordon Highlanders will relieve the 7th Middlesex Regt., in Support.

2. The Battalion will move by Light Railway.
   Entraining point :- Road spur, 600 yards W of HERMAVILLE.
   Capacity of a truck :- 27.
   Detraining point :- WAILLY.

   Battalion will parade, ready to move off, at 4.50 pm in the order, Battn. Hd qrs., Band, D, C, B, A, Coys. Head of column to be at the junction of BLACK WATCH and ABERCROMBIE STREETS ("C" Coys billets)

3. Lewis Guns and drums, dixies, Signalling gear, mess kits, etc, will be loaded on limbers at O.R. by 4 pm, and conveyed to the Station.
   Limbers will be at the detraining Point to carry these to the line.

4. Further orders will be issued at the detraining point.
   Guides. 2 per Battn. Hdqrs. 1 per Coy Hdqrs, and 1 per Platoon will meet the Battalion at the detraining point.

5. All defence schemes, maps and stores will be taken over and receipts given. Lists will reach Battn. Hdqrs. by 10 am 16th.

6. Completion of relief to be wired at once to Battn. Hdqrs. H. 16. d. 9. 6. by code words "G. 15 received"

7. ACKNOWLEDGE.

(Signed) G, P, Geddes, Capt & Adjt.
5th Battn. The Gordon Highlanders.

Distribution :-
Copies 1 - 4 O.C. Coys.
5, L.G.O. 6, R.S.M.

7. Signals, 8,

SECRET

VII.

5th Battalion, The Gordon Highlanders

OPERATION ORDER No. 25.

By

Lt. Col. J.B.WOOD, D.S.O., M.C. Cmdg.

20th August,
1918

1 The 8th Seaforth Highlanders will relieve the 5th Gordon Highlanders to-morrow, 21st August, 1918. On relief the 5th Gordon Highlanders will relieve the 4/5th Black Watch in the front line in accordance with O.O. No 26.

2 Dispositions:

"A" Coy Gordons will be relieved by "D" Coy Seaforths.
"D" " " " " " " "B" " Gordons.
"C" " " " " " " "C" " Seaforths.
"B" " " " " " " "B" " "
Battn. Hdqrs. " " " " Battn. Hdqrs. Seaforths.

"A" Coy. Seaforths will not relieve any Company of Gordons, and will require no guides.

"B" Coy. Gordons require no guides.

Relief will be carried out in the above order and must be completed by 8.30 pm.

3 Guides.

1 per platoon, 1 per Coy H.Q. from each of "A", "B" & "C" Coys and 1 for Battn H.Q. will rendezvous under Lt. Macdonald at the Junction of TELEGRAPH HILL SWITCH AND DAB LANE (M.16.b.2.0) at 7.15 pm.

4 All movement will be by trenches. The greatest care must be taken to avoid the relief being observed by the enemy.

5. All trench stores, tools, petrol tins, defence schemes etc., will be handed over and receipts forwarded to O.R. by 9 am, 22nd.

6 Completion of relief will be wired to Battn. H.Q. by the Code Words "Your GH/20 received".

7 ACKNOWLEDGE.

G.P. Geddes
Capt & Adjt.,
5th Battn. The Gordon Highlanders.

Distribution

Copies Nos 1 – 4 O.C. Coys.
No 5 I.O.
6 Signals
7 R.S.M.
8 8th Seaforths
9 Details
10 War Diary
11 File

SECRET

5th Battn, The Gordon Highlanders.

OPERATION ORDER No 26

BY

Lt. Col. W. B. WOOD, D.S.O, M.C. Cmdg.

20th August, 1918

1 The 5th Gordon Highlanders will relieve the 4/5th Black Watch in the front line, Right Brigade, to-morrow night, 21st/22nd August.

2 Dispositions:

"A" Coy. Gordons will relieve "D" Coy Black Watch in the right front

"D" " " " " "C" " " " " " Centre Front.

"C" " " " " "A" & "B" " " " " Left Front.

"B" " " " " "D" Coy Gordons and become Reserve Coy.

Battn. Hdqrs. " " " Battn. Hdqrs. Black Watch at (M.22.d.0.1)

3 Guides:

To be arranged between O.C. Coys concerned. Time 9 pm.

4 Advanced party of 1 Officer and 1 N.C.O., per Coy. and 1 N.C.O. from Battn. Hdqrs. will proceed to take over stores and accommodation etc, before 6 pm.

5 Trench stores, esplosive stores, tools, petrol tins, defence schemes, maps etc, will be taken over and receipts forwarded to O.R. by 9 am, 22nd.

6 Completion of relief to be reported to Battn. Headqrs. by Code Words "BUNG-OH".

7 ACKNOWLEDGE.

G P Geddes
Capt & Adjt.
5th Bn. Gordon Highlanders.

Distribution.
Copies 1 - 4 O.C. Coys
5 I.O.
6 Signals
7 R.S.M, 8 8th Black Watch, 9 Details
10 War Diary, 11 File.

SECRET

5th Battn, The Gordon Highlanders
OPERATION ORDER No. 27
by
Lt. Col. J. E. WOOD, D.S.O., M.C. Comdg.

22nd August, 1918.

1 The 5th Gordon Highlanders will be relieved in the front line tonight, 22nd/23rd August, by the 31st Canadian Battalion.
The destination of Battalion after relief, will be notified later.

2 Dispositions:

	Canadians										
1 Coy.	Canadians	will	take	over	from	"A"	Coy	Gordons	(Right Front)
1 "	"	"	"	"	"	"B"	"	"	(Centre Front)
1 "	"	"	"	"	"	"C"	"	"	(Left Front)
2 Platoons	"	"	"	"	"	"D"	"	"	(Reserve)

Battn. Hdqrs. Canadians will be at present Support Battn. Hdqrs. M. 16. d. 9. 5.

3 Guides.

1 guide per platoon, 1 per Coy Hdqrs, and 2 for Battn. Hdqrs. will rendezvous at Battn. Hdqrs. at 8 pm under 2nd Lt. R. B. Strathdee. Guides will then proceed to Bde. Hdqrs. where they will meet the incoming Battalion at 8.30 pm.

4 All defence schemes, maps, aeroplane photographs, trench stores, petrol tins, etc, will be handed over and receipts forwarded to Orderly Room, by 12 noon, 23rd inst.

5 1 limber per Coy and 2 for Battn. Hdqrs. will be at their respective Coy. Hdqrs. and at Battn. Hdqrs. at 9.15 pm to convey Lewis Guns and drums, signalling gear, dixies, Officers' mess kits etc, to billets.

6 Completion of relief will be reported to Battn. Hdqrs. by wire by the Code Words "NO CAN DO". Arrival at Billets will also be reported.

7 ACKNOWLEDGE.

Capt & Adjt.
5th Battn. The Gordon Highlanders.

Distribution

Copies 1 - 4 O. C. Coys.
5 L. G. O.
6 R. S. M.
7 T. O. & Q. M.
8 31st Canadian Battn.
9 M. O.
10 File.
11 Signals.

8. HONOURS AND AWARDS.

Under authority granted by His Majesty the King, the Field Marshall C. in C, has awarded the Military Cross to the undermentioned Officers for gallantry in action.

The Commanding Officer expresses his congratulations to the recipients.

Lieut. R.W.Youngson.
2/Lt. F.W.Lovie.

The undermentioned N.C.O's and men have been awarded decorations for acts of gallantry in the field.

The Commanding Officers expresses his congratulations to the recipients.

Military Medal.

5140	Cpl.	J.Peart.	
202494	Pte. (L/C)	F.Harrison.	
S/8890	Pte.	W.Ballantyne.	
S/7065	Pte. (L/C)	R.Clague.	
41090	Pte.	A.Fraser.	
266529	"	W. Will.	
241229	"	J.Sutherland.	
26598	" (L/C)	G.Watt.	(Attd. T.M.B.)

Officers Commanding Companies will ensure that the awards of French decorations for recent operations in the French Ara.are duly recorded in the A.B.64 of the recipient.

(Signed) G.P.Geddes, Capt & Adjt,
5th Battalion, The Gordon Highlanders.

War Diary

SECRET

XI.

5th Battn. The Gordon Highlanders.

OPERATION ORDER No. 28.

By

Lt.Col. J.B.[illegible], D.S.O., M.C., Cmdg.

24th August, 1918.

1. The 5th Gordon Highlanders will relieve the 11th Manchester Regiment in the Right Sub-sector of the [illegible] (Right) Sector, to-day, 24th August.

2. Dispositions.

"B" Coy. Gordons will relieve "P" Coy. Manchesters in the Right Front. Coy.H.Q. Q.30.b.55.55
"D" " " " " "S" Coy. Manchesters in the Right Centre. Coy. H.Q. Q.30.b.40.80
"A" " " " " "Q" " Manchesters in the Left Centre. Coy.H.Q. Q.24.b.20.05
"C" " " " " "R" " Manchesters in the Left Front. Coy.H.Q. Q.24.b.55.55.
Bn.H.Q. " " " Bn.H.Q. Manchesters at Q.24.c.0.3. (Junction of PONT ST. and CURZON ST.)

Relief will be carried out in the above order.

3. Guides.
1 per platoon and 1 for Bn.H.Q. will be at WELLINGTON POST, Q.25.b.2.2. at 3.30 pm.

4. Battalion will parade ready to march off in the order indicated in para. 2 at 2 pm, and march to the entraining point, CUP SIDING, Q.11.d.7.8.
Entraining will commence at 2.30 pm.
O.C.Coys. and L.G.O. will arrange to reconnoitre the route to this point.

Detraining Point. BULLY GRENAY BRIDGE, R.2.c.0.2.
There will be five trains per Battn., of 6 trucks each.
Accommodation for 30 per truck.

Route from Detraining Point. Via side of Railway to WELLINGTON POST. Trench to be entered at Q.26.a.6.8, thence via Q.20.d.2.8 - NORTHERN UP - VILLAGE LINE SWITCH.

5. All movement to the Entraining Point will be by Companies at 100 yards interval.
East of BRACQUEMONT - platoons at 200 yards interval.
East of WELLINGTON POST - Sections at 50 yards interval.

6. All trench stores, defence schemes, maps, air photographs etc., will be taken over and carefully checked. Receipts will be forwarded to O.R. by 6 am August, 25th.

7. Completion of relief will be reported to Bn. H.Q. by the code words "SAD NEWS".

8. ACKNOWLEDGE.

(Signed) G.F.Geddes, Capt., & Adjt.
5th Battn. The Gordon Highlanders.

Distribution.
Copies 1 - 4✓: O.C.Coys.
5✓: I.O. 6✓ L.G.O.
7✓ 2nd in command. 8✓ Q.M. 9✓ T.O. 10✓ R.S.M. 11✓ Signals.
12✓: 11th Manchesters. 13 : War Diary. 14 : File.

Issued through Signals 11 am.

War Diary

SECRET

XI A.

5th. BATTN. THE GORDON HIGHLANDERS

Operation Order No. 29
by
Lieut-Colonel J. E. Wood, D.S.O., M.C., Comdg.

27th. August 1918

1 The 5th. Gordon Highlanders will be relieved by the 4/5th. Black Watch in the Right Sub-section of the Right Sector tomorrow 28th. Aug. On relief the 5th. Gordon Highlanders will become Support Battn. and be disposed as follows:-
B & D Coys. MAZINGARBE.
A Coy. TENTH AVENUE from NORTHERN SAP to QUARRY DUMP. Coy. H.Q. G.23.b.4.
C Coy. LONE TRENCH, Coy. H.Q. G.17.d.o.1.
Bn. H.Q. G.22.b.95.75.

Altered see further War Diary. BJhl

2 Dispositions
B Coy. Gordons will be relieved by D Coy. B.W. (Rt. Front)
D " " " " " " C " " (Rt. Centre)
A " " " " " " B " " (Left Centre)
C " " " " " " A " " (Left Front)

3 Guides
For D Coy. B.W. - at Junction of CHALK PIT ALLEY & TENTH AV. at 6 p.m.
" C " " - " " " POSEN ALLEY " " " at 6 p.m.
" B " " - " " " VENDIN ALLEY " " " at 5.30 pm
" A " " - " " " VENDIN ALLEY " " " at 5.45 pm
1 guide per platoon and 1 per Coy. H.Q. No guide required for Bn. H.Q. 1 Officer to be in charge of each Coy's guides. Guides must reconnoitre routes beforehand.

4 Advanced parties.
A & C Coys: 1 Officer per Coy. and 1 N.C.O. per platoon will report to their opposite Coy. H.Q's before 2.30 p.m.
B & D Coys: 2 N.C.O's per Coy. will report to 2/Lt. STRATHDEE at Bn. H.Q. at 11 a.m. and proceed to Rear H.Q. MAZINGARBE.

5 All trench stores, defence schemes, work in progress etc. will be handed over and taken over and receipts forwarded to O.R. by 10 a.m. 29th. August.

6 Completion of relief will be reported to Bn. H.Q. by the Code Words "GOOD NEWS". Arrival in new area will also be reported.

7 Acknowledge.

G.A. Geddie

Capt. & Adjt.
5th. Battn. The Gordon Highlanders.

Distribution
1 - 4: Coys.
5: 2nd. in Command
6: M.O.
7: Signals
8: Q.M. & T.O.
9: R.S.M.
10: 4/5th B. W.
11: W.D.
12: File

XII.

6. EXTENSION OF LEAVE.

O.C.Coys will bring to the notice of all ranks that applications for extension of leave should be addressed to the Officer in Charge of Records, PERTH, or to the WAR OFFICE, LONDON. On no account should they be addressed to the Commanding Officer of the Battalion.

7. HONOURS AND AWARDS.

The undermentioned Officer has been awarded the MILITARY CROSS for acts of gallantry in the field.

Lieut. J.T.Reid.

The undermentioned N.C.O's and man, have been granted the following awards for acts of gallantry in the field.

DISTINGUISHED CONDUCT MEDAL

No. 3/13186 Sgt. Iveson, J.
" 2021 " Raphael, W.

BAR TO MILITARY MEDAL.

No. 242456 Pte. Thomson, D. M.M.

8. POTATOES - THEFT OF.

XVII Corps R.O. 837 is republished for information:-
"A large number of claims have been received from the
"inhabitants for potatoes alleged to have been stolen
"by British soldiers.
"In future the offence of theft of potatoes or other
"vegetables from inhabitants will be severely dealt with.
"This order is to be repeated in the orders of all units".

9. PHOTOGRAPHY.

No Officer, soldier or other person subject to Military Law is permitted to be in possession of a camera or to take photographs unless he has been issued with the necessary permit signed by the Adjutant General. Such permits are only granted in very exceptional cases.

This order will be promulgated to all troops arriving in this country, and will be republished periodically in the orders of units.

Any Officer or soldier or other person subject to Military Law who disobeys this order will be placed in arrest and the case will be reported to the Headquarters of the Army or Lines of Communication Area.

10. DEFENCE AGAINST GAS.

Casualties were recently caused to troops in billets owing to their having left their small box respirators in huts. The shells in this instance were Yellow Cross 1 with apparently the same proportion of H.E. as an ordinary shell. Troops should be warned against judging gas shells by their low burst. On the

War Diary

SECRET

XIII.

O.C.
"A", "B", "C" & "D" Coys.,
Q.M. & R.S.M.

1. "C" Coy less 1 platoon will move up to-night to [illegible] Avenue. Move to be completed by 10 pm.
On completion of this move, "C" Coy will come under command of Major F.J.O.Moffat, D.S.O., M.C., [illegible] LOCALITY, who will arrange accommodation.

2. "C" Coy will parade ready to march off at 8 pm.

<u>Route.</u> PHILOSOPHE - LAMBERT TRACK - [illegible] TRENCH.

<u>Intervals.</u> 100 yards between platoons.

3. A limber will be at "C" Coys huts at 7.30 pm to convey Lewis Guns, dixies, mess kits etc., to the end of [illegible] TRENCH.

4. Completion of move will be reported to Major Moffat.

(Signed) C.F.[illegible], Capt., & Adjt,
5th Battalion, The Gordon Highlanders.

30th August, 1918.

Lieut. Colonel.

CONFIDENTIAL.

Vol 41

WAR DIARY

FOR

THE MONTH OF

SEPTEMBER

1918

VOLUME No. 41

D. G. Gordon. Lieut-Colonel,
Commanding 5th Battalion, The Gordon Highlanders.

Instructions regarding War Diaries and Intelligence Summaries are contained in F. S. Regs., Part II. and the Staff Manual respectively. Title pages will be prepared in manuscript.

WAR DIARY
or
INTELLIGENCE SUMMARY.
(Erase heading not required.)

Army Form C. 2118.

Place	Date	Hour	Summary of Events and Information	Remarks and references to Appendices
In the field.	1.9.18		The battalion paraded for Divine Service in the morning the remainder of the day was observed as a holiday. A party of officers & N.C.O's went up the line to reconnoitre the sector the bn was to move into the following day.	
	2.9.18.		The forenoon was devoted to baths and the afternoon the bn moved up to the left sector of the brigade to relieve the 8th Seaforths, as per O.O. No. 30 attached. Bn HQrs was located in Tenth Avenue from there forward all movement was done by tunnels, which are lighted up with electric lights all the way. "C" Coy took over HAY LOCALITY in the front line, "A" Coy were in immediate support, "B" Coy were in reserve in TENTH AVENUE, & "D" Coy were on detachment in LONE LOCALITY. The accommodation was very good throughout all ranks were very cheered with the prospects. Bn order No. 60 giving list of promotions etc is attached.	O.O. No. 30. attached. Appx No. I. Bn order No. 60. attd. Appx No. II.
	3.9.18		The day passed quietly enough, but a general state of alarm existed as the enemy were believed to be withdrawing [illegible]	[illegible]

Army Form C. 2118.

Instructions regarding War Diaries and Intelligence Summaries are contained in F. S. Regs., Part II. and the Staff Manual respectively. Title pages will be prepared in manuscript.

WAR DIARY
or
INTELLIGENCE SUMMARY.

(Erase heading not required.)

Place	Date	Hour	Summary of Events and Information	Remarks and references to Appendices
In the field.	3.9.18.		to withdraw on this front because of the operations north & south of him in this sector. The outcome of this was that strong enterprising patrols were to be sent out to try & establish touch with him. He certainly did not appear to be in position in either his front or support lines, & GREASE TRENCH appeared to be his nearest habitation.	
	4.9.18		There was quite a lot of enemy movement to be observed throughout the day & some felt that he had not at present vacated his forward areas. Otherwise the day passed quietly with occasional shelling & at night a little livelier M.G. activity. Patrols were active all night on the bn front as well as on the fronts of the left (8th A & S.H.) & right (4/5 B.W.) battalions. All reported enemy in position though not in his front positions. O.O. No 31 issued in case of an advance by the bn.	O.O. No. 31 attached Appx No. [illegible]
	5.9.18.		As there still was no positive information concerning the enemy a small raiding party was prepared to visit the X roads at H.13.c.7.5, S.W. of HULLUCH church, where some work	[illegible]

Instructions regarding War Diaries and Intelligence Summaries are contained in F. S. Regs., Part II. and the Staff Manual respectively. Title pages will be prepared in manuscript.

WAR DIARY
or
INTELLIGENCE SUMMARY.
(Erase heading not required.)

Army Form C. 2118.

Place	Date	Hour	Summary of Events and Information	Remarks and references to Appendices
In the field.	5.9.18.		had been reported to be in progress the two previous nights. The operation was to be supported by a Stokes bombardment under the command of 2/Lt. Law of "C" Coy, zero hour was fixed at 10 P.M. The operation came off successfully but no enemy were to be seen, the party received no molestation whatsoever.	O.O. No 32 attached. Appx. No IV.
	6.9.18		The Black Watch on our right were to raid a German post dugout post on the north side of POSEN LOCALITY, our people had to participate by sending out a strong reconnoitring patrol between HICKS + HANDON Alleys supported by a Stokes mortar bombardment. The operation came off at 10 P.M. but neither party had any success. The Artillery barrage was excellent, the enemy retaliation rather heavy, shells of all calibres being fired principally on the tunnel entrances.	
	7.9.18		The weather turned wet, stormy showers, heavy showers of rain came down. Two patrols were out during the early part of the night one on the [illegible] [illegible] to the south side of the	[illegible]

WAR DIARY
or
INTELLIGENCE SUMMARY.
(Erase heading not required.)

Army Form C. 2118.

Instructions regarding War Diaries and Intelligence Summaries are contained in F. S. Regs., Part II. and the Staff Manual respectively. Title pages will be prepared in manuscript.

Place	Date	Hour	Summary of Events and Information	Remarks and references to Appendices
In the field	7.9.18		craters in front of HAY LOCALITY. Reports confirmed the suspicions that the enemy did not hold either of his two front lines and that GREASE TRENCH was his first line of resistance.	
	8.9.18.		The day commenced with a raid at 1 A.M. by the 13th Royal Scots on our left; for the rest the day passed peacefully. Four patrols went out at night on a patrol scheme intending the third enemy line was to be reconnoitred for practically the whole distance on the Bn. front. The three southern patrols were unable to secure their objectives because of a party of 30 of the enemy who were directly in their way, the patrol furthest north moved up to the trench (GREASE) but was unable to enter it owing to strong wire. It was however discovered to be occupied. Lord Dudley Gordon assumed command of the Battn.	
	9.9.18		Another wet squally day. An inter company relief took place in the afternoon "C" Coy in the front line being relieved by "B", returning to 10th AVENUE, "A" Coy relieved by "B" returning to LONE LOCALITY.	O.O. No 275 attached. Appx No. V. [illegible signature]

D. D. & L., London, E.C. (10340) Wt W5300/P713 750,000 3/18 E 2688 Forms/C2118/16.

Instructions regarding War Diaries and Intelligence Summaries are contained in F. S. Regs., Part II. and the Staff Manual respectively. Title pages will be prepared in manuscript.

WAR DIARY
or
INTELLIGENCE SUMMARY.
(Erase heading not required.)

Army Form C. 2118.

Place	Date	Hour	Summary of Events and Information	Remarks and references to Appendices
In the field.	10.9.18		Patrolling at night was the only activity. A patrol to the [illegible] of the craters discovered rather an interesting [illegible] those lying in the Mains Lane with a fairly taut wire running [illegible] from the enemy lines. The patrol were suspicious of this & [illegible] marking the spot with a newspaper. They [illegible] to be some diabolical device of the enemy's, preferred to leave it to professional [illegible] inspection. Instructions were received that	Bde O.O. No 30[illegible].
	10.9.18		the 45th Bde on our left was to move forward to occupy the enemy forward positions and we were to extend our line to the left.	Appx No VI
	11.9.18		An extension as per appendix attached was made in the forenoon, the frontage covered by the Bn. now being about 2000 yds. "A" Coy moved to the extreme left from LONE LOCALITY, where they relieved a coy of the Royal Scots (see Appx) in the crater land E of the QUARRIES. We now held with 6 platoons what the Royal Scots manned with a strong coy.	O.O. No 36 attached Appx No VII. R.S. O.O. attached Appx No VIII

D. D. & L., London, E.C. (10340) Wt W5300/1713 750,000 3/18 E 2688 Forms/C2118/16.

Instructions regarding War Diaries and Intelligence Summaries are contained in F. S. Regs., Part II. and the Staff Manual respectively. Title pages will be prepared in manuscript.

WAR DIARY
or
INTELLIGENCE SUMMARY.
(Erase heading not required.)

Army Form C. 2118.

Place	Date	Hour	Summary of Events and Information	Remarks and references to Appendices
In the field.	11.9.18		the whole of 'A' & 1/2 'B' being called upon to do this. Later instructions were received to prepare to push out posts at dawn the following morning to form a defensive flank for the Royl Scots, who were establishing themselves to the E & N.E. of the QUARRIES. We had to string out posts from DEVON LOCALITY to the N corner of the QUARRIES (Ref. & map of QUARRIES attached)	Map of QUARRIES attached. Appx No. VIII A
	12.9.18		The operation came off about 4.30 A.M. after a heavy fall of rain during the night, the objectives were all secured though we were not able to establish the post intended in GRASSE TR; because of stiff opposition from the enemy whose presence was not quite expected where he showed himself to be. The Royl Scots were also reported to have established their posts & the QUARRIES were in our hands. Everything remained peaceful until the afternoon when a barrage was opened on the new posts. Enemy bombers came forward. From thence onwards there was fluctuating fighting, our people were constantly moving forward & being driven back, until finally at nightfall our people	[illegible signature]

Instructions regarding War Diaries and Intelligence Summaries are contained in F. S. Regs., Part II. and the Staff Manual respectively. Title pages will be prepared in manuscript.

WAR DIARY
or
INTELLIGENCE SUMMARY.
(Erase heading not required.)

Army Form C. 2118.

Place	Date	Hour	Summary of Events and Information	Remarks and references to Appendices
In the field	12.9.18		were all back in our front line though the Royal Scots reported that their posts were still in position. Orders were received from Brigade to reoccupy these posts. For this purpose "A" Coy & ½ of "B" Coy were detailed, the remainder of the Bn. less one Coy (D) returning to MAZINGARBE upon relief by the 15th Black Watch. The men were all very tired through but cheerfully submitted to the fresh operation. The rain and ground [illegible] made the conditions very trying. The whole of this operation was performed by the men of what is known as "Peaceful Penetration".	
	13.9.18		Except for heavy shelling on the newly occupied posts the day passed without further incident. Lt Bean was killed in the morning by a shell in DEVON LOCALITY where his platoon had taken up their positions. The command of the sector passed to the O.C. Black Watch at mid day. The remainder of the Bn were relieved at night & returned to MAZINGARBE.	
	14.9.18		Bn. had baths & spent the day in cleaning up with a few short Coy parades. Everybody much elated with the news of ally	

D. D. & L., London, E.C. (10540) Wt W5300/P713 750,000 3/18 E 2888 Forms/C2118/16.

Instructions regarding War Diaries and Intelligence Summaries are contained in F. S. Regs., Part II. and the Staff Manual respectively. Title pages will be prepared in manuscript.

WAR DIARY
or
INTELLIGENCE SUMMARY.
(Erase heading not required.)

Army Form C. 2118.

Place	Date	Hour	Summary of Events and Information	Remarks and references to Appendices
In the field	14.9.18.		American advances down in the St MIHIEL salient.	
	15.9.18		Church parade in the morning. Orders received for training with tanks on the morrow.	Appx No. IX.
	16.9.18		The Bn were up early to move to MARQUEFELLES FARM, where the practice attack was to take place. The object of the scheme was to show us the limitations of a tank & how the infantry & tanks should cooperate to make an attack successful. This proved very instructive though the scheme was rather too ambitious for the state of training the men were in. The operation was done in the forenoon & then again after the dinner hour, when the Corps Commander (Gen. Holland. 1st Corps) was present. Bn returned to billets at C.R.M. after having spent a very enjoyable day in the best of autumn weather.	Bn operation order No 38 attached. Appx No. 10.
	17.9.18		Relieved the Seaforths in the right sector of the Bde. "D" Coy moving into HAY LOCALITY, "B" into M. L. of R., "C" into 10th AVENUE, "A" into LONE LOCALITY. This was exactly the sect. we occupied last time when we moved in, & now we found it the right sector of the Bde, whereas when we came into this [illegible]	O.O. No. 38A. attached Appx No. XI. [illegible]

Instructions regarding War Diaries and Intelligence Summaries are contained in F. S. Regs., Part II. and the Staff Manual respectively. Title pages will be prepared in manuscript.

WAR DIARY
or
INTELLIGENCE SUMMARY.
(Erase heading not required.)

Army Form C. 2118.

Place	Date	Hour	Summary of Events and Information	Remarks and references to Appendices
In the field	17.8.18		sector of the front from the ARRAS area it was the left sector of the Brigade. The evening & night passed in the usual way, except	
	18.9.18		that the right brigade (46th) did the raid in the afternoon, when gas projectors were also let off.	
	18.9.18		Bn HQ moved from LONE LOCALITY into DUMP TUNNEL where a new HQ had been prepared. There was general quiet on the bn front during the day, at night two patrols went out to prove our superiority in NO MANS LAND, the enemy front line. [illegible] too bright for enterprising patrol work.	
	19.9.18		The 1/8th A. & S. H., we were informed, were to snatch some enemy posts in the neighbourhood of FOSSE ALLEY at 5.15 A.M. on the [illegible] night. The operation came off & turned out successful. The enemy were observed forming up for a counter attack on the Black Watch [illegible] near the QUARRIES at 10 A.M. about a minute after, [illegible] caused our fire, completely [illegible] him by surprise, scattering his place. 18 pdrs fired 1400 rounds & 4.5's also during the enemy attempt, & his losses must have been very heavy. Active patrolling at night.	[illegible]
	20.9.18		A very quiet & normally peaceful day. Weather beautifully warm though	

D. D. & L., London, E.C.
(10340) Wt W5300/1713 750,000 3/18 E 2688 Forms/C2118/16.

Instructions regarding War Diaries and Intelligence Summaries are contained in F. S. Regs., Part II. and the Staff Manual respectively. Title pages will be prepared in manuscript.

WAR DIARY
or
INTELLIGENCE SUMMARY.
(Erase heading not required.)

Place	Date	Hour	Summary of Events and Information	Remarks and references to Appendices
In the field	21.9.18		There was nothing of any consequence on the bn front, though the news from MACEDONIA and ST QUENTIN fronts was very cheering to all ranks. Patrols were active during the night. Both our and enemy bombing machines were frequent passengers overhead, the night being ideal for bombing.	
	22.9.18		Instructions to the effect that the Bde boundaries had been changed were received the resultant effect of this on us was we had to take over DEVON LOCALITY. There was also to be an inter coy relief on the same day, so the new dispositions became as follows "C" Coy in DEVON LOCALITY, (left boundary DEVON ALLEY) "B" Coy in HAY LOCALITY, "A" Coy in M... of R., "D" Coy in 10th AVENUE. The afternoon turned wet but the clouds cleared away, the moon came out at night. The Seaforths relieved the Black Watch on our left.	Bde O.O. No 311 attached Appx No. XII.
	23.9.18		The morning passed peacefully but the afternoon at 4 a gas projection N of HOLNON [illegible] on the enemy's [illegible] supported by an artillery bombardment took place. The gas did not appear very effective as shortly afterwards two prisoners [illegible] themselves	Bn [illegible] gas attack [illegible] Appx No [illegible]

WAR DIARY
or
INTELLIGENCE SUMMARY.
(Erase heading not required.)

Army Form C. 2118.

Instructions regarding War Diaries and Intelligence Summaries are contained in F. S. Regs., Part II. and the Staff Manual respectively. Title pages will be prepared in manuscript.

Place	Date	Hour	Summary of Events and Information	Remarks and references to Appendices
In the field	23.9.18		over the parapet in exactly the same place that the gas was projected. The enemy commenced his retaliation 10 minutes after zero & continued for a long time though no losses were inflicted on the Bn. Patrols [illegible] at night [illegible] attempting to enter GRANSA TR [illegible] investigate the effects of the gas. It was hindered by the enemy [illegible] [illegible] our [illegible] [illegible] [illegible] enemy [illegible] could be seen firing their M.G.s from the enemy trenches.	
	24.9.18		A quiet & peaceful day with only normal activity. Patrolling at night.	
	25.9.18		The only departure from the usual activities was some enemy 3 kites being [illegible] by [illegible] planes from [illegible], [illegible] which the enemy persistently [illegible] himself. This is entirely a monopoly for the British Army [illegible]. [illegible] was [illegible] by the enemy at HAY LOCALITY but escaped with slight injuries thanks to his [illegible], & was able to remain on duty.	
	26.9.18		A great stir in the morning when a sergeant of the 17th Regt 26th Div. was found in DEVON LOCALITY. He	[illegible]

D. D. & L., London, E.C. (10340) Wt W5300/P713 750,000 3/18 E 2688 Forms/C2118/16.

Instructions regarding War Diaries and Intelligence Summaries are contained in F. S. Regs., Part II. and the Staff Manual respectively. Title pages will be prepared in manuscript.

WAR DIARY
or
INTELLIGENCE SUMMARY.
(Erase heading not required.)

Army Form C. 2118.

Place	Date	Hour	Summary of Events and Information	Remarks and references to Appendices
In the field.	26.9.18		cross examination by Lieut. H. Greene M.C. it appeared he was an Alsatian who had deserted. He was very much inclined to talk & gave away a lot of valuable information as Corps [illegible] to listen to it as he certainly appeared to take great pleasure in decrying the Germans, & was quite convinced the Allies would triumph completely in the Spring. The news of the Palestine victory & the Bulgarian defeat was [illegible] to him. He stated as [illegible].	
	27.9.18		9th Black Watch relieved the Bn in the right sector during the afternoon & the Bn less "C" Coy, who were retained as a garrison for LE RUTOIRE locality, returned to MAZINGARBE, the last Coy coming in by 7.30 P.M. To further "Comradeship" amongst the officers of the Bn a mess for the officers was decided upon, the [illegible] in the Avenue formerly occupied by the Portuguese was taken over. The Black Watch had done the same, & it is hoped that all three battalions of the Brigade will adopt the same thing, [illegible] them forming the mess. At the moment there are very few comforts in the mess but [illegible] tables should very [illegible] be forthcoming with the assistance of that 'jack of all trades' — THE PIONEER.	[illegible]

Instructions regarding War Diaries and Intelligence Summaries are contained in F. S. Regs., Part II. and the Staff Manual respectively. Title pages will be prepared in manuscript.

WAR DIARY
or
INTELLIGENCE SUMMARY.
(Erase heading not required.)

Army Form C. 2118.

Place	Date	Hour	Summary of Events and Information	Remarks and references to Appendices
In the field.	28.9.18		The forenoon & part of the afternoon were devoted to baths, in the late afternoon the men spent their time in playing football.	
	29-30 9.18		Coy parades in the morning & in the afternoon of the 29th the Bn played the 9th Gordons in soccer being defeated by 7-3. [illegible] were sent up the line to supply working parties for the forward ammunition dumps. They returned the following day i.e. 30th having suffered very heavily on the [illegible] [illegible] [illegible] [illegible]	[illegible] orders [illegible] Appendix XV.
			A copy of the letter sent by the G.O.C. 17th French Corps to G.O.C. 15th Divn. is attached. This relates to the memorial erected in honour of the 15th Divn. by the French at BUZANCY.	
			Strength & casualty summary for September attached.	
			[illegible signature]	

D. D. & L., London, E.C.
(10340) Wt W5300/P713 750,000 3/18 E 2688 Forms/C2118/16.

Second Army No. A1496/39

VII Corps.

1.- The attached printed copy of a letter written by the Field Marshal, Commanding-in-Chief, to the Army Commander on the disbandment of the 8/10th Gordon Highrs. is forwarded.

2. Will you kindly forward it to the Battalion as it is thought the Commanding Officer may wish to place it with the official records of the Battalion.

3. Kindly acknowledge receipt.

Headquarters,
Second Army.
15th August, 1918.
AHB

J. L. Chaytor
Lieut. Colonel,
A.A.G., Second Army.

SPECIAL ORDER

BY

GENERAL SIR H. S. HORNE, K.C.B., K.C.M.G.,

COMMANDING FIRST ARMY.

The following letter from the General Officer Commanding, 17th (French) Division, to the General Officer Commanding, 15th Division, is published for the information of all ranks:—

27th August, 1918.

Mon Général.

After relieving your Division in the pursuit on the Vesle, I established my Headquarters at Buzancy. I found there the traces still fresh of the exploits of your Scottish soldiers, and the officers of my staff were able to see clearly what hard fighting you had had to gain possession of the village, and above all, of the park.

Wishing to leave on the spot some lasting tribute to the bravery of your soldiers, I entrusted to one of my officers, Lieutenant Réné Puaux, the task of erecting there, with the material at hand, a small monument emblematic of the homage and admiration of my Division for yours.

This monument has on it a medallion on which are inscribed thistles and roses, and beneath, the words:—

" *Here the noble thistle of Scotland will flourish*
for ever among the roses of France ";
and beneath,
" *17th French Division*
to
15th (Scottish) Division."

This monument was erected on the highest point of the plateau, where we found the body of the Scottish soldier who had advanced the farthest (on 28th July, 1918—Buzancy).

The photograph of this monument has appeared in the last number of the journal *L'Illustration*. I thought you would be glad to have a few copies of the photograph, which I send you herewith. They convey to you, together with the memories which I have kept of our short meeting at Vierzy, the expression of my esteem and my admiration for your valiant Division.

Will you please accept, dear General, the expression of my sincere regards.

(Signed) C. GASSOINS.

(Général de Division C. GASSOINS, Commanding 17th (French) Division).

I am confident that this testimony of the true feeling of comradeship which exists between our ally and ourselves will be highly appreciated by all ranks of the First Army.

General,
Commanding First Army.

First Army Headquarters,
15th September, 1918.

PRINTED IN FRANCE BY ARMY PRINTING AND STATIONERY SERVICES. PRESS A—9/18

105

Lieut

D S McDonald

WAR DIARY
or
INTELLIGENCE SUMMARY.

(*Erase heading not required.*)

Instructions regarding War Diaries and Intelligence Summaries are contained in F. S. Regs., Part II. and the Staff Manual respectively. Title pages will be prepared in manuscript.

Place	Date	Hour	Summary of Events and Information	O	OR	O	OR
30 · 8 · 18			Effective Strength			40	794
Increase							
Reinforcements from Base				1	13		
T/Capt G Cowper crossposted from 9th Bn Gordon Hghs				1			
				2	13		
Decrease							
Lieut G. T Haddow crossposted to 9th Gordons				1			
Wounded					2		
Struck off Strength on being taken on establishment of 44th Infantry Brigade Headquarters					1		
Wounded (Gas Shell)					1		
Evacuated Sick					7		
Over 7 days in F.A (sick)					11		
To U.K. for transfer to M.G.C. Lieut J.D.G. Stewart				1	-		
				2	22		
Difference between Increase & Decrease						-	9
6. 9. 18 Effective Strength						40	785
Increase							
Reinforcements from Base				-	15		
" Lieut Colonel The Lord Dudley Gordon D.S.O				1	-		
				1	15		
Decrease							
Lieut G Dean, Killed in Action 13 9 18				1			
Wounded in Action				-	6		
Evacuated Sick				-	11		
Over 7 days in F.A. (Sick)				-	7		
Died of Wounds				-	1		
				1	25		
Difference between Increase & Decrease						1	10
13 9 18 Effective Strength						40	775

Summary of Events and Information	O	OR	O	OR
13. 9. 18 Effective Strength			40	775
Increase				
Reinforcements from Base	-	29		
Transfer to Battn from Connaught Rangers	-	1		
	-	30		
Decrease				
Wounded in Action	-	3		
Evacuated Sick	-	8		
Over 7 days in F.A. (Sick)	-	2		
Major F. J. A. Moffat. D.S.O. to U.K. for duty	1	-		
	1	13		
Difference between Increase & Decrease			1	17
20. 9. 18. Effective Strength			39	792
Increase				
Reinforcements from Base	-	15		
Rejoined from Hospital	-	4		
	-	19		
Decrease				
Wounded in Action	-	2		
Evacuated Sick	-	1		
Over 7 days in F.A. Sick	-	3		
Difference between Increase & Decrease			-	13
27. 9. 18 Effective Strength			39	805

D. D. & L., London, E.C. (A8004) Wt. W2771/M2731 750,000 5/17 Sch. 52 Forms/C2118/14

Army Form C. 2118.

WAR DIARY
or
INTELLIGENCE SUMMARY.
(Erase heading not required.)

Instructions regarding War Diaries and Intelligence Summaries are contained in F. S. Regs., Part II. and the Staff Manual respectively. Title pages will be prepared in manuscript.

Casualties for September 1918

Place	Date	Hour	Summary of Events and Information	Remarks and references to Appendices
			No 313017 Pte Cuthbert C Wounded 12 9 18	
			20548 " Innes J do 13 9 18	
			3421 " Scott P do 2 9 18	
			240603 " Strachan C do 3 9 18	
			263004 " Robb A do 6 9 18	
			5892 Russell F do 6 9 18	
			11751 " Kinley C4 Killed 10 9 18	
			Lieut Dean G do 13 9 18	
			290603 Pte Urquhart A Wounded 8 9 18	
			243614 " Hardie J do 7 9 18	
			22751 " Pirie A do 12 9 18	
			291485 " Armstrong J do 12 9 18	
			291778 " West WA do 12 9 18	
			201352 " Anderson S do 12 9 1[illegible]	
			291380 " Naismith C do 12 9 18	
			23278 " Porter JW do 12 9 18	
			3/7773 Sellars A do 20 9 18	
			2nd Lieut Haig AW MM do (at duty) 24 9 18	

D. D. & L., London, E.C.
(10340) Wt W5300/P713 750,000 3/18 E 2688 Forms/C2118/16.

5th Battn, The Gordon Highlanders.

OPERATION ORDER No. 30.

By

Lt. Col. J.B.WOOD, D.S.O., O.C. Cmdg.

1st September, 1918.

1. The 5th Gordon Highlanders will relieve the 8th Seaforth Highlanders in the Left Sub-section of the Brigade Front to-morrow, 2nd September.

2. DISPOSITIONS.

"C" Coy.	Gordons will relieve	"B" Coy.	Seaforths	in	front line.
"A" "	" " "	"C" "	"	"	Immed. Support
"B" "	" " "	"A" "	"	"	Support.
"D" "	" " "	"A" "	Gordons	"	Reserve (TENTH AVENUE)
Bn.H.Q.	" " "	Bn.H.Q.	Seaforths	in	TENTH AVENUE, just S. of HAY ALLEY.

Relief will be carried out in the above order.

3. GUIDES.

(1) O.C.'s "A" & "C" Coys will make their own arrangements ~~with their own arrangements~~ with their opposite numbers about guides and times.

(2) "D" Coy will require no guides.

(3) 1 guide per platoon for "B" Coy., and 2 for Bn.H.Q. will be at PHILOSOPHE CrossRoads, G.20.a.3.3 at 2 pm.

4. Reserve platoon of "C" Coy will march off at 1.30 pm and report to "C" Coy Hdqrs prior to relief.

"B" Coy. and Bn.H.Q. will march off at 1.40 pm.

"D" Coy will march off at 1.50 pm.

5. The greatest precautions must be taken to prevent the relief being observed by the enemy.

All movement East of PHILOSOPHE must be by trenches.

6. All haversacks and Officers' valises will be dumped at Q.R. by 12 noon, and collected by the T.O.

7. Advanced parties of 1 N.C.O. per Coy and 1 N.C.O. for Bn.H.Q will proceed in the morning to take over stores.

8. Lists of stores taken over will be forwarded to Bn.H.Q. by 9 am, 3rd September.

9. Completion of relief will be wired to BnH.Q. by Code Words "Sick Report NIL".

10. ACKNOWLEDGE.

(Signed) G.P.Geddes, Capt., & Adjt,
5th Battalion, The Gordon Highlanders.

Distribution:-

Copies 1 - 4 : O.C.Coys. 5 : Major Moffat. 6 : Capt. Cowper. 7 : T.O. & Q.M. 8 : I.O. 9 : L.G.O. 10 : R.S.M. 11 : Sigs. 12 : 8th Seaforths. 13 : War Diary. 14 : File.

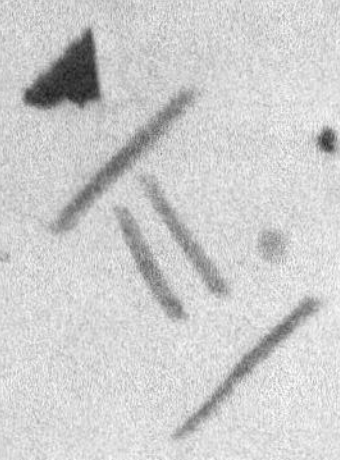

5th Battn. The Gordon Highlanders.

BATTALION ORDER No. 30. PartII

By

Lt.Col. J.B.WOOD, D.S.O., M.C. Cmdg.

1st September, 1918.

1. EXTRACT from Appointments, Commissions, etc., approved by The Field-Marshal, Commanding-in-Chief, The British Armies in France.

"Captain J.R.Hay to be secd. for duty as Comdt. 37th Divl. Reception Camp, and to be acting Major whilst so employed, to fill establishment, 23rd July, 1918."

2. STRENGTH (INCREASE).

The undermentioned reinforcements joined Unit from Base on 20/8/18 and are posted to Coys as stated:-

"A" Coy. No. 40204 L/C. Mason, A.
"A" " " S/11837 Pte. Cochrane, A.
"D" " " 235282 " Thompson, J.H.

The undermentioned reinforcements joined Unit from Base on 1/9/18 and are posted to Companies as under:-

"A" Coy. No. 235345. Pte. Barclay, A.
"A" " " 240732. " Ferguson, G.
"C" " " 240011.C.Q.M.S. English, [illegible]
"C" " " 268304 ~~Pte.~~L/C. McEwan, A.
"D" " " 43820 L/C. Mitchell, H.J.

3. STRENGTH (INCREASE) Officers.

2nd Lieut. E.Wilson-Smith joined from Base on 30/8/18, and is taken on strength of the Battalion and posted to "A" Coy.
2nd Lieut. A.G.Tindall joined from Base on 1/9/18, and is taken on strength of the Battalion and posted to "C" Coy.
T/Captain Gordon Cowper having been cross posted from the 9th Battalion, Gordon Highlanders with effect from 1/9/18, is taken on the strength of the Battalion, and assumes command of "C" Coy from this date.
(Authy:- A.G's No. A/17979 d/10/7/17 and A.G/2158/3654(o) d/21/8/18)

4. STRENGTH (DECREASE).

"C" Coy. No. 17733, Pte. Arnott, J, is taken on establishment of 44th Infantry Brigade.
(Authy:- War Office letter 121/France/2588(SD2) d/4/8/18 5515 (o)

5. LEAVE TO LOURDES.

"B" Coy. S/10741 Col. Crook, [illegible] granted leave to Lourdes from 3/9/18 to 12/9/18.

SHEET -2- No. 60 Part 11. 1/9/1 8.

6. ADMISSIONS TO F.A.

"C" Coy.	235395.	Pte.	Sutherland,	J.	Admitted sick	28/8/18.
"C" "	41407	"	Fadian,	A.	" "	29/8/18.
"C" "	23215	"	Jackson,	[illegible]	" "	30/8/18.
"B" "	23248	"	Holdsworth,	G.	" "	"
"B" "	13209	Cpl.	Wilson,	A.	" "	"
"B" "	230189	Pte.	~~Hde~~ Hyde,	H.	" "	1/9/18.

7. LEAVE.

The undermentioned N.C.O's and men having been granted leave to United Kingdom from dates stated against their names are entitled to ration allowance accordingly:-

	263043	Pte.	Mitchell,	A.	From 18/3/18	To 4/4/18.
"B" Coy.	5712	Cpl.	Sinclair,	T.	" 3/9/18	" 17/9/18.
"A" "	2251	Pte.	Lowrie,	J.	" 3/9/18	" 17/9/18.
"D" "	240444	CQMS.	Johnston,	J.	" 3/9/18	" 17/9/18.
"C" "	14358	L/C.	Rettie,	W.L.	" 3/9/18	" 17/9/18.
"A" "	7529	RSM.	Smith,	W.L.	" 3/9/18	" 17/9/18.

8. CASUALTY.

44th T.M.B. No. 23091 Pte. McDonald, J. Wounded in action 29/8/18.

9. REJOINED FROM F.A.

"D" Coy. 290703 Pte. G.Barnett, 30/8/18.

10. CORRIGENDA.

Ref. B.O. No. 49, para. 1 of 9/8/18 "for 10086 Pte. R. Cooper" read S/18058, Pte. R. Couper.

Ref. B.O. No. 57, Part 11, para 5 "Promotions & Appointments" should read:-

To be Corporal Paid.
"D" Coy. 15932 L/C Brown, G, vice Sewell to U.K. d/22/7/18.

11. PROMOTIONS AND APPOINTMENTS.

To be Corporals Paid.
"D" Coy. 374 L/C. Shaw, A. to complete establishment 9/8/18.
"D" " S/7933 " Davidson, A." " " "

To be Lance Corporals Paid.
"D" Coy. 203031 Pte. Duff, R. To complete establishment 9/8/18
"D" " 260186 " Mansfield.A." " " "
"D" " 242211 " Bremner, G. " " " "

12. SUSPENSION OF SENTENCE.

The Brigadier Commanding 44th Infantry Brigade, has further suspended the sentence of
3350 Pte. J.Lindsay, "B" Coy.
and directs that it be brought up for further reconsideration on the 10/10/18.

(Signed) G.P.Geddes, CaptO.Adjt,
5th Battn, The Gordon Highlanders.

W. DIARY

SECRET

5th Battn, The Gordon Highlanders,

OPERATION ORDER No. 31

By

Lieut. Col. J. B. WOOD, D.S.O. M.C. Cmdg.

Reference Map 44Q N.W.

4th September, 1918

1 Operations elsewhere may cause the enemy to withdraw on our front. The enemy must not be allowed to withdraw unnoticed, and every effort must be made to maintain touch.

2 In the event of a general advance being ordered, the Brigade will advance according to boundaries on maps issued herewith.
4/5th Black Watch on right.
5th Gordons on left.
8th Seaforths in reserve.
8th Argyl and Sutherland Highlanders will be on our left.

3 The advance will be by bounds as shown on maps referred to, and will be carried out as per diagram attached.
"C" Coy on right.
"A" " " left
"B" " in support
"D" " " reserve.

4 When first objective has been reached, "A" & "C" Coys will each send out strong fighting patrols towards the second objective, remainder of these Coys consolidating first objective. O.C. Coys will, thereafter, continue the advance, if possible, without further reference to Hdqrs.
O.C. "B" Coy will detail two platoons to mop up that part of Hulluch in Battalion sector, remainder will consolidate on Puits No. 13 bis.
O.C. "D" Coy will detail two platoons to garrison Hay locality which will not leave it without orders from Battn, Hdqrs.
Remainder of "D" Coy will remain in tunnel near eastern exits and await orders

5 It must be impressed on all ranks that the advance will be pressed irrespective of the flanks, regular lines are not necessary and independence of action by parties, however small, and individuals is to be encouraged. Enemy forts holding out must be dealt with by bold outflanking movements.

6 O.C. front Coys will each detail a liaison patrol of 1 N.C.O. and 2 O.R. to maintain touch with units on their flanks.

7 Two T.M's will be attached to the Battalion.
Artillery support will be obtained when required through Liason Officer at Battalion Headquarters.
One section of M.G's will take up position on or near Puits 13 Bis on capture of second objective, and form a protective barrage or give covering fire for further advance.
A party of 3rd Australian Tunnelling Coy will be attached for examining dugouts and roads for "booby traps". Instructions previously issued about "booby traps" will again be explained to all ranks and strictly adhe red to.

8 Bombs etc, will be issued as per appendix.

9 Battn, Hdqrs, will be in Carpe Post where reports will be rendered.

A. G. Copeland Lieut & A/Adjt

MOGK

SHEET -2- O.O. No. 31 4/9/18

Distribution

Copies 1 - 4 : Coys
5 : Brigade
6 : A & S. H.
7 : B. W.
8 : Seaforths
9 : Diary
10 : Rear
11 : File
12 : Spare.

A P P E N D I X TO O. O. No 31

Bombs No 23
100 per Company.
No 27 (White phosphorous smoke bomb)
"A" & "C" Coys 4 each.
"B" Coy 8
M. S. K. (Teat gas bombs)
"B" Coy 12
S. O. S. 5 per Coy.

Ground Flares 50 per Coy.

N. B. It must be clearly understood that flares will only be lit by the forward troops, and only when called for by contact planes.

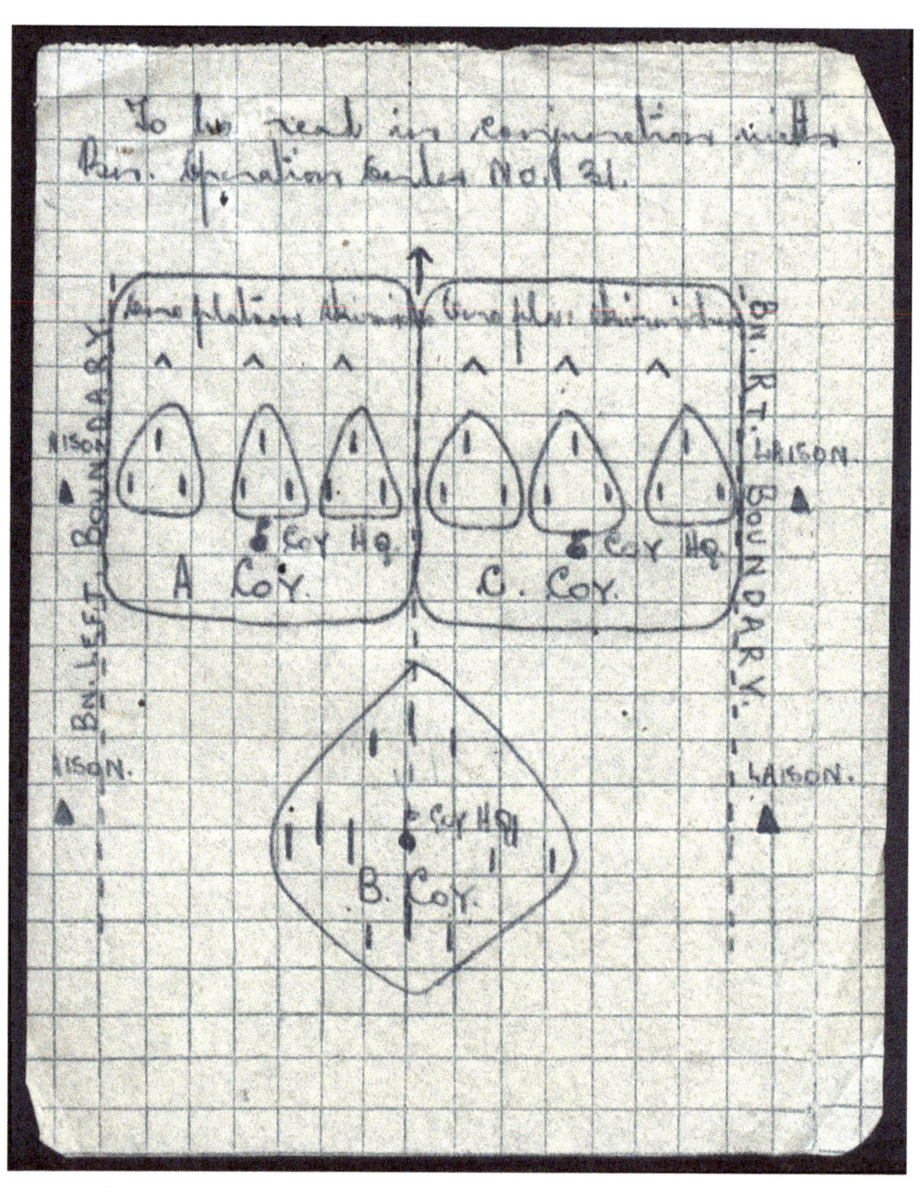

To be read in conjunction with Bn. Operation Orders No. 31.
BN. LEFT BOUNDARY.
AISON.
A COY.
COY HQ.
C. COY.
COY HQ.
BN. RT. BOUNDARY.
LAISON.
LAISON.
B. COY.
COY HQ.

IV.

SECRET

H O G E

O P E R A T I O N   O R D E R   No 32 5/3/18

by

Lt Col J.R. [illegible] D.S.O. M.C. Cmdg

Reference Map Sheet, France, 44A, N.E.3

1 Lieut Lo[illegible] and 10 other ranks of "C" Coy will raid the cross roads at N.13.c.7.5 tonight.

2 Party will assemble at N.13.c.20.30 (junction of front line and road) at 9.30 pm, move out to cross roads at N.13.c.45.40 (in No Man's Land)

3 Light Trench Mortar Battery will fire 20 rounds rapid on objective and then lengthen range to Hilda trench between N.13.c. and 13.d. Raiding party will immediately rush in, secure prisoners and find out what sort of work is in progress at cross roads mentioned in para 1.

4 Signal that trench mortar fire has lengthened will be by Green Very Light - Trench Mortar will then fire 20 rounds slow fire on Hilda trench above mentioned.

5 Arms Rifles and bayonets, 50 rounds S.A.A., 2 bombs per man and 2 spare bombs.

6 ZERO hour, 10 pm.

7 ACKNOWLEDGE.

A.D. Copland Lieut & A/Adjt,
H O G E

Distribution

Copies 1-4 : Coys 5 : [illegible]
6 : [illegible] 7 : [illegible]
8 : JOHN 9 : File
10 : War Diary, 11 : Spare

SECRET Copy No 5

OPERATION ORDER No 33

MOGE

8th September, 1918

1 Inter Company relief as per Warning Order 7th inst, will be carried out at 5 pm to-day

2 **Dispositions:-** As per Warning Order of 7th

3 **Route :-** "B" Coy will move up to position via HULLUCH TUNNEL, "C" Coy on relief will move back by same route

"D" Coy will relieve via VENISON ALLEY and "A" Coy will move back by the same route

4 Details of relief will be arranged by O's. C. Coys.

5. All trench stores, maps etc, will be handed over and receipts taken and sent to Hdqrs by 10 am 9th inst. All work in hand will be handed over

6 Completion of relief will be wired to this Office by means of the cod word "BON"

7 ACKNOWLEDGE

A.D. Copland. Lieut & A/Adjt,
MOGE

Distribution :-

Copies 1 - 4 : Coys, 5 : I.O, 6 : L.G.O, 7 : Signals
8 : Q.M. & T.O., 9 : R.S.M. 10 : File,
11 : War Diary, 12 : Spare

VI ....

War Diary

SECRET.   Copy No. 3

44th Highland Brigade Order No. 305.

Reference Map -
Sheet 44A. N.W.3.   10th Sept. 1918.

1. Bde. Order No. 304 is cancelled and the following substituted.

2. The 45th Brigade, tonight 10/11th, is to occupy the QUARRIES G.12.a. and establish a line of posts on the N.E. side of the QUARRIES, connecting the present front line about G.12.d.4.8. to the existing post at G.5.d.7.1.

The 16th Division on the Left are advancing their line to-morrow, Sept.11th.

3. The 44th Brigade has been ordered to extend to the Left and take over from the 45th Brigade, as far North as G.12.a.0.0.

4. The Brigade Boundary will then run along the road, running S.W. through G.6.d., G.12.b. and a., (road inclusive to 44th Bde.), G.12.a.60 00., G.12.a.0.0., thence to G.11.d.40.00., G.11.c.20.00. thence to original boundary at G.16.b.85.70.

5. The 5th Gordon Highrs. will take over the front as far North as the above boundary, (an additional 2-Coy. frontage), by 12 NOON tomorrow, 11th instant, exclusive of any post which may be established by the 45th Brigade between G.12.d.4.8. and the QUARRIES in to-nights operation. The relief of such a post would be impossible in daylight and further orders will be issued as to its relief tomorrow night.

6. Arrangements will be made between C.Os. concerned.

7. One Coy. of the 9th Gordon Highrs. will relieve the Coy. of the 5th Gordon Highrs. now in LONE LOCALITY, and will come under the orders of the O.C. LONE LOCALITY.

This relief will be completed by 9 A.M. tomorrow, Sept.11th.

The Coy. of the 5th Gordon Highrs. thus relieved will then be at the disposal of the O.C. 5th Gordon Highrs. to help occupy the new front being taken over.

8. O.C. 5th Gordon Highrs. will notify this H.Q. of dispositions of troops on completion of move.

9. Completion of move will be reported to this H.Q. by use of code phrase "YOUR B.M.123 RECEIVED AT ______". - 12 noon.

10. ACKNOWLEDGE.

Issued thro'
Signals -

[signature]
Major,
Brigade Major,
44th Infantry Brigade.

DISTRIBUTION - List B, plus -

No.13. 9th Gordon Highrs.
14. O.C. LONE LOCALITY.
15. File.
16. G.O.C.
17. S.C.
18. War-Diary.
19. O.C. 44th Bde. Signal Section.

DIARY

VII.

SECRET

Copy No

OPERATION ORDER No 35

by

5th Battn, The Gordon Highlanders

Ref Map Sheet 44A N.W.3

11th September, 1918

1 Operation Order No 34 (issued to "B" & "D" Coys) of 10th inst, is cancelled and the following substituted.

2 The 45th Brigade, during the night of 10/11th, is to occupy quarries G.12.a and establish a line of posts on the North East side of the quarries, connecting the present front line about G.12.d.4.8. and the existing post on G.5.d.7.1

3 The 44th Brigade has been ordered to extend to the left and take over from the 45th Brigade as far North as G.12.a.0.0

4 The Brigade boundary will then run along the road running southwest through G.6.d., G.12.b. and a. (road inclusive to 44th Brigade), G.12.a.60.00, G.12.a.0.0., thence to G.11.d.40.00, G.11.c.20.00, thence to original boundary on G.16.b.85.70.

5 "A" Coy, HOGS and 2 platoons of "D" Coy will take over the front as far north as the above boundary (an additional 2 Company frontage) exclusive of any posts which may have been taken by the 45th Brigade in last night's operations, between G.12.d.4.8 and the quarries. "D" Coy HOGS will arrange to take over CAMP POST from "B" Coy, HOGS. This relief will be completed by 12 noon to-day, 11th.

6 One Company of the 9th Gordons will relieve "A" Coy 5th Gordons in LONE LOCALITY by 9 am to-day.

7 2 Platoons of "D" Coy will relieve "A" Coy, 13th Royal Scots
2 " " "A" " " " "B" " " " "
2 " " "A" " " " a portion of "D" Coy Royal Scots

8 <u>Guides</u> Guides as follows will be supplied:-
For "A" Coy 9th Gordons, 1 guide per platoon, and 1 for Coy. H.Q. from "B" & "D" Coy, 13th Royal Scots will be at HAY ALLEY entrance to tunnel at 9 am to-day.
For "D" Coy, 2 guides of "A" Coy, 13th Royal Scots will be at same place at 9 am to-day.

9 Details of Relief will be arranged between Officers concerned.

10 All trench stores will be handed over and receipts exchanged and forwarded to this Office by 4 pm to-day.

11 O's.C Coys will notify this Office of dispositions of troops on completion of move.

12 Completion of move will be reported to this Office by means of code phrase "Ten tins received"

13 ACKNOWLEDGE

A.S. Copeland Lieut & A/Adjt.,
5th Battn, The Gordon Highlanders

11th September, 1939

Distribution :-

Copies 1 - 3 : O's.C "A", "B", "C" Coys
4 : HQ
5 : War Diary
6 : File

2 men to look after their stores. These men will be responsible for loading stores on the return ration train and for unloading same at Kingsbridge Station. "C" Coy will make their own arrangements re mess kits, etc
N.C.O. in charge of Canteen will detail one man to remain behind in charge of stores.

7 TRANSPORT

The Transport Officer will arrange to collect all stores and deliver to Companies in Mazingarbe. He will supply one limber per Coys and one for Bn Hd qrs and Orderly Room boxes.

8 ROUTINE

All maps, Trench Stores, Work-in-hand etc, will be handed over and receipts exchanged, signed copies of which will be sent to this Office by 9am 28th inst.

9 RELIEF

Completion of relief will be wired to this Office by means of the code phrase "one available"

10 ACKNOWLEDGE

A.D. Copeland Lieut & A/Adjt,
5th Bn The Gordon Highlanders

Distribution :-

Copies Nos 1 - 4 : O's C Coys
5 : C.O.
8 : 4/5th B.W.
10 : R S M
6 : M.O. W.D.
7 : QM & T.O
9 : Lt Ky
11 : File

VIII

SECRET.

13 Bn the Royal Scots. Copy No. 6

Operation Order No 100.

1. A & B Coys will side slip to the left to day being relieved by the 1/5 Gordon Hrs in accordance with attached table A' after which these Coys will relieve 6 Cameron Hrs in accordance with attached table B.

2. On relief the Bn boundaries will be:–

RIGHT. Road running NE and SW. through squares G6 b and d, and G12 a and b (inclusive to 44 Bde) to G12 a 6.0. – thence due west to G12 a 00. (post at G12 a 4.1 inclusive to 45th Bde) – G11 d 5.0. – due west to G11 c 2.0 – G16 b 90.75. thence original boundary.

LEFT. G6 c. 0.0. – G11 b 55.55 – G11 b 10.40. (SLAG VIEW inclusive to 6 Cameron Hrs) G11 b 00.40 (STUDIO 2 inclusive to 13 Royal Scots) – G11 a 45.40. – G16 a 9.9. (MANNING Coy Area inclusive to 10 Royal Scots)

②

thence HULLOCH-VERMELLES ROAD
(inclusive to 6th Cameron Hrs)

3. 'D' Coy 13th Royal Scots will be relieved by the Gordon Hrs in accordance with table 'A': on relief O.C. 'D' Coy will make his own arrangements as regards accommodation in the TUNNEL.
He can temporarily retain his Coy Cook house and Coy mess.

4(a) Reliefs in accordance with table 'A' will be notified by wire to Bde HQ by using code word "SPEY"
(b) Reliefs in accordance with table B will be notified by wire to BHQ by using the code-word 'TWEED'

5. The platoons of A & B Cos presently attached to 'D' Coy will rejoin their Coys on relief.

6 Coys will arrange for Cooks, orderly men and servants to proceed after breakfast to the new area and take over cooking arrangements.

7 A & B Coys on relief will proceed to their new areas via LIMBER TRENCH and MANNING TUNNEL

8 All trench stores etc will be handed over and taken over and receipts will be sent to BHQ by 8pm to-day.

9 OC 'A' Coy will arrange to relieve a post at present manned by the 6 Camerons at G12 a 40.70. as soon after dark as possible and will arrange with out going unit for a guide for this post. The post will consist of 1 NCO. and 10. Other Ranks and they will have a hot meal before starting This is a permanent post

4

and will be relieved every 24 hours.

R.A.P will move to R.A.P at junction of OB1 and STANSFIELD ROAD. Personnel will be rationed with 'B' Coy. and the M.O. will mess with 'B' Coy Officers Mess.

11 The Commanding Officer will see OC's A B & D Coys. at 'D' Coy HQ at 7 am to-day.

11-9-18.

Captain
Adjt. 13' R. Scots.

Copies Nos 1 to 4 OC. Cos.
Copy No 5 M.O.
6 1/5. Gordon Hrs.
7 6 Camerons.
8 File
9 Q.M.
10. War Diary.

TABLE 'A'

UNIT RELIEVED.	UNIT RELIEVING	GUIDES No.	RENDEZVOUS	TIME
The whole of 'A' Coy R. Scots	2 platoons 'B' Coy and Coy HQ 1/5 Gordon Hrs.	1 per platoon + 1 for Coy. HQ (3 guides)	HALE ENTRANCE to TUNNEL.	9 am
The whole of 'B' Coy R. Scots	2 platoons 'A' Coy + Coy HQ 1/5 Gordons	Do. 3 guides	Do	Do.
Part of 'D' Coy Royal Scots	2 platoons 'A' Coy 1/5 Gordons	1 per platoon 2 guides	Do	Do

Table 'B'

UNIT RELIEVING	UNIT RELIEVED	NEW AREA.
'B' Coy Royal Scots	Coy 6' Cameron Hrs	MANNING AREA
'A' Coy Royal Scots	2 platoons + Coy HQ of 6' Cameron Coy	STUDIO AREA

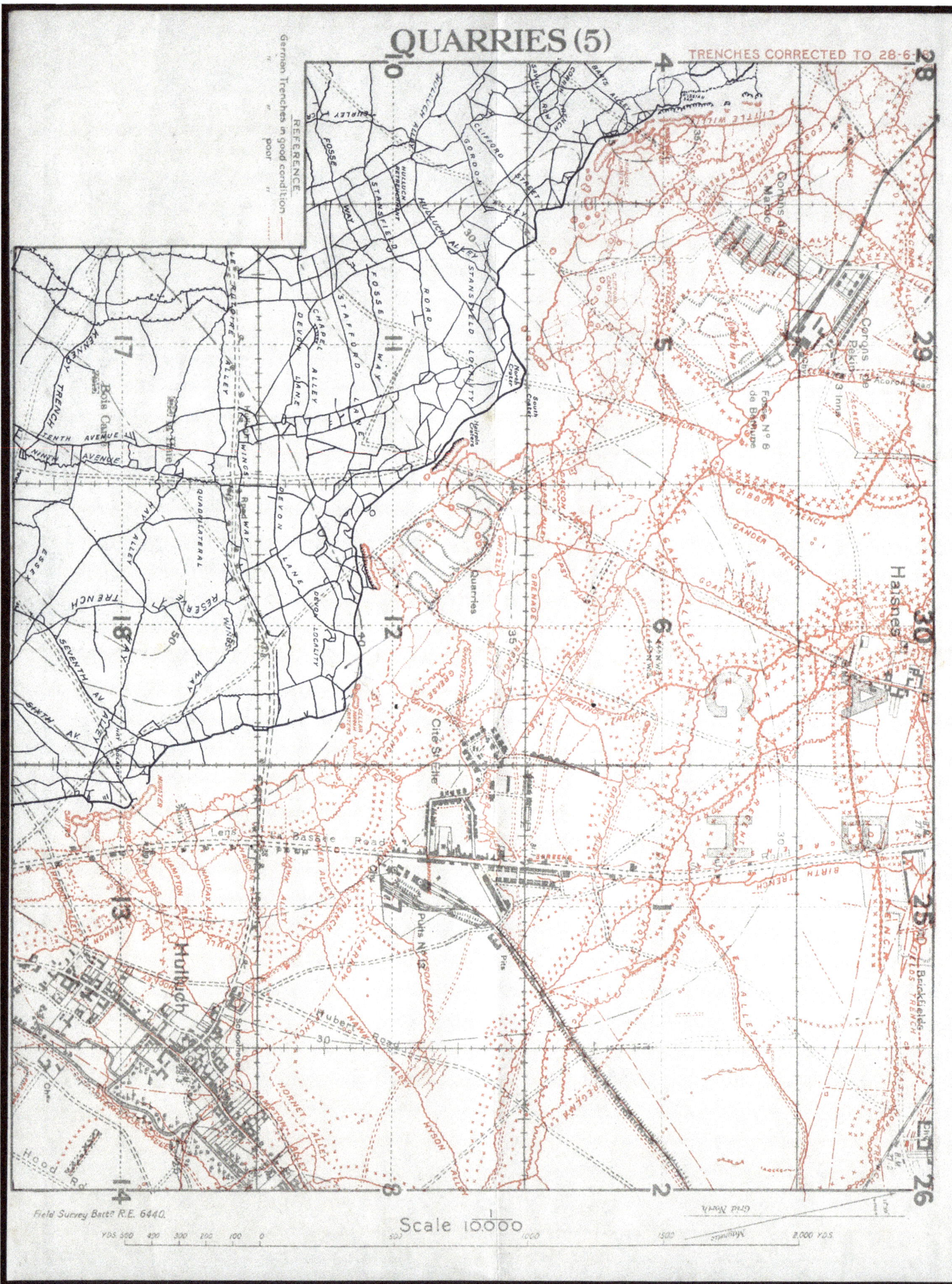
QUARRIES (5)
TRENCHES CORRECTED TO 28-6-
REFERENCE
German Trenches in good condition
" " poor "
Quarries
Cité St Elie
Hulluch
Haisnes
Lens Bassée Road
Puits No 12
Fosse No 8 de Béthune
Corons de Pekin
Corons de Maroc
Hood Rd
Hulluch Road
Bois Carré
Schoolhouse
Pits
KENNEDY TRENCH
TENTH AVENUE
NINTH AVENUE
SEVENTH AV
SIXTH AV
QUADRILATERAL
RESERVE TRENCH
DEVON LANE
CHAPEL ALLEY
STAFFORD LANE
FOSSE WAY
STANSFIELD ROAD
HULLUCH ALLEY
GORDON ALLEY
CLIFFORD STREET
GIBBON TRENCH
GANDER TRENCH
GOAT TRENCH
BIRTH TRENCH
HORNET ALLEY
Field Survey Battn R.E. 6440.
Scale 1/10,000
YDS 500 400 300 200 100 0 500 1000 1500 2,000 YDS
Grid North
Magnetic

44th Brigade G.11/8

5th Gordon Highrs.

IX.

W. Dacey

Reference Map -
Sheet 44.A.

1. 1/5th Gordon Highrs. will carry out training tomorrow, 16th Sept. with a section of the Tank Corps, which is at MARQUEFFLES FARM (R.26.a.).

2. Rendezvous at R.26.d.8.7. at 10-0 A.M., 16th instant.

3. Five copies of the scheme for demonstration are forwarded herewith.

4. The Battalion will be out for the whole day; cookers and dinners should be taken.

5. Distances to be preserved on the march are 100 yards between companies and 100 yards between Battalion and Transport.

[signature]

Major,
A/Brigade Major,
15-9-18. 44th Infantry Brigade.

X

War Diary

5th Battalion, The Gordon Highlanders.
OPERATION ORDER No.38.
By
Lieut-Colonel, The Lord Dudley Gordon, D.S.O. Cmdg.

SECRET. Copy No. 12

15th September, 1918.

Ref. Sheet 44B 1/40,000

1. INTENTION. The 5th Gordon Highlanders will carry out training tomorrow, 16th September, with a section of the Tank Corps.

2. SCHEME. As attached.

3. PARADE. The Battalion will form up in mass formation on the football ground, behind Orderly Room, ready to move off at 7.30 am. All men will parade except the men on fatigue (less 8.15 pm fatigue), Orderly Room staff, sick, (including inoculated) and 2 police. The Signal Section will take signalling lamps and flags. 2 Orderlies will have cycles. Headquarters (less detailed above) will parade with their Companies.

4. ORDER OF MARCH. Signal Section, Band, "A", "B", "C" & "D" Coys. Band will change Companies at each halt.

5. PARADE STATES. Will be collected on parade.

6. DRESS. Fighting Order, Tam o shanters. Company Commanders will be mounted. "B" & "D" Coys will take Lewis Guns.

7. TRANSPORT. 2 Limbers will be at Orderly Room at 6.45 am to take Lewis Guns. These limbers may be used for Officers mess kits. Cookers and Officers' mess cart will accompany the Battalion ~~at cross roads at~~ One water cart will join the Battalion at cross roads at Pt SHINS R26 5.8 this will be filled at Transport Lines. 2 Water duty men will accompany limbers, and join the water cart at that point. 2 cooks only are allowed with cookers on the line of march. The water cart will be at cross roads at 8. am

8. GUIDE. Lieutenant D.S.Macdonald will guide the Battalion to destination.

9. ACKNOWLEDGE.

(Signed) A.D.Copland, Lieut & A/Adjt.,
5th Battalion, The Gordon Highlanders.

Issued at 8.30 pm.

Distribution:-

Copy No 1 : Commanding Officer.
2 - 5 : O's C. Coys.
6 : Intelligence Officer.
7 : Signals.
8 : L.G.O.
9 : T.O. & Q.M.
10 : R.S.M.
11 : Sgt. Cook.
12 : War Diary.
13 : File.

War Diary

O's C. All Coys, Signalling Officer, L.G.O., R.S.M., Drum Major.

S.O/1

SPECIAL ORDER.

When route marching, before halting, the Commanding Officer will blow a whistle; this is a caution only. On the second blast of the whistle, Company Commanders will give the word of command "Halt". When the battalion is marching with intervals between Companies which make it impossible to hear the whistle, Companies will conform to the movements of the Company in front.

When Companies are halted, Company Commanders will see that men are properly covered off, with 2 paces interval between section of fours, as soon as this is so, they will be told to fall out on the right of the road. When the 10 minutes halt is completed, the "Advance" will be sounded on the bugle; on this sounding, all men will fall in in their places, with arms slung, care being taken to keep 2 paces interval between section of fours. Files will be changed over, that is to say, the left file will move to the right. Platoon Commanders will stand outside the ranks until their platoons are properly covered off ready to move. When ready to move they will fall in in their places. The Company Commander will place himself in such a position that his word of command can be heard by the whole Company. On the "Advance" being sounded on the bugle, Company Commanders will give the word of command "Quick March" without waiting for the Company in front.

Particular ~~Proper~~ care must be taken that the men keep the proper interval between section of fours when halting, and do not close up when falling in to resume the march. During the halt the road must be kept absolutely clear, not only by men, but by Officers and horses. Officers may fall out on the left side of the road, but must not stand in the centre. When passing through villages, there will be no smoking, and caps must be worn straight and not on the back of the head. When passing General Officers' cars etc., the usual compliment will be paid. On the word "Eyes right" or "Eyes Left", every man will remain with his head turned in the named direction until the word "Eyes Front" is given. Men must be taught to keep their mouths shut when doing this, and to look straight into the eyes of any Officer being saluted.

(Signed) A.D.Copland, Lieut & A/Adjt,
5th Battn, The Gordon Highlanders.

15th September, 1918.

War Diary XI

SECRET. 5th Battn, The Gordon Highlanders. Copy No. 5

OPERATION ORDER No. 38.

16th September, 1918.

1. INTENTION.
The 5th Gordon Highlanders will relieve the 8th Seaforth Highlanders in the right sub-sector of the Brigade front to-morrow, 17th inst.

2. DISPOSITIONS.
"D" Coy Gordons will be the front line Company.
"B" " " " " " M.L.R. "
"C" " " " " " Tenth Avenue "
"A" " " " " " Lone Locality "

3. ROUTE.
By Rutoire or Chapel Alley at discretion of Os.C. Coys.

4. GUIDES.
No guides will be supplied.

5. TIME.
The Battalion will move off at 12.30 pm.

6. RELIEF.
Relief must be completed by 5 pm. Completion will be wired to this Office by means of the code phrase "One rifle damaged".

7 BAGGAGE.
All mess kits, etc, will be dumped, ready for loading, at Battalion Orderly Room at 12 noon.
Transport Officer will arrange to collect. Arrangements same as last relief.

8. ROUTINE.
All trench stores, maps aeroplane photographs, work in hand, etc, will be handed over and receipts exchanged, these will be sent to this Office by 9 am on 18th inst.
O.C.Coys will proceed to Headquarters, 8th Seaforth Highlanders, one hour before the Battalion marches off, and take over dispositions etc.

9 ACKNOWLEDGE.

(Signed) A.D.Copland, Lieut & A/Adjt
5th Battalion, The Gordon Highlanders.

Issued at 10 pm
Distribution:- Copies 1 - 4 : Os.C.Coys.
5 : I.O.
6 : L.G.O.
7 : Q.M. & T.O.
8 : S.O.
9 : R.S.M.
10 : 8th Seaforths.
11 : File.

SECRET. Copy No. 3

XII War Diary

44th Infantry Brigade Order No. 311.

Reference Map -
Sheet 44A. N.W.3.

20th Sept. 1918.

1. The boundaries of the 44th Brigade will be amended to run as follows :-

BRIGADE SOUTHERN BOUNDARY. - H.13.d.0.5. - G.18.d.0.8. - G.17.d.9.2., thence due West to G.15.d.9.2.

BRIGADE NORTHERN BOUNDARY. - G.6.a.6.0. - G.12.a.0.9.(Road inclusive) - G.11.a.0.3. - G.10 a.0.3. - G.9.b.0.5. - G.8.d.8.0. - G.8.c.0.0. (46th Brigade will continue to occupy the Battn. H.Q. in CHAPEL ALLEY, G.11.c.3.3.).

INTER-BATTALION BOUNDARY. DEVON LANE, inclusive to Right Battn. from G.12.d.05.75. to where it crosses the road at G.11.d.95.15. thence South to road junction, G.17.b.95.84. and then West along VERMELLES - HULLUCH Road. The post at G.12.central will be inclusive to left Battalion.

2. The above adjustments will be made on Sept.22nd and night 22/23rd, in conjunction with the Bde. relief laid down in Bde. Order No. 301.

3. Reliefs will be carried out as follows :-

(a). One Coy. 13th Royal Scots will relieve the Coys. of the 5th Gordon Highrs. and 4/5th Black Watch in LONE LOCALITY.
The Coy. of the 4/5th Black Watch thus released will relieve one Coy. of 7/8th K.O.S.B. in LA RUTOIRE LOCALITY.
Upon completion the command of LONE LOCALITY will pass to 45th Brigade.

(b). The Coy. of the 5th Gordon Highrs. from LONE LOCALITY will relieve the Right Coy. of the 4/5th Black Watch in DEVON LOCALITY.

(c). The 8th Seaforth Highrs. will relieve the two remaining Coys. of the 4/5th Black Watch and all troops of the 46th Inf. Bde. as far North as the new Bde. boundary.

(d). One Coy. 9th Gordon Highrs. will relieve a Coy. of the 7/8th K.O.S.B. in the CROSSWAY portion of LA RUTOIRE LOCALITY.

4. H.Q. 8th Seaforth Highrs. will be at G.17.a.8.8.

5. All details of reliefs will be arranged between C.Os. concerned.

6. Trench stores, programmes of work, air photos, defence schemes, etc. will be taken over by 8th Seaforth Highrs.

7. O.C. T.M. Battery will arrange reliefs of all guns affected.

8. Completion of reliefs will be wired by code phrases to this H.Q. as under :-

(a). Relief of LONE LOCALITY - "Your B.M.123 received at __".
(b). " Black Watch Right Coy. by 5th Gordons Coy. - "Your B.M.456 received at __".
(c). Relief of Black Watch Seaforth Highrs. - "Your B.M.789 received at __".
(d). Relief of 8th Seaforths complete - "Your B.M.222 received at __".
(e). Relief of T.Ms. complete - "Your B.M.321 received at __".

8. (f). Relief of RUTOIRE - CROSSWAY LOCALITY - "Your B.M. 333 received at __".

9. LA RUTOIRE - CROSSWAY LOCALITY will be garrisoned by -
 1 Coy. - Support Battalion.
 1 Coy. - 9th Gordon Highrs. (P).
 2 Sections - R.E.

The senior officer will assume command of locality defence.

10. ACKNOWLEDGED /R.64.

Issued thro' Signals -
7-30 A.M., 21st.

Major,
A/Brigade Major,
44th Infantry Brigade.

DISTRIBUTION -

List A, plus -
No.30. 9th Gordon Highrs.(P).

War Diary XIII.

O.C. "A", "B", "C" & "D" Coys.

1 Gas projectors will be discharged, if weather conditions are favourable, on the 23rd September, with artillery co-operation.

2 Map of targets, danger and precautionary zones, may be seen at Orderly Room. Within the danger zone all troops will be withdrawn and tunnel entrances closed from zero until an Officer of "C" Company R.E. reports area cleared. Within the precautionary zone, all troops will keep under cover and will wear their respirators from zero until areas affected are reported clear. All "B" Coy and extreme right of "A" Coy will thus be withdrawn.

3 Lewis Gun positions outside the Precautionary zone, as fixed by the Commanding Officer, will be manned and fire brought to bear on trenches [illegible] & [illegible], and enemy support lines between these two trenches, [illegible] TRENCH & [illegible] TRENCH, so as to catch the enemy manning his parapet, as soon as artillery barrage lifts off.

4 15th Battalion Machine GUN Company to co-operate and put down a barrage on [illegible] TRENCH and between [illegible] & HIGH WALLERS.

5 Gas projectors are to be fired at zero plus 7 minutes.

6 Zero will be 4.30 pm, 23rd September.

7 Watches will be synchronised by an Officer from Brigade Hdqrs at Bn. Hdqrs at 12 noon, 23rd September.

8 Code words to be used in connection with operation will be notified later.

9 ACKNOWLEDGE.

A D Copland Lieut. / Adjt,
5th Bn, The Gordon Highlanders.

22nd September, 1918

War Diary

XIV.

SECRET

Copy No 5

5th Battn, The Gordon Highlanders

OPERATION ORDERS No 40

26th September, 1918

1 INTENTION

The 4/5th Black Watch will relieve the 5th Gordon Highlanders in the right sub-sector, tomorrow 27th inst.

2 DETAIL

(a) "B" Coy Black Watch will relieve "B" Coy 5th Gordons
"C" " " " " " "C" " " "
"D" " " " " " "A" " " "
"A" " " " " be relieved by "C" Coy 5th Gordons in Le Rutoire locality and will then relieve "D" Coy 5th Gordons in Tenth Avenue.

(b) "C" Coy 5th Gordon Highlanders, on completion of relief, will come under the command of O.C. Le Rutoire Locality, Coy Hdqrs will be in Le Rutoire Farm at G 15 [illegible]. Lieut [illegible] will assume command of "C" Coy, and will arrange to relieve the guard of 4/5th Black Watch on Lone locality, just S of Philosophe, consisting of 1 N.C.O. & 3 men.

(c) Capt G Cooper, 5th Gordons will assume command of Le Rutoire [illegible] locality with Hdqrs in Avenue, Mazingarbe. He will take over from Major A.J. Stewart, D.S.O., 2nd in command 4/5th Black Watch.

3 GUIDES

"A", "B" & "C" Coys will send one guide per platoon & one for Coy Hdqrs to be at junction of Limber Trench & Tenth Avenue by 3 pm. "D" Coy will send one per platoon & one for Coy Hdqrs to junction of Limber Trench & Tenth Avenue by 5 pm. Guides for "C" Coy, one for Coy Hdqrs & one per platoon will be at junction of Limber Trench & Tenth Avenue at 4 pm.

4 ROUTE

"B" Coy will move back by Hulluch Tunnel, Limber Trench, Chapel Alley thence to Vermelles. "C" Coy will move back by Hulluch Tunnel, Limber Trench thence to Le Rutoire. "D" Coy will move back by Limber Trench, Chapel Alley thence to Vermelles. "A" Coy will move back by Hay Alley, Tenth Avenue, Limber Trench thence to Vermelles.

5 ADVANCE PARTY

O. C. "A" Coy will detail the following parties to report at Bn Hdqrs not later than 8 am on the 27th inst. :-
(1) 1 N.C.O. & 16 men for work on dugouts at Northern Huts.
(2) 1 N.C.O. & 3 men for Brigade Bomb Store guard.
(3) 1 N.C.O. & 3 men for Anti Aircraft Team at Bde Hdqrs

They will carry rations with them, which will be cooked by 4/5th Black Watch; they will report to Black Watch Orderly Room, Mazingarbe on arrival.

Lieut J. McKay will be responsible for marching down this party, and will hand them over to Black Watch. He will take over billets for the Bn, at Mazingarbe

6 BAGGAGE

All surplus mens kits, [illegible], officers stores, etc, will be dumped not later than 4.30 pm at Hay Dump. Each Coy will detail

XV.

O.C.
"A", "B", "C" & "D" Coys, SECRET. G.1
Q.M., T.O., I.O. & R.S.M.

1 "B" Coy will proceed in full fighting order (haversacks to be left out) to the Right Battalion Area this afternoon, and report to the O.C. 4/5th Black Watch (Right Battn) on arrival.

Parade ready to march off at 5 pm and march by platoons at 100 yards interval. All movement to be by trench.

2. The company will be at the disposal of the O.C. 4/5th Black Watch for carrying ammunition from HAY SIDING to HAY LOCALITY, where an advanced Battalion Dump will be formed at H.13.a.1.0.

The work is to be completed to-night 29th/30th, and the company will remain thereafter in the Right Battn Area. It will still remain under the orders of O.C.5th Gordon Highlanders for tactical purposes.

O.C. 4/5th Black Watch will arrange accommodation.

3. Haversacks and officers valises will be dumped at "B" Coys Store Hut by 3.30 pm, and collected by the T.O.

4. Rations for to-morrow and thereafter, will be loaded at CUP SIDING and conveyed by train with the rations of the Right Battn, to POSEN DUMP, where ration party will meet the train.

5. O.C."D" Coy will take over all guards furnished by "B" Coy before 2.30 pm.

6. O.C."B" Coy will report by wire, location of his Headquarters, and will report his dispositions by 9 am to-morrow.

7. ACKNOWLEDGE.

(Signed) G.P.Geddes, Capt & Adjt,
5th Battalion, The Gordon Highlanders.

29th September, 1918.

C O N F I D E N T I A L.

Vol 44

W A R   D I A R Y.

****

FOR THE MONTH

OF

O C T O B E R.

1918.

V O L U M E 42

****

J B Wood

Major,

Commanding 5th Battalion, The Gordon Highlanders.

1/11/1918.

Instructions regarding War Diaries and Intelligence Summaries are contained in F. S. Regs., Part II. and the Staff Manual respectively. Title pages will be prepared in manuscript.

WAR DIARY
or
INTELLIGENCE SUMMARY.
(Erase heading not required.)

Army Form C. 2118.

Place	Date	Hour	Summary of Events and Information	Remarks and references to Appendices
In the field.	1.10.18		The day was devoted to company parades in the afternoon the Bn played the South Africans at soccer but were beaten. O.O. No 41 issued concerning relief of Bn on the next day. Weather very cold.	O.O. No. 41 attached. App No. I.
	2.10.18		About 8 A.M. a wire was received from Bde to say the long anticipated withdrawal had commenced. This meant the relief was cancelled. The Bn were ordered to stand by ready to move forward. The order finally came through at 19.00 hours the Bn moved forward as the Bde reserve. "A" Coy went into the [illegible] — the scene of their former success — the remaining three coys were distributed along the M.W. of R. in the tunnels & dugouts between DEVON & HAY LOCALITIES. There were also numerous Black Watch [illegible] congregated here with the result that everybody was very crowded.	
	3.10.18		Spent the day in the same place. Working parties were supplied to the R.E.s for road repairs etc. The rear areas were now a literal ant's nest of activity. A couple of lorries in their eagerness to get forward became ditched on the VERMELLES – HULLUCH Rd. The enemy had left behind numerous booby traps and [illegible] [illegible] but the [illegible] were up to their tricks [illegible]	[illegible]

Instructions regarding War Diaries and Intelligence Summaries are contained in F. S. Regs., Part II. and the Staff Manual respectively. Title pages will be prepared in manuscript.

WAR DIARY
or
INTELLIGENCE SUMMARY.
(Erase heading not required.)

Army Form C. 2118.

Place	Date	Hour	Summary of Events and Information	Remarks and references to Appendices
In the field	3.10.18.		very capable in dealing with them. A noticeable feature of the enemy defences was the number of tank mines he had placed along the wire in front of the VENDIN – HAISNES line & the M.I. [illegible] These were however soon stripped. The enemy line now appeared to run conformably to the [illegible] of the [illegible]. See map attached.	Map of WINGLES vicinity attached.
	4.10.18		Instructions were received to relieve the [illegible] after all arrangements had been made in [illegible] of the relief completed [illegible] orders were received to relieve the M.O.S.B.'s. This meant the Bde was to side slip, as the B.W. advanced, the [illegible] M.O.S.B.'s were not very clear concerning their dispositions but with the assistance of guides [illegible] the disposition of the [illegible] was [illegible] as per map (WINGLES 1.) The enemy appeared to be [illegible] the canal except on the MEURCHIN – WINGLES RD [illegible] a post was suspected at H.6.d. 50.45. Here the [illegible] the [illegible] Bn HQ being at H.8.a. 70.70.	
	5.10.18		"C" Coy on the right attempted to push through the wood on the MEURCHIN RD shortly after dawn after encountering some resistance [illegible] fire from [illegible], owing to the [illegible] being heavily	M.G. [illegible]

D. D. & L., London, E.C. (10340) Wt W5300/P713 750,000 3/18 E 2688 Forms/C2118/16.

Instructions regarding War Diaries and Intelligence Summaries are contained in F. S. Regs., Part II. and the Staff Manual respectively. Title pages will be prepared in manuscript.

WAR DIARY
or
INTELLIGENCE SUMMARY.

(Erase heading not required.)

Army Form C. 2118.

Place	Date	Hour	Summary of Events and Information	Remarks and references to Appendices
In the field	5.10.18		[illegible] ½ coy had to fall back [illegible] killed [illegible]	
	6.10.18		[illegible]	
	7.10.18		[illegible]	[illegible]

(10140) Wt W5300/1713 750,000 5/18 E 2668 Forms/C2118/16.

Army Form C. 2118.

Instructions regarding War Diaries and Intelligence Summaries are contained in F. S. Regs., Part II. and the Staff Manual respectively. Title pages will be prepared in manuscript.

WAR DIARY
or
INTELLIGENCE SUMMARY.
(Erase heading not required.)

Place	Date	Hour	Summary of Events and Information	Remarks and references to Appendices
In the field	7.10.18		An inter coy relief as per O.O. attached took place in the evening "B" & "D" Coy relieving "A" & "C" on the left & right respectively.	O.O. No 43. attached Appx. No. II.
	8–10th 10.18.		During this period the enemy made every effort to let us know he was still in position constantly shelling our forward areas & using a lot of gas on HULLUCH & vicinity. At night his M.G.'s were fairly active & fires could be seen behind his lines. Explosions in the back areas were also being continually heard everything pointed to a further withdrawal. Floods were increasing behind our lines but there was always a dry line of communication. 2/Lt [illegible] was killed at dawn on the 8th back at Coy HQrs ("D") by a shell. The enemy only appeared to have one battery situated on the eastern outskirts of MEURCHIN with which he did all his shelling from wide front. During this period the 16th Div. were on our left & the 8th Seaforths on our right. "A" Coy relieved "D" Coy on the right front on the evening of the 10th. The sluice valve causing the flood opened by Col. Gordon was closed at night there was no further flow into the [illegible] surrounding our companies.	O.O. No 44 attached Appx No. III.
	11.10.18			[illegible]

Instructions regarding War Diaries and Intelligence Summaries are contained in F. S. Regs., Part II. and the Staff Manual respectively. Title pages will be prepared in manuscript.

WAR DIARY
or
INTELLIGENCE SUMMARY.
(Erase heading not required.)

Army Form C. 2118.

Place	Date	Hour	Summary of Events and Information	Remarks and references to Appendices
In the field	15.10.18		had withdrawn when the information passed back to the Corps the Regt received permission to cross. Before the R.E.'s were up "C" Coy had planked the canal were over & "A" Coy had in the absence of the R.E.s constructed the southern bridge. Both Coys ("C" "D") were soon over & established bridgeheads. MEURCHIN was clear of the enemy. In the afternoon the red line was reached & patrols pushing forward found about 15 of the enemy at MAGENTA. (See map for red line MAGENTA — MEURCHIN 1.) The advance rested on this line for the night with "B" Coy forming the outposts. The advance was to continue in the early morning up to the blue line shown on the map.	Map MEURCHIN 1 attd Appx No. V
	16.10.18		[illegible] came under [illegible] at light [illegible] the advance was continued. Slight opposition was met with from the Fosse de ST BARBE the enemy having a M.G. with some riflemen posted there. There was considerable [illegible] from the rifle range. The 18 pdrs of which a battery was attached to us, soon dispersed them. "B" Coy then pushed on right up to the objective where positions were taken up. Two M.G.'s from CAMPHIN were [illegible]	[illegible signature]

D. D. & L., London, E.C. (10540) Wt W5300/P713 750,000 3/18 E 2688 Forms/C2118/16.

Instructions regarding War Diaries and Intelligence Summaries are contained in F. S. Regs., Part II. and the Staff Manual respectively. Title pages will be prepared in manuscript.

WAR DIARY

or

INTELLIGENCE SUMMARY.

(Erase heading not required.)

Army Form C. 2118.

Place	Date	Hour	Summary of Events and Information	Remarks and references to Appendices
In the field.	11.10.18		The day was very hazy & cold. The enemy were very quiet. Arrangements which had commenced for crossing the canal where the conditions were favourable were being consolidated. The bn were to have two foot bridges at its disposal on the first day.	
	12.10.18		Except for an attack on VENDIN-LE-VEUIL by the 9th Royal Scots in the afternoon the day passed very quietly. Attack was a complete success. [illegible] prisoners were secured with light losses to the Scots. 2/Lt [illegible] & 2 O.R's were slightly wounded in the early part of the evening by a rifle grenade.	
	13.10.18		Enemy artillery & T.M's showed an activity a little above normal. The day was cloudy, the visibility decidedly bad. "D" Coy relieved "C" & 1st [illegible] "B" [illegible]	O.O. No. 45 attached. App. No. IV [illegible]
	14.10.18		There was a lot of gas shelling during the day & a large amount of movement was observed on the edge E of MEURCHIN. Loud shouting & heavy explosions were heard during the night.	
	15.10.18		2/Lt [illegible] with a couple of men after hearing explosions in MEURCHIN finding the [illegible] enemy positions abandoned crossed the road bridge [illegible] the village. [illegible] did the same further south. Both patrols reported the enemy [illegible]	[illegible]

(10340) Wt W3500/P713 750,000 3/18 E 2688 Forms/C2118/16. D. & S. L., London, E.C.

Instructions regarding War Diaries and Intelligence Summaries are contained in F. S. Regs., Part II. and the Staff Manual respectively. Title pages will be prepared in manuscript.

WAR DIARY
or
INTELLIGENCE SUMMARY.
(Erase heading not required.)

Army Form C. 2118.

Place	Date	Hour	Summary of Events and Information	Remarks and references to Appendices
In the field.	16.10.18		outskirts. Later the shelling went further back towards our lines & a very large proportion of it was Blue X gas. CARVIN which had been found clear of the enemy was heavily shelled during the afternoon & evening, during which 1 O.R. was killed & 2/Lt. [illegible] was severely wounded. Orders were received later to push on to the next objective (E of ENNEGOURT) but owing to confusing & contradictory orders the line was only advanced about 1000× in the direction of the village. "A" Coy then became the outpost Coy & the remaining Coys were distributed between the line & the trenches E of ST. BARBE. Instructions were received from BDE that the 46th Bde would relieve us in the early morning & pass through to the next objective, leaving the outpost line here to be consolidated.	O.O. No. 47 attached Appx No VI
	17.10.18		"C" Coy of the 13th Royal Scots relieved "A" Coy or rather passed through them at 06.30 hours & the Bn then moved into billets in CARVIN. The day was then spent in furnishing quarters & constant streams of men were to be seen loaded with chairs, mattresses, etc. etc.	[illegible]

D. D. & L., London, E.C. (10340) Wt W5300/P713 750,000 3/18 E 2888 Forms/C2118/16.

Instructions regarding War Diaries and Intelligence Summaries are contained in F. S. Regs., Part II. and the Staff Manual respectively. Title pages will be prepared in manuscript.

WAR DIARY
or
INTELLIGENCE SUMMARY.
(Erase heading not required.)

Army Form C. 2118.

Place	Date	Hour	Summary of Events and Information	Remarks and references to Appendices
In the field	17.10.18		long since that the men were in such glee. There was absolute quiet all day. Our efforts to find the Royal Scots appeared to induce some ahead like a previous line. The Bn. was warned at first to be prepared to move at six hours notice but this was later cancelled. CARVIN showed signs of recent civilian occupation was in good condition. The Huns had not, it appeared, had time to perform much frightfulness though the interior of the church was littered with chairs, tables, altar etc., disgracefully defiled. Some civilians from a neighbouring village came in and informed us that we should find several more further on. He was also able to give some valuable information concerning the enemy withdrawal.	Warning order attached App. No VII
CARVIN	18th		The Battalion remained here till the forenoon of the 18th when orders were received to move to the BOIS D'EPINOY, about 2½ Kilos N. of CARVIN. The Transport and Qm. Stores had joined the Battalion at CARVIN and from this forward, we moved as a complete unit. The wood proved to be quite an interesting place and had been used by the Bosche as an ammunition dump. The shelters erected for his ammunition	A.G. Copeland Lt. W.O. attached APP. No VIII

D. D. & L., London, E.C. (10340) Wt W5300/P713 750,000 3/18 E 2688 Forms/C2118/16.

Instructions regarding War Diaries and Intelligence Summaries are contained in F. S. Regs., Part II. and the Staff Manual respectively. Title pages will be prepared in manuscript.

WAR DIARY
or
INTELLIGENCE SUMMARY.
(Erase heading not required.)

Army Form C. 2118.

Place	Date	Hour	Summary of Events and Information	Remarks and references to Appendices
BOIS D'EPINOY	18th		provided excellent shelter for the Battalion.	
DO.	19th		Orders for a further move forward were received on the early morning of the 19th. MERIGNIES was the destination. Here, the Battalion was billeted and the men were in the best of spirits. The civilians were delighted when we arrived and were eager to tell us of the treatment they had received whilst in captivity. They were extremely kind to the men and altogether a very pleasant evening was spent here. We were constantly hearing that the forward units were continuing the advance and consequently we were always in a state of readiness to move forward.	ADC
MERIGNIES.	20th		We left MERIGNIES on the forenoon of the 20th and billeted on the Eastern outskirts of CAPPELLE. The roads at this time were in very bad condition but in spite of this the marches were carried out exceedingly well. There again, the people were delighted to see us. All the houses were in splendid condition & there was no evidence of any wanton destruction by the Boche. The civilians had been employed on the land and	W. Order attached. APP. No IX.

D. D. & L., London, E.C. (10340) Wt W5300/P713 750,000 3/18 E 2888 Forms/C2118/16.

Instructions regarding War Diaries and Intelligence Summaries are contained in F. S. Regs., Part II. and the Staff Manual respectively. Title pages will be prepared in manuscript.

WAR DIARY
or
INTELLIGENCE SUMMARY.
(Erase heading not required.)

Army Form C. 2118.

Place	Date	Hour	Summary of Events and Information	Remarks and references to Appendices
CAPPELLE			it was purely an agricultural district with little or no evidence of Bosch occupation.	a.o.c.
Do.	21st.		On the morning of the 21st we continued our advance. This time, our destination was DÉRODERIE about 14 kilo. N.W. of CAPPELLE. The roads were still in very bad condition and in many places, mined, but the Battalion completed the march without a single man having fallen out. The villagers turned out and cheered us as we arrived. The kindness they showed here was exceptional and they did everything in their power for the comfort of the troops. Before night had fallen, villagers and troops were the best of friends and our stay in DÉRODERIE promised to be very pleasant indeed.	Map Sheet 44. Belgium and Part of France a.o.c.
DERODERIE	22nd		It now became known that we were likely to be here for a few days. The day was given over to cleaning up and resting. The enemy had taken up positions on the other bank of the River ESCO a formidable obstacle & likely to hold us up	Map Sheet 44. Belgium and part of France

D. D. & L., London, E.C.
(10340) Wt W5300/P713 750,000 3/18 E 2688 Forms/C2118/16.

Army Form C. 2118.

Instructions regarding War Diaries and Intelligence Summaries are contained in F. S. Regs., Part II. and the Staff Manual respectively. Title pages will be prepared in manuscript.

WAR DIARY
or
INTELLIGENCE SUMMARY.

(Erase heading not required.)

Place	Date	Hour	Summary of Events and Information	Remarks and references to Appendices
			some time. The Brigade had now come into support with this unit as Battalion in reserve.	ADC
DÉRODERIE	23rd / 28th		During this time training was carried out. The men were in splendid form and carried out their work in ~~[illegible]~~ a very pleasing manner. They had benefited by the rest of these few days and were looking remarkably well. Some very successful games of rugby & soccer were played, both by officers and men, and a platoon championship in soccer was arranged, play for which commenced to-day.	
			Very little activity had been shown by the enemy and although we were now within range of his artillery little or no shelling took place in our vicinity.	ADC
DÉRODERIE	29th		Orders to relieve the 7/8th Bn. K.O.S.B's. in Front Brigade reserve were issued to-day. (O.O. No 52). The relief was carried out by day and completion reported by 4.30 pm. The dispositions were as follows 'A' Coy. at PETIT RUMES about C.7.a.3.3. 'B' Coy. BASSE RUE about C.8.c.9.0. 'C' Coy. at Cross Roads C.14.a.4.0. 'D' Coy. M. DE CLERMAY about C.8.c.0.3.	O.Order attached APP. No X ADC

(20340) Wt W5300/P713 750,000 3/15 D. D. & L., London, E.C. E 2688 Forms/C2118/16.

Instructions regarding War Diaries and Intelligence Summaries are contained in F. S. Regs., Part II. and the Staff Manual respectively. Title pages will be prepared in manuscript.

WAR DIARY
or
INTELLIGENCE SUMMARY.
(Erase heading not required.)

Army Form C. 2118.

Place	Date	Hour	Summary of Events and Information	Remarks and references to Appendices
			Battalion Headquarters remained at DÉRODERIE.	Map Sheet 44 Belgium & Part of France.
	30th		Nothing worthy of note happened during the day. Usual training was carried out	A.D.C.
	31st		Company Parades were carried out.	A.D.C.

J. B. Wood Major
Cmdg. 5th Gordon Highrs

D. D. & L., London, E.C.
(10340) Wt W5300/P713 750,000 3/18 E 2688 Forms/C2118/16.

Strength October 1918

WAR DIARY
or
INTELLIGENCE SUMMARY.
(*Erase heading not required.*)

Army Form C. 2118.

Instructions regarding War Diaries and Intelligence Summaries are contained in F. S. Regs., Part II. and the Staff Manual respectively. Title pages will be prepared in manuscript.

~~Place~~ Date	Date / Hour / Summary of Events and Information	O	OR	O	OR
27.9.18.				39	805
	INCREASE				
	Reinf. from Base.	-	16		
	Rejoined from Hosp.	-	2		
	Taken on Str from 8/10 Gordon Highlanders.	-	1		
		-	19		
	DECREASE				
	To UK for Commission	-	1		
	Transferred to 9th Gordon Hgh.	-	2		
	Evacuated (sick)	-	4		
	Struck off Strength. (Sick on leave to UK)	-	1		
	Over 7 days in FA Sick	-	3		
	Struck off Strength posted to 1st Gordons.	-	1		
5/10/18		-	12	39	812
	INCREASE				
	Reinf. from Div. Recpt Camp.	2	5		
	DECREASE				
	Killed in action	2	15		
	Wounded "		4		
	Evacuated sick		6		
	over 7 days in FA sick		7		
12/10/18		2	32	39	785

Date	Summary of Events and Information	O	OR	O	OR
12/10/18				39	785
	INCREASE				
	Joined from Div. Recp. Camp	1	10		
	At Div. Recpt Camp taken on Strength.	1	7		
		2	17		
	DECREASE				
	Cross posted to 9th Gordons.	.	1		
	Wounded	2	13		
	Evacuated Sick	-	3		
	Over 7 days in FA Sick	-	13		
19/10/18		2	30	39	772
	INCREASE				
	Cross posted from 9th Gordon Highlanders.	-	1		
	Joined from Div. Reception Camp.	3	7		
		3	8		
	DECREASE				
	Evacuated Sick	-	2		
	Over 7 days in FA Sick	-	13		
26/10/18		-	15	42	765

A6945 Wt. W11422/M1160 35,000 12/16 D. D. & L. Forms/C./2118/14.

Instructions regarding War Diaries and Intelligence Summaries are contained in F. S. Regs., Part II. and the Staff Manual respectively. Title pages will be prepared in manuscript.

Army Form C. 2118.

WAR DIARY
or
INTELLIGENCE SUMMARY.
(Erase heading not required.)

Casualties October 1918

Place	Date	Hour	Summary of Events and Information	Remarks and references to Appendices
			No 233049 Pte Gardiner W Wounded 14 10 18 No 7846 Pte Fraser A Wounded	10 10 18
			62560 " Milliken D do 13 10 18 203031 L/c Duff R do	10-10-18
			302618 " Hodge R do 13 10 18 42466 Pte Dixon I do	10 10 18
			2nd Lieut Haddon W J do 13 10 18 8197 " Stewart A do	10 10 18
			2nd Lieut Buchanan A H Killed 5 10 18 17666 " Tappin A do	10 10 18
			2nd Lieut Tindall A G do 8 10 18 S/10121 " Carey A do	11 10 18
			No 40448 Cpl Antonelli J Wounded 5 10 18 271174 " Urie D do	11 10 18
			235353 L/c Henderson J do 5 10 18 22786 " Kerr J do	11 10 18
			23243 Pte McGuire J do 5 10 18 23250 " McBrier J Killed	5 10 18
			201489 " Moir A do 5 10 18 22704 Sinclair A do	10 10 18
			40187 L/c Parsons R do 5 10 18 20826 Arnott R do	10-10-18
			235358 Pte Thomson D do 5 10 18 22398 McArthur J do	10 10 18
			8533 Cpl Barker H do 5 10 18 62573 " Elder G Wounded	5 10 18
			241646 Pte Gharge H do 5 10 18 13785 Jackson J do	5 10 18
			S/176 Sgt Glendinning I do 5 10 18 300587 King J do	6 10 18
			242498 L/c McLachlan J do 10 10 18 330040 Gorrie S do	6-10-18

A6945 Wt. W11422/M1160 350,000 12/16 D. D. & L. Forms/C./2118/14.

Instructions regarding War Diaries and Intelligence Summaries are contained in F. S. Regs., Par. II. and the Staff Manual respectively. Title pages will be prepared in manuscript.

Army Form C. 2118.

WAR DIARY
or
INTELLIGENCE SUMMARY.
(*Erase heading not required.*)

Casualties October 1918

Place	Date	Hour	Summary of Events and Information	Remarks and references to Appendices
			No 41140 Pte Jordan A Wounded 10 10 18 No 42066 Pte Dixon [illegible] Died of wounds	15 10 18
			302340 " Cane G do 11 10 18 2nd Lieut Haig MM AW do	17 10 18
			62592 " McInnes M do 11 10 18	
			23220 " Bellamy J do 14 10 18	
			2nd Lieut Haig AW do 16 10 18	
			290289 Pte Hutchison J do 15 10 18	
			17684 L/Cpl Butchart G do 17 10 18	
			23254 Pte Semple A do 17 10 18	
			241873 " McLachlan C do 14 10 18	
			22669 " Brown C Killed 17 10 18	
			13506 " Pyper D Wounded 14 10 18	
			325326 " Watt P do 8 10 18	
			202597 " Thomson J do 8 10 18	
			203614 " Hardie J do 4 10 18	
			202691 " Southern A do 4 10 18	
			5182 " Bain L do 17 10 18	

A6945 Wt. W11422/M1160 350,000 12/16 D. D. & L. Forms/C./2118/14.

SECRET. Copy No. 7

5th Battalion, The Gordon Highlanders.

OPERATION ORDER No. 41.

1st October, 1918

1 The 5th Gordon Highlanders will relieve the 8th Seaforth Highlanders in the Left Sub-Section to-morrow, 2nd inst.

2. DISPOSITIONS

"A" Coy Gordons will relieve "B" Coy Seaforths in the Right Front
Coy Hdqrs G.12.a.7.3.

"D" " " " " "C" " Seaforths in the Left Front.
Coy Hdqrs G.11.b.90.65

"B" " " " " "A" " Seaforths in the Support Front.
Coy Hdqrs G.11.c.6.5

"C" " " " " "D" " Seaforths in the Res. Front.
Coy Hdqrs G.11.a.3.0.

Battalion Headquarters at G.17.a.6.8

3. The Battalion will parade ready to march off, at 2 pm in the order, "A" & "B" Coys, Battn. Hdqrs, "D" Coy, and march off by platoons at 100 yards interval.

4. GUIDES.

5 per Coy for "A", "B" & "D" Coys and 2 for Battn. Hdqrs, will be at the Western end of CHAPEL ALLEY, G.8.d.1.5. at 2.30 pm.

O.C. "C" Coy will make his own arrangements about guides.

As "D" Coy cannot relieve by daylight, they will be accommodated in STANSFIELD ROAD, West of the Reserve Coy Area, until 7.15 pm, when one guide per post will report to O.C. "D" Coy.

5. Advanced parties as detailed in the WARNING ORDER of to-day, will proceed this afternoon, and thoroughly reconnoitre the line, and the tunnel system.

6. Lists of trench stores, maps, work in hand, etc., taken over will be forwarded to Battn Hdqrs by 10 am, 3rd October.

Disposition sketches will reach Battn Hdqrs at the same hour.

7. Completion of relief will be wired to Battn Hdqrs by the Code Phrase "Your GH/30 RECEIVED AT ......"

8. ACKNOWLEDGE.

(Signed) G.P.Geddes, Capt & Adjt,
5th Battalion, The Gordon Highlanders.

Distribution:-

Copies Nos 1 - 4 : O.C.Coys.
5 : T.O.
6 : Q.M.
7 : I.O.
8 : Signals.
9 : 44th Brigade.
10 : 8th Seaforths.
11 : War Diary.
12 : File.

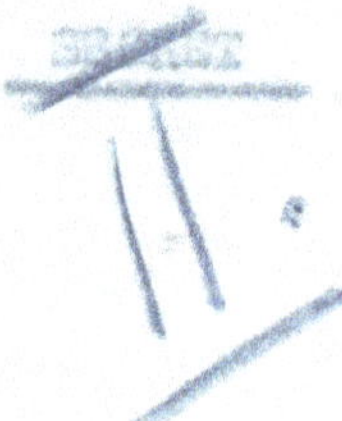

Copy No

5th Bn., The Gordon Highlanders.

O P E R A T I O N   O R D E R   No. 43.

7th October, 1939

1 The following inter-company reliefs will be carried out to-night, commencing at dusk :-
"B" Coy will relieve "A" Coy as Left Front Coy.
"D" " " " "C" " " Right " "
On relief. "A" Coy will withdraw to Support and "C" Coy to Reserve.
Arrangements for guides etc to be made by O.C. Coys concerned.

2 On completion of relief, Captain W.S.Kemp, M.C., will assume command of the Outpost Line, with H.Q. at Left Coys H.Q., D.22.d.8.2

3 "A" and "C" Coys will send advanced parties this afternoon to take over accommodation from "B" and "D" Coys, respectively.

4 The guard of 1 N.C.O. and 3 at Bn.H.Q., at present provided by "D" Coy, will be relieved by a similar guard from "C" Coy at 1530 hours.

5 Completion of relief will be wired to Bn.H.Q. by the Code Phrase "Your GH/21 received at ....".

6 ACKNOWLEDGE.

G.P.Geddes
Capt & Adjt.,
5th Battalion, The Gordon Highlanders.

Distribution :-

Copies Nos.		
	1-4	O.C. Coys.
	5	Details.
	6	Signals.
	7	R.S.M.
	8	44th Brigade.
	9	M.O.
	10	File.

SECRET

Copy No 10

5th Battn, The Gordon Highlanders.

OPERATION ORDER No. 44

10th October, 1918

1 The following inter-company relief will be carried out tonight, commencing at dusk.
"A" Coy will relieve "D" Coy as Right Front Company.

2 On completion of relief "D" Coy will withdraw to Support.

3 All arrangements to be made by O.C. Coys concerned.

4 Arrangements for rations will remain the same.

5 Completion of relief will be wired to Bn. H.Q. by the Code Words "Your GH/21 received at........."

6 ACKNOWLEDGE.

G.P. Geddes

Capt & Adjt,
5th Battn, The Gordon Highlanders.

Distribution:-
Copies Nos 1 - 4 : O.C. Coys.
5 : R.S.M.
6 : Signals
7 : 8th Seaforths.
9 : Details.
10 : W.D.
11 : File.

SECRET

6th Battn, The Gordon Highlanders. Copy No. 12

OPERATION ORDER No. 45

17th October, 1918.

1 The following inter-company relief will be carried out to-night, commencing at dusk:-
"D" Coy will relieve "A" Coy as Right Front Coy.
"C" " " " "B" " " Left " "

2 On relief "A" Coy will withdraw to Support and "B" to Reserve.

3 All arrangements to be made between O.C. Coys concerned.

4 Rations for "C" & "D" Coys will arrive at 1800 hours, for "A" & "B" Coys at the usual time.

5 Completion of relief to be wired to Battn. H.Q. by the code phrase "Your GH/2 2 received at ...."

6 ACKNOWLEDGE.

Capt & Adjt.
6th Battn, The Gordon Highlanders.

Distribution:-
Copies Nos 1 - 4 : O.C. Coys
5 : Major [illegible]
6 : I.O.
7 : L.G.O.
8 : Signals
9 : Q.M.
10 : T.O.
11 : R.S.M.
12 : W.D.
13 : 44th Brigade.
14 : File.

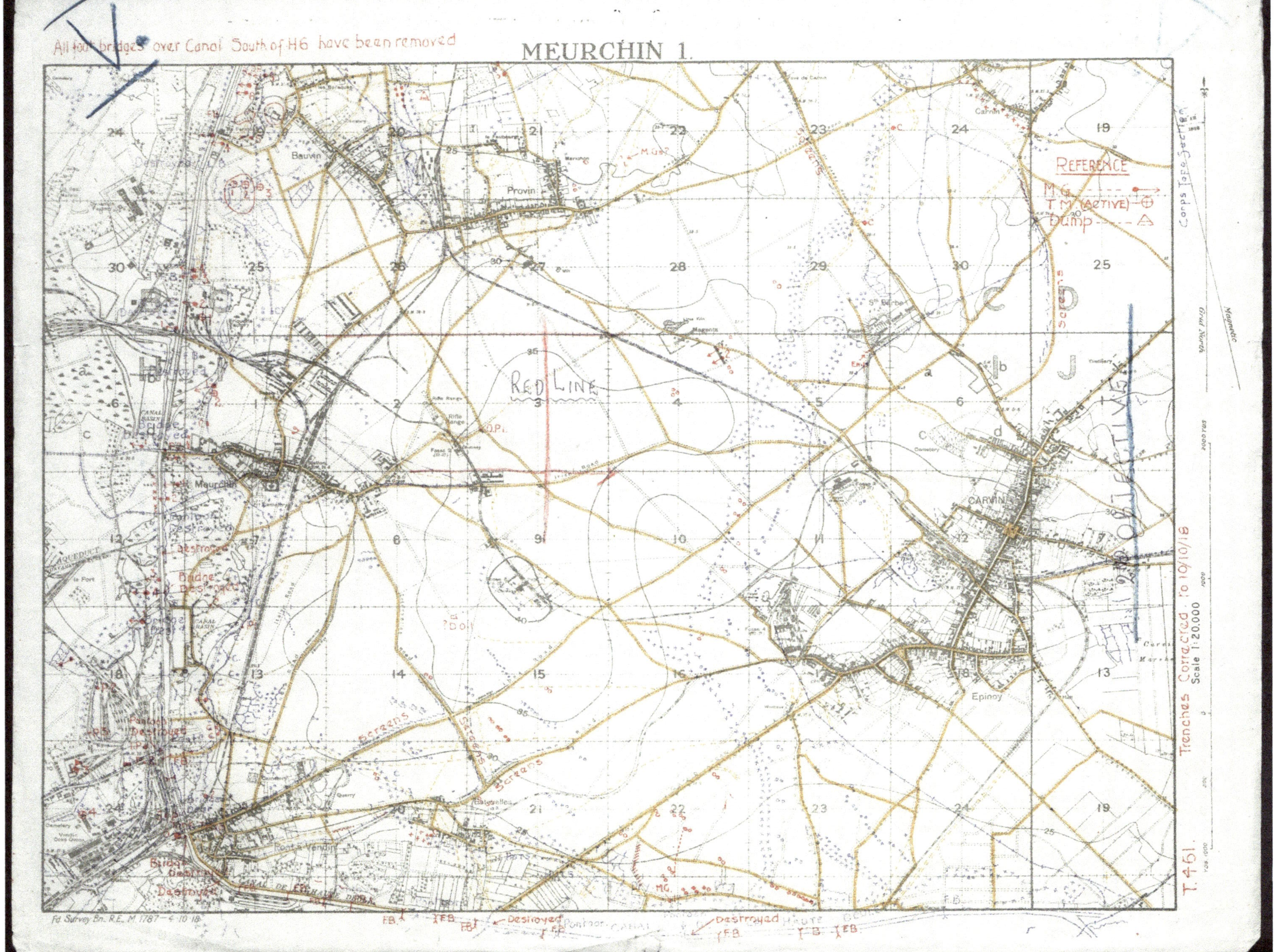

MEURCHIN 1.

All foot bridges over Canal South of H6 have been removed
Corps Topo Section
REFERENCE
M.G. - - - -
T.M. (ACTIVE)
Dump - - - -
RED LINE
OBJECTIVE
Trenches Corrected to 10/10/18
Scale 1:20,000
T.461.
Grid North
Magnetic
Bauvin
Provin
Meurchin
CARVIN
Epinoy
Carvin
Ste Barbe
Magenta
Bataville
Port à Vendin
Quarry
Aqueduct
le Port
Canal Basin
Bridge Destroyed
Pontoon Destroyed
Destroyed
Screens
Rifle Range
O.P.
F.B.
Canal de la Haute Deule
Fd Survey Bn. R.E. M 1787 – 4-10-18.

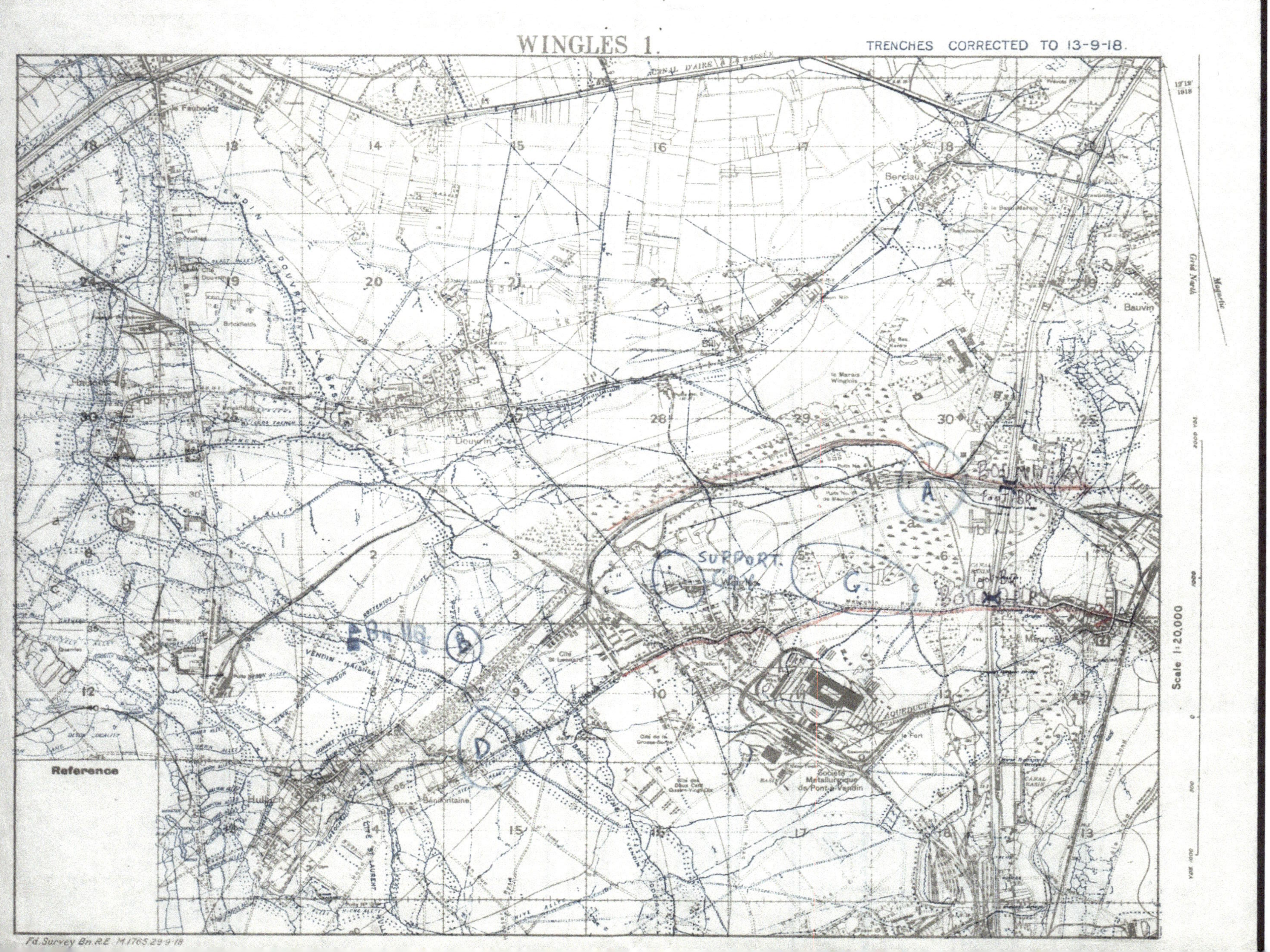
WINGLES 1.
TRENCHES CORRECTED TO 13-9-18.
Berclau
Bauvin
Billy
Douvrin
Hulluch
Bénifontaine
Cité St Laurent
Société Métallurgique de Pont-à-Vendin
SUPPORT
Reference
Scale 1:20,000
Grid North
Magnetic
Fd. Survey Bn. R.E. M.1765 29-9-18

Reference Sketch on back.

To

1. My {Platoon / Company} has reached

(Mark position on map or give map reference).

and is consolidating.
has consolidated.
is ready to advance.

2. I am (not) in touch with on right.
and (not) with on left.

3. I am held up at {by wire. / by M.G. fire. / by rifle fire.}

4. Enemy's artillery is firing on
from

5. I have sent forward patrols to

6. I estimate {my casualties at / my strength at}

7. I need
boxes S.A.A.
Lewis gun drums
Bombs
Rifle Grenades
Stokes Shells
Very Lights
Ground Flares
Stakes
Coils wire
Tins water
Rations
(at once)
(to-night)

8. I intend to

9. (General remarks on position and strength of enemy. Number of prisoners taken and identifications, if known).

Time	Name	Rank
Date	Platoon	Coy.
	Battalion	

Strike out all that is not applicable and forward at once to Bn. H.Q.

SECRET.

Copy No. 9

5th Battn, The Gordon Highlanders.
O P E R A T I O N O R D E R No. 47.

16th October, 1918.

1 "B" Coy will send guides to Battn. H.Q. at once. at J.1.c.20.53.

2 "A" Coy will move up and relieve "B" Coy, immediately consolidation is completed.

3 "D" Coy will return to their former billets.

4 "C" Coy will occupy billets vacated by "A" Coy. O.C. "C" Coy will send parties to reconnoitre position of billets forthwith.

5 On relief "B" Coy will retire to billets in the village.

6 Completion of relief and arrival in billets will be reported to Battn. H.Q. by the code phrase " Your CH/23 received at......"

7 ACKNOWLEDGE.

G.P. Geddes
Capt & Adjt,
5th Battn, The Gordon Highlanders.

Distribution :-
Copies Nos 1 - 4 : O.C. Coys.
5 : 2nd in Command.
6 : R.S.M.
7 : Signals.
8 : L.G.O.
9 : I.O. for War Diary.
10 : File.

VII.

SECRET

Copy No 7

5th Battn, The Gordon Highlanders.
W A R N I N G   O R D E R

17th October, 1918

1 The Advanced Guard of the 40th Brigade now well forward. Outpost of "A" Coy will withdraw at once to Billets.

2 Companies will be prepared to move off at short notice. Probable time of moving will be wired as soon as possible.

3 ACKNOWLEDGE.

Capt & Adjt,
5th Battn, The Gordon Highlanders.

Distribution :-
Copies Nos 1 - 4 : O.C. Coys.
5 : R.S.M.
6 : Signals.
7 : I.O. for War Diary.
8 : File.

Secret.

VIII

6th Battalion, The Gordon Highlanders.

WARNING ORDER.

1. The Battalion will form up in mass outside the CHURCH ready to march off at 0945 hours to-morrow the 18th instant.

2. Officers' valises and otger retinue of the transport will be ready to collect at Battalion and Company Headquarters at 0830 hours.

3. Further details will be issued later.

17th October, 1918.

Lieut-Colonel,
Comdg. 6th Battalion, The Gordon Highlanders.

Distribution.

Copies 1 - 4 : O.C. Coys.
5 : Qr Mr.
6 : T.O.
7 : R.S.M.
8 : Signals.
9 : Headquarters Mess.
10 : File.

No7

5th Battalion The Gordon Highlanders.
OPERATION ORDERS No.48

Ref. Map :- 44A N.E. 1/20,000 18/10/18.

1. The 15th Division will continue the advance tomorrow. The objective is a line East of CARDONNERIE (exclusive) WATTINGS -CAPPELIE-TEMPIEUVE (exclusive). The 44th Brigade will follow in reserve. Destination - Huts in J.15a and b.

2. Starting point - The CHURCH. Time - 1000 hours. The battalion will pass the starting point in the following order Bn.H.Qrs. A,B,D,C Coys.

3. 1st Line transport less cookers and water carts will march Brigaded. Cookers and water carts will march in rear of C Coy. Pack animals will march in rear of Coys.

4. Advance party with bicycles, consisting of Lieut.Copland, C.Q.M.S.s and one N.C.O. mounted from transport will report at Bn.H.Qrs. at 0900 hours. They will report to the Staff Captain at CROSS ROADS J.15b.15.90. at 0930 hours. Advance party will meet the Battalion at J.9.c.00.75.

5. Distances of 200 yards to be maintained between Coys.

6. Halts will be 10 minutes to the clock hour.

7. ACKNOWLEDGE.

Issued at 06.30 hours.
18/10/18.

(Sgd) G.P.GEDDES, Captain & Adjt.
5th Battalion The Gordon Highlanders.

Copies to :-

No.1/4 O.C.Coys.
5 Q.M. and T.O.
6 Signals.
7 Lt.Copland.
8 R.S.M.
9. File
10. War Diary.

SECRET.

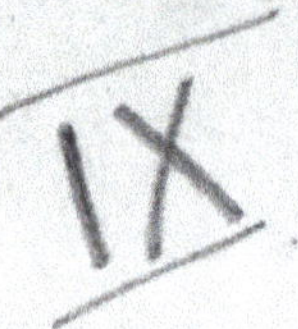

O.C.Coys, R.S.M. & T.O.

WARNING ORDER.

1. Probable Starting Times to-morrow:-

Battn, H.Q. ,,,,...........	0845 hours.
"D" Coy	0847 "
"A" "	0849 "
"B" "	0851 "
"C" "	0853 "

Starting Point. Road Junction, F.29.c.9.0.
O.C.Coys must calculate carefully the time they will take to reach the Starting Point.

2. Valises, Mess kits etc, of Battn,H.Q., "A" & "C" Coys will be stacked at Q.M.Stores, those of "B" & "D" Coys at "D" Coy.H.Q. by 0745 hours.

3. The usual billetting parties will report to Lieut.Copland at Orderly Room at 0800 hours.

G.P. Geddes.
Capt & Adjt,
5th Battn, The Gordon Highlanders.

Issued through Signals 2200 hours.

20th October, 1918.

SECRET

Copy No. 11

APP. NoX

5th Battalion The Gordon Highlanders.

OPERATION ORDER No. 52

29/10/1918.

1. The 5th Bn. The Gordon Highlanders will relieve the 7/8th K.O.S.B.s as Reserve Battalion of the Front Brigade today 29th October, 1918.

2. Dispositions.
   Coys. will relieve opposite Coys. which are located as under :-

   "A" Coy. ... PETIT RUMES about C.7.a.8.3.
   "B" Coy. ... BASSE RUE, about C.8.c.9.0.
   "C" Coy. ... CROSS ROADS, C.14.a.4.0.
   "D" Coy. ... M. de CLERMAY, about C.8.c.0.3.
   Bn.H.Q. ... Will remain at present location.

3. Guides.
   One per Coy. will report to their respective Coy.H.Q. at 1445 hours.

4. All movement to be by platoon. at 100 yards interval.

5. The Alert Zone.
   Box respirators will be carried in the "Alert" position and steel helmets worn East of the N. and S. Grid Line between C.7 and C.8.

6. Transport and Q.M. Stores will move under their own arrangements to CROSS ROADS, GUIGNIES, C.3.c.7.5.

7. Completion of relief to be reported to Bn. H.Q. by runner.

8. ACKNOWLEDGE.

G.P. Geddes
Capt.& Adjt.

5th Bn. The Gordon Highlanders.

Distribution.

List "A"
plus 7/8th K.O.S.B.s

Issued through Signals at 1100 hrs

SECRET.

ADMINISTRATIVE INSTRUCTIONS.

(In conjunction with Operation Orders..No.52)

1. Rations, if received before 1300 hours, will be distributed before Coys. move off.
   Otherwise, they will be distributed in the new area.

2. Cookers and L.G. limbers will proceed and remain with their Coys.

3. Officers' Valises and Mess Kits will be dumped at each Coys H.Q. by 1330 hours, when G.S. Wagons will collect.

4. The R.A.P. will be established at -- to be notified later.

G.A. Geddes

Capt & Adjt,
5th Battalion, The Gordon Highlanders.

29/10/18.

5 Gordon Hrs
WR 45

CONFIDENTIAL.

WAR DIARY.

FOR THE MONTH

OF

NOVEMBER.

1918

VOLUME 43.

D. G. Gordon Lieut-Colonel,

1/12/18. Commanding 5th Battalion, The Gordon Highlanders.

Instructions regarding War Diaries and Intelligence Summaries are contained in F. S. Regs., Par. II. and the Staff Manual respectively. Title pages will be prepared in manuscript.

WAR DIARY
or
INTELLIGENCE SUMMARY.
(*Erase heading not required.*)

Army Form C. 2118.

Place	Date	Hour	Summary of Events and Information	Remarks and references to Appendices
DÉRODERIE	1/11/18 To 8.11.18		During this period, the usual parades were carried out and the football competition continued. On the first of the month, orders in the event of further withdrawal of the enemy, were issued. About 0950 hours on the 8th the code word "SUSPECTED" was received from Brigade (See App No I) and all preparations were made for a move at very short notice. 'B' Company immediately moved forward to take over the outpost line held by the 8th Seaforth Highlanders. Later in the day, the code word "GONE" came through. The Battalion was now ready to go forward, and orders were issued accordingly.	APP. No I. APP No II. a.b.c. APP No III APP No IV
DO	9.11.18		The order to move was issued on the early morning of the 9th, the destination being HOLLAIN about eight kilometres East of DÉRODERIE	MAP SHEET 44 A.P.P. No V a.b.c.
HOLLAIN	9.11.18		The Battalion arrived at HOLLAIN about 1230 hours and remained there till 1000 hours the following morning. Dispositions in the event of further move, were issued.	APP. VI. a.b.c.

A6945 Wt. W11422/M1160 35,000 12/16 D. D. & L. Forms/C./2118/14.

Army Form C. 2118.

Instructions regarding War Diaries and Intelligence Summaries are contained in F. S. Regs., Par. II, and the Staff Manual respectively. Title pages will be prepared in manuscript.

WAR DIARY
or
INTELLIGENCE SUMMARY.
(*Erase heading not required.*)

Place	Date	Hour	Summary of Events and Information	Remarks and references to Appendices
HOLLAIN	10.11.18		It was known that the Battalion had to move forward from HOLLAIN on the night of the 9th, but as no orders were received to this effect, no move was made till the morning of the 10th, and then, without any written order. During the night, the other units of the Brigade had moved far forward and it was therefore necessary for the Battalion, to make what was really a two days march, in order to get again in touch. Consequently, the Battalion left HOLLAIN and set off for TOURPES, North East of HOLLAIN and about 25 kilometres distant. This march was completed by 1830 hours that night, and not a single man had fallen out.	a.D.C. MAP SHEET 38
TOURPES	11/11/18.		Operation Orders to the effect that the Battalion would pass through the 8th Seaforth Highlanders were issued.	APP. No VII.
			The first Company left TOURPES at 0630 hours on the morning of the 11th and thereafter we became front line Battalion. About 11.20 am, we were moving over open	

A6945 Wt. W11422/M1160 350,000 12/16 D. D. & L. Forms/C./2118/14.

Instructions regarding War Diaries and Intelligence Summaries are contained in F. S. Regs., Par. II, and the Staff Manual respectively. Title pages will be prepared in manuscript.

WAR DIARY
or
INTELLIGENCE SUMMARY.
(Erase heading not required.)

Army Form C. 2118.

Place	Date	Hour	Summary of Events and Information	Remarks and references to Appendices
			country just West of, and in sight of CHIÈVRES, when news of the armistice was brought. Rumours had been circulating during the morning, and the news wasn't altogether unexpected, but when it was given out officially, the men cheered and sang. It was altogether a strange picture. The Companies were moving forward, with outposts well ahead, and on receipt of the news, the Battalion seemed to assemble at lightening speed, and continued the march in column of fours, whistling and singing. Not a shot had been heard and no Bosche had been encountered. We were now close on CHIÈVRES and instructions were issued for the Battalion to billet there. A billeting party went on ahead. The reception at DÉRODERIE has already been written about but, it was as nothing compared to the reception	A.L.

Instructions regarding War Diaries and Intelligence Summaries are contained in F. S. Regs., Par. II. and the Staff Manual respectively. Title pages will be prepared in manuscript.

WAR DIARY
or
INTELLIGENCE SUMMARY.
(*Erase heading not required.*)

Army Form C. 2118.

Place	Date	Hour	Summary of Events and Information	Remarks and references to Appendices
			given to the Battalion at Chievres. The streets were lined by civilians who cheered us as we passed and handed us all sorts of gifts. In the afternoon a guard of honour headed by the town band waited on Major Wood, who was then in command, and he along with other officers from Headquarters was marched to the Town Hall, where he was officially received by the Mayor Mons Emille Doems, and acclaimed hero of the town (see app N° 8). After the ceremony a minute was entered in the town records and signed by each of the officers present. It was altogether a remarkable day and the wildest scenes of enthusiasm on the part of both civilians and soldiers were witnessed.	APP. N° 8. aDC aDC
CHIEVRES	12.11.18		The day was given over to cleaning up. B Company remained in outpost line at HOYES which had been taken up on the afternoon of the 11th.	

A6945 Wt. W11422/M1160 35,000 12/16 D. D. & L. Forms/C./2118/14.

Instructions regarding War Diaries and Intelligence Summaries are contained in F. S. Regs., Par. II. and the Staff Manual respectively. Title pages will be prepared in manuscript.

WAR DIARY
or
INTELLIGENCE SUMMARY.
(*Erase heading not required.*)

Army Form C. 2118.

Place	Date	Hour	Summary of Events and Information	Remarks and references to Appendices
CHIEVRES	13.11.18		A message of congratulation was received from The Chairman	
			of the Aberdeenshire Territorial Force Association to which	APP. X
	14.11.18		Major Wood replied (App X) Parades as usual were	
			carried out. B Company were relieved in the outpost	
	15.11.18		line by D Company 10th Scottish Rifles and withdrew to	APP XI
			billets in Chievres (App IX) The move detailed in appendix	
			9 was cancelled and the Battalion remained in Chievres	ADC
	16.11.18		Parades as usual were carried out. A detachment	
	17.11.18		attended thanksgiving service in Church. The Commanding	
			Officer and officers present marched to the Town Hall	
			and were received by the Mayor. To commemorate	
			the entry of the Battalion into Chievres it was decided	ADC
			to present to the town the Battalion Flag. The Battalion	
			formed up in the Grande Place and after the flag	
			had been blessed by the Padre (Capt The Rev B J Whiteside)	
			the Commanding Officer in a fitting speech handed it	

A6945 Wt. W11422/M1160 35,000 12/16 D. D. & L. Forms/C./2118/14.

Instructions regarding War Diaries and Intelligence Summaries are contained in F. S. Regs., Par. II. and the Staff Manual respectively. Title pages will be prepared in manuscript.

WAR DIARY
or
INTELLIGENCE SUMMARY.
(Erase heading not required.)

Army Form C. 2118.

Place	Date	Hour	Summary of Events and Information	Remarks and references to Appendices
CHIEVRES	17.11.18		to the Mayor who received it on behalf of the townspeople after the ceremony the Commanding Officer was received by the Mayor. A pamphlet on the presentation of the colours will be forwarded with Diary of December	
	18.11.18		The Battalion was inspected by the Divisional Commander Major General HL Reed VC CB CMG.	ADC
	19.11.18 to 25.11.18		Usual parades were continued and the football competition decided 15 Platoon D Company winning. Batt. Parade was held on 25th.	
	26.11.18		The Battalion was inspected by the G.O.C. Brigade.	
	27.11.18 to 30.11.18		Usual parades were held.	

APP. No I

SECRET. K/3.

O.C. All Coys,
L.G.O., T.O & Q.M., Signals & R.S.M.

1. In the event of a further enemy withdrawal the 15th Division is to secure small bridge-heads as soon as possible at the River crossings at ANTOING, and also to establish posts on the right bank of L'ESCAUT FIEUVE as far South as BRUYELIE, to cover the Road leading from BRUYELIE to ANTOING. These posts will be approximately 500 yards East of the River.

2. The 44th Infantry Brigade will be prepared to advance under cover of the above posts as soon as they are established, and to secure a bridge-head on the line VEZONCHAUX-BOURGEON-FONTENOY-GUERONDE.

3. The above advance will be carried out, on receipt of orders from Brigade Hdqrs., as follows:-

(a) The Front Battalion (4/5th Black Watch) will cross the River in or near V.21.c. and secure the line VEZONCHAUX-BOURGEON (both inclusive)

(b) The Support Battalion (8th Seaforth Highlanders) will cross in or near V.15 and secure the line FONTENOY-GUERONDE (both inclusive), and, in the event of the troops of III Corps on their left being unable to cross, will throw back a defensive flank to the river.

(c) The dividing line between Battalions will be the Road V.15.d.3.2 - V.22.a.4.9. - FONTENOY - all inclusive to the left Battalion.

4. On receipt of Code Word "SUSPECTED", the 5th Gordon Highlanders, less "B" Coy, will stand to, ready to move at very short notice.
"B" Coy will relieve the Front Battalion in the present outpost line, South of BRUYELLE (exclusive). Coy.H.Q. will be established at WEZ VELVAIN CHATEAU.

5. On it being established that the enemy have withdrawn, the Code Word "GONE" will be issued and the following action will be taken:-

(a) 4/5th Black Watch and 8th Seaforth Highlanders will assemble in artillery formation West of LANNOY CHATEAU, and West of MERLIN respectively.

(b) The 5th Gordon Highlanders will remain in present position

6 On receipt of the Code Word "SUSPECTED", blankets and officers' valises will be stacked at each Coy.H.Q. under a guard of 3 O.R's. Transport Officer will collect and dump at Q.M.Stores.

(Signed) G.P.Geddes, Capt & Adjt,
5th Battalion, The Gordon Highlanders.

1/11/18.

APP No II

Army Form C. 2123.
(In books of 100.)

"C" FORM.
MESSAGES AND SIGNALS.

No. of Message ....

Prefix SB Code 0924 Words 16	Sent, or sent out.	Office Stamp.
Received from VADW By D Burnett	At .... m.	Dolu 8.11.18
Service Instructions VADW Pty	To	
	By	

Handed in at VADW Office 0924 m. Received 0950 m.

TO Dolu

*Sender's Number.	Day of Month.	In reply to Number.	AAA
BM454	8		
Suspected	aaa	addsd	affiliated
units	acknowledge		reptd
VOSE	JURA	BAVA	BASO
BARA			

OR83

FROM VADW

PLACE & TIME

* This line, except A A A, should be erased, if not required.

(3287) Wt. W54/P738. 691,000 Pads. 2/18. A.P.Ltd. (E2263)

App No III

"C" FORM.
MESSAGES AND SIGNALS.

Army Form C. 2123.
(In books of 100.)
No. of Message

Prefix SM Code 1100 Words 28

Received from VADW By DB

Service Instructions
VADW

Sent, or sent out.
At m.
To
By

Office Stamp.
Doh
8.11.18

Handed in at Office m. Received m.

TO Doh

*Sender's Number.	Day of Month.	In reply to Number.	AAA
BM455	8	—	
GONE	aaa	addsd	affiliated
units	acknowledge	reptd	
VOSE	JWRA	BAVA	BASO
BARA			

FROM
PLACE & TIME VADW 1050

* This line, except AAA, should be erased, if not required.

(3287) Wt. W54/P738. 691,000 Pads. 3/18. A.P.Ltd. (E2062)

O. C. All Coys. L. T. M.

APP. No IV

1. GONE.

2. O.C. Coys will draw from the transport at once, flares to complete to one per man.

3. All men who will leave the battalion to proceed on leave up to and including the 13th inst, will report at once at the Q. M. Stores and remain with them.

The following officers will be left out and sent to Q. M. Stores at once:-

'A' Coy Lieut. Bain.
'B' . Capt. Watt
'C' . Lieut West
'D' . " Muir

4. Lewis Gun Limbers and pack animals will be sent at once to the Transport Lines.

O. C. Coys will be responsible for this.

Cookers will be sent to the Transport on receipt of orders to move forward.

5. Remainder of rations for the day will be carried on the man.

6. Lewis Guns and S.A.A will be carried on the man.

7. Full marching order will be worn.

8. ACKNOWLEDGE.

(Signed) G. P. Geddes, Capt. & Adjt.
5th Battn. Gordon Highrs.

8/11/18.

"C" Form.

Army Form C. 2123.
(In books of 100.)

MESSAGES AND SIGNALS. No. of Message..........

Prefix..........Code.........Words..........	Received.	Sent, or sent out.	Office Stamp.
£ s. d. Charges to Collect	From.......... By..........	At..........m. To.......... By..........	
Service Instructions.			

APP. V

Handed in at.......................Office..........m. Received..........m.

TO: O.C. A. C. D Coys. T.O. L.G.O. Lt Copland. R.S.M.

*Sender's Number	Day of Month	In reply to Number	AAA
G 13	9	—	

The	Battn	will	moves
up	to	HOLLAIN	this
morning	via	JOLLAIN	MERLIN aaa
Coys	will	move	off as
follows	Bn Hq.	and	A Coy
at	0645	C and	D
Coys	at	0700	aaa
1 Officer per		coy	will
report	to	Lt Copland	at
X Roads	D.7.a	55 at	0730
to	arrange	billets	aaa
T.O.	will	arrange	to
collect	mess	kits aaa	Lewis
Guns	will	be	carried
on	limbers	aaa	All
Transport	will	report	to
B.T.O	at	HOLLAIN	STATION

FROM

TIME & PLACE

*This line should be erased if not required.

C. & R. 7300. Wt. W14832/M1523 100,000. 3/17. (E930). Forms C/2123.

Army Form C. 2123.
(In books of 100.)

"C" Form.

MESSAGES AND SIGNALS. No. of Message..................

Prefix..........Code.........Words.......... £ s. d. Charges to Collect	Received. From.................. By..................	Sent, or sent out. At..................m. To.................. By..................	Office Stamp.
Service Instructions.			

Handed in at..Office..........m. Received..................m.

TO

*Sender's Number	Day of Month	In reply to Number	AAA
by	0900	hours	aaa
Arrival	in	billets	and
location	of	Coy	H.Q.
will	be	reported	at
once	to	Bn. HQ.	aaa
Acknowledge.			

FROM

TIME & PLACE

*This line should be erased if not required.

C. & R. 7300. Wt. W14832/M1523 100,000. 3/17. (E930). Forms C/2123.

349

Secret

APP. VI

K/141

OC Coys
7.30

In event of advance east from line VEZONCHAUX FONTENOY divisional boundaries will be:-

On right. - D20a central – D12 c.00 – E10 c.00. – F5a.05 thence due east.

On left. Y9 d 0.0 – W3a.00. – X.5 central thence due east.

59th Division will be on right and 55 Division on left.

15 Division is advancing on two Bde front. 44th Inf Bde on right and 46th Inf Bde on left boundary being line BOURGEON – WASMES both inclusive to 44th Inf Bde.

(Sgd) G.P. Geddes Capt.
Adjt.
5 Gordon Highlanders

9/11/18.

393

APP. VII

O.6 A B C D Coys T.O I.O
Sigs. + RSM

9/16

1. The 15th Div. will continue the advance today 11th Nov. with 44 Bde on right & 46th Bde on left.
5th Gordons Hrs will pass through 8th Seaforths on right and 7/8th KOSBs will pass through 4/5 BW on left.

2. Objective: X Roads O36.d.2.3 – high ground just East CHIEVRES-HOVES.

3. The 5th Gordon Highlanders will pass the Starting point S 14 a. 8.8 as follows:–

D Coy	0630
C "	0632
BHQ	0634
B Coy	0635
A "	0637

Route:– ELLIGNIES – T 26 c 6.2 – X Roads T 21. 3 4.

4. Method of Advance from HUISSIGNIES
(a) D Coy on the left and C Coy on the right will cross the BLATON CANAL at the most suitable places between the Bde boundaries (see para 5). The lock at T 17 d 9.2 and Bridge at T 12 b.22 are

are still reported intact.
On crossing canal D & C Coys will establish a bridgehead line running along road from PONT STANNANNE – CHAPEL at U 13 c 6.2 – Road running SW to ROUMONT.
D Coy will push out patrols to EM de la GRANDEUR and C Coy to BOIS de VILLE

4 (c) Until the above Bridgehead line is secured B & A Coys will remain under cover near Lock No 15 and the Church respectively.
On D & C Coys reporting that the above line is secured B & A Coys will cross the Canal & pass through D & C Coys respectively in Artillery formation and make good the final objectives referred to in para 1.
B & A Coys will push out patrols to WESTERN outskirts of BRUGELETTE & BAUFFE.

5. Boundaries
IV Bde :- TONGRE (exclusive) CHIEVRES (inclusive) BRUGELETTE (exclusive)
5 Bde :- BELOEIL – BAUFFE (both exclusive)
Inter Coy :- Continuation of road from LADEUZE to CHAPEL

6. Bn HQ will be established at Church HUISSIGNIES. They will move to T 24 b 4 9 when the advance from

pon Bridgehead line commences
Coys must keep in touch by visual
& Semaphore.

4/ ACKNOWLEDGE

(Sgd) Capt raaj
Capt raaj

0530
11.11.18

[illegible] Gordon Highlanders

Operation Order No. 1

SECRET

APP No 9.

12 Nov 1916

1. The 5th Gordon [illegible] will be relieved by the 10[illegible] today 12th Nov. as follows:-

B Coy. [illegible] will be relieved by D Coy [illegible]

A " " " B " R.

C " " " C " S.R.

D " " " A " S.R.

Relief will commence about 1500 hours. Completed Coys will [illegible] in TONDRES.

Route [illegible] U x a. 9.3 - [illegible] U.1.c.7.4 - [illegible] T.12 b.4.2.

2. [illegible] limbers, cookers [illegible] will march back with their Coys.

3. [illegible] 9.12 of [illegible]

4. [illegible] of relief will be [illegible] to Bn. H.Q.

5. Billeting party will [illegible] T.12.d.2.2.

6. Acknowledge.

[illegible] Capt. [illegible]
5 Gordon Highlanders

[illegible] O.C.s.
I
T.O. [illegible]

G. 12

O.C. All Coys.
R.S.M.

The Battalion will be relieved at dusk by the 1st Bn Sco. Rifles & will withdraw to TONGRES.

Coy Qm. Sergeants will report to Lieut McCosland at Orderly Room at 2.15 pm with bicycles.

Valises of A & B Coys will be collected at 1400 hours prompt. Those of C & D Coys at 1500 hours.

Details of relief to follow

G Meiklejohn Capt & Adjt
2 Gordon Highlanders

12.11.1918.

Cancelled.

"C" FORM.

MESSAGES AND SIGNALS.

(In books of 100.)

No. of Message..........

Prefix SM Code 1825 Words 61

Received from ... By ...

Service Instructions

ABERDEEN MO. RNF

Sent, or sent out. At ... m. To ... By ...

Office Stamp. Done 13-11-18

APPX

Handed in at ABERDEEN Office 1825 m. Received 2330 m.

TO Officer cmdg 5th Gordons
France

Sender's Number.	Day of Month.	In reply to Number.	AAA
—	13	—	

The county of Aberdeen territorial force association hereby congratulate you and all ranks under your command on the successful termination of hostilities aaa They are sensible of the deep devotion to duty and the great sacrifice made and feel proud of the splendid work done by your battn during the war

B.O.

FROM MELLIS: CHAIRMAN

PLACE & TIME OF ASSN

The above line, except A A A, should be erased, if not required.

... P738. 691,000 Pads. ...

The message of generous
and heartening appreciation
which you have sent to
the Battalion on behalf of the
County of Aberdeen T.F.
association has greatly
touched all ranks. I beg
you to convey to them
our deep gratitude and thanks.

OC 8/10 Battn
Gordon Highlanders

Forwarded

Please acknowledge receipt

For the War Diary

T. T. Busy.

Major.

Daag VII Corps

16/8/18

VII CORPS.
D.A.A.G.
No. A/6338/2
Date 16/8/18

ZUYKERKUE

MAP TO ACCOMPANY 44TH Bde G Notes No 54.

G H **SECRET.**

12 7 9

18 13

24 19

REFERENCE.

DANGER ZONE SHOWN IN	RED.
PRECAUTIONARY ZONE " "	BLUE
TARGETS	GREEN.

SHEET 44 NW.3. SCALE 1/10,000.

CONFIDENTIAL
****

5 Gordon Hrs

A/507 V8246

W A R D I A R Y

****

FOR THE MONTH OF DECEMBER

1 9 1 8

****

V O L U M E No. 44

****

25/1/19

D. G. Gordon Lieut.Colonel,

Commanding 5th Bn.The Gordon Highlanders.

Army Form C. 2118.

Instructions regarding War Diaries and Intelligence Summaries are contained in F. S. Regs., Part II. and the Staff Manual respectively. Title pages will be prepared in manuscript.

WAR DIARY
or
INTELLIGENCE SUMMARY.
(*Erase heading not required.*)

Place	Date	Hour	Summary of Events and Information	Remarks and references to Appendices
CHIÈVRES	1.12.18 to 5.12.18		During this period, the usual parades were carried out. On the 2nd a Brigade Gymkhana was held, which was attended by both soldiers and civilians.	A.D.C.
	5th to 7th		On the 5th, ten officers and one hundred men proceeded to WILLAUPUIS to represent the Battalion on the occasion of the King's visit. On arrival they were billeted in the CONVENT there. At 0900 hours on the morning of the 7th the detachment paraded and marched to their position on the main LEUZE-PERUWELZ Road. His Majesty arrived about 1115 hours and proceeded on foot through the ranks and was given an enthusiastic welcome by each unit in turn. During the afternoon, the detachment returned to CHIÈVRES.	APP. No I. A.D.C.
	8th.		Church Parade was held in the Concert Hall. In the afternoon, the Battalion XV played a Rugby Football match against a Combined XV. of Black Watch and Seaforths. Result 3-nil for the Battalion.	A.D.C.

A6945 Wt. W11422/M1160 350,000 12/16 D. D. & L. Forms/C./2118/14.

Army Form C. 2118.

Instructions regarding War Diaries and Intelligence Summaries are contained in F. S. Regs., Par. II. and the Staff Manual respectively. Title pages will be prepared in manuscript.

WAR DIARY
or
INTELLIGENCE SUMMARY.
(Erase heading not required.)

Place	Date	Hour	Summary of Events and Information	Remarks and references to Appendices
CHIÈVRES	9.12.18 to 10.12.18		Usual parades were carried out. A football match between officers of the Battalion and officers of 4/5th Black Watch, arranged for the afternoon of the 10th, had to be cancelled owing to the weather.	A.D.C.
"	11.12.18.		A party of 34 miners left the Battalion to-day, being the first party to leave for demobilization. Owing to rain parades were held in billets during the day.	A.D.C.
"	12.12.18.		The second party of miners numbering 31, left Battalion for demobilization today. On account of rain parades were held in billets by Company's to-day.	J.McB.
"	13.12.18.		Parades under Company arrangements were carried out as usual. A Battalion concert was held at 1730 hrs attended by both soldiers & civilians.	J.McB.
"	14.12.18. to 16.12.18		Nothing of special interest occurred during this period.	A.D.C.

A6945 Wt. W11422/M1160 35,000 12/16 D. D. & L. Forms/C./2118/14.

Instructions regarding War Diaries and Intelligence Summaries are contained in F. S. Regs., Par. II. and the Staff Manual respectively. Title pages will be prepared in manuscript.

WAR DIARY
or
INTELLIGENCE SUMMARY.
(Erase heading not required.)

Army Form C. 2118.

Place	Date	Hour	Summary of Events and Information	Remarks and references to Appendices
CHIÈVRES	17.12.18		The Battalion moved at 0902 hours, to SOIGNIES.	1/40,000 & BRUSSELS 1/100,000 APP 2 aDC
SOIGNIES	18.12.18		Battalion moved at 0810 hours to ITTRE, being staging area in the move forward.	aDC APP 3
ITTRES	19.12.18 20.12.18		Usual parades were carried out.	aDC
Do	21.12.18		To day, the battalion Colours were trooped. A full battalion parade, for the trooping, was held in the grounds of the CHATEAU at ITTRE.	
ITTRE	22.12.18		The Battalion moved forward to HIVELLES (SHEET BRUSSELS 1/100,000)	App 4 aDC
HIVELLES	23/24		On the 23rd, the day was devoted to cleaning up and parades commenced on the 24th.	aDC
Do	25th		No training was carried out. R.C. services were held at 0900 hours & C of E at 0700 and 0800 hours.	
Do	26th		Training recommenced under Company arrangements	aDC
Do	27th		B & C Coys carried out route marches, whilst A & D Coys attended baths.	aDC

A6945 Wt. W11422/M1160 350,000 12/16 D. D. & L. Forms/C./2118/14.

Instructions regarding War Diaries and Intelligence Summaries are contained in F. S. Regs., Part II. and the Staff Manual respectively. Title pages will be prepared in manuscript.

WAR DIARY
or
INTELLIGENCE SUMMARY.
(*Erase heading not required.*)

Army Form C. 2118.

Place	Date	Hour	Summary of Events and Information	Remarks and references to Appendices
NIVELLES	28/12/18		B & C Coys bathed, A & D Coys carried out Route marches	ADC
Do	29/12/18		Divine service was held in the Brigade Hall for Presbyterians, R.C. service was held in Church, & C of E in the Cinema.	ADC
DO	30/12/18		Parades as usual were carried out.	ADC
Do	31/12/18		Parades as usual. Latter part of the forenoon was devoted to Company Route marches. No holiday was observed. During the month, football & Rugby matches were arranged & played off	ADC ADC

A6945 Wt. W11422/M1160 35,000 12/16 D. D. & L. Forms/C./2118/14.

Instructions regarding War Diaries and Intelligence Summaries are contained in F. S. Regs., Part II. and the Staff Manual respectively. Title pages will be prepared in manuscript.

WAR DIARY
or
INTELLIGENCE SUMMARY.

(Erase heading not required.)

Army Form C. 2118.

Place / Date / Hour / Summary of Events and Information	O	OR	O	OR
30·11·18. Effective Strength			50	934
Increase				
Reinforcements from Base	-	62		
Decrease				
Lieut M.C. WRIGHT, M.C. to U.K. Sick	1	-		
" J.C. RUSSELL to 2nd Army Musketry School	1	-		
To Transportation Troops Depot Base	-	3		
" 14th (P) Bn Northumberland Fusiliers	-	1		
Taken on establishment of 44th T.M.B.	-	5		
Evacuated Sick	-	3		
	2	12		
Difference between Increase & Decrease			2	50
7·12·18. Effective Strength			47	984
Increase				
Joined from Base 2/Lieut. I. McPHERSON	1			
" " " " J.E. DIXON	1			
" " " Other Ranks	-	12		
	2	12		
Decrease				
Miners to U.K. for Demobilization	-	60		
Evacuated Sick	-	4		
	-	64		
Difference between Increase & Decrease			2	52
14·12·18. Effective Strength			49	932

Summary of Events and Information	O	OR	O	OR
14·12·18. Effective Strength			49	932
Increase				
Joined from Base	-	3		
Decrease				
Evacuated through being 7 days in F.A.	-	11		
Difference between Increase & Decrease			-	8
21·12·18 Effective Strength			49	924
Increase				
Joined from 15th Div Reception Camp	-	10		
Decrease				
Lieut J.U.E. BARRON to U.K. sick	1	-		
To Base for Transfer to Home Establishment		1		
Evacuated Sick	-	7		
To Concentration Camp for Demob. Lt. GRANT	1	-		
" " " Other Ranks	-	43		
	2	51		
Difference between Increase & Decrease			2	41
28·12·18. Effective Strength			47	883

D. D. & L., London, E.C. (A8004) Wt. W.771/M2 31 750,000 5/17 Sch. 52 Forms/C2118/14

APP. No I

CO. 4 Coy.

Orders for Royal Visit of 7th December, 1918.

1. Party representing the Battalion on the occasion of His Majesty The King's Visit, will parade in the PLACE ST JEAN ready to march off at 0845 hours to-morrow.
The Band will also parade and go with the detachment.

2. ~~[illegible]~~ Full Marching Order, 20 rounds S.A.A., no Box Respirator or Steel Helmet

3. Officers for Parade.
The following officers will parade with the detachment:-
Captains Cowie, Kemp and Watt.
Lieuts. West and ~~[illegible]~~.
2nd Lieuts. ~~[illegible]~~, Irvine, Pirrie, Leslie and Barron.
R.S.M. W.L.Smith, D.C.M. will proceed with the detachment.
The officers detailed above will take servants.
2 servants will remain behind and come on with the baggage wagon.

4. Names of men attached herewith are for parade.

5. Baggage.
Officers valises will be stacked outside Battn.H.Q. Mess ready for loading by 0830 hours.
Blankets will be rolled in bundles of ten, properly labelled and stacked at the same time and place.
Band packs will also be dumped.

6. O.C.Coys will arrange ~~[illegible]~~ that loading parties are detailed to load these articles.

7. "B" Coy's cooker will accompany the detachment and will be prepared to serve dinner on the march.

8. O.C.Coys will make arrangements to send sufficient messing kit for their officers.

9. Sgt.Dathie will detail a cook for the officers. and two cooks for O.R's.

10. Major F.J.C.Moffat, D.S.O. will assume command of the Battalion.
2nd Lieut.R.B.Strathdee will assume duties of Adjutant.

11. C.S.M.Inglis, M.M. will take over the duties of R.S.M.

12. ACKNOWLEDGE.

Distribution:- O.C.Coys. (Sd) A.D.Copland, Lieut. A/Adjt,
Q.M.T.O. R.S.M. Pipe M/ 6th Battalion, The Gordon Highlanders.
5/12/18.

APP No I

K.P./2.

APP. MOT.

All Officers
R.S.M.
Pipe Major

(1) Parade tomorrow will be at X22.a.4.3 (on South of Road 200 yards S.E of MAIRIE)

One marker will report to Brigade Major at 0900 hours.

One marker will report to DAAG at F.H.Q. 4.5 at 0930 hours

The band will parade with detachment and will fall out on reaching X.22.d.4.5.

The Brigade Major's billet is No. 112, opposite MAIRIE.

(2) The detachment will parade outside the Convent, by Companies, at 0830 hours tomorrow morning for inspection.

The band will parade at that time with detachment.

After the inspection the detachment will form up, facing the Convent ready to move off by 0900 hours.

(3) Dress. Walking out Dress

NCOs Belts & side-arms

Other Ranks belts

Officers will wear Balmorals

4. Procedure on arrival of the King

Troops will be formed up as close together as possible and not less than five deep on both sides of the Road, Officers in front.

All troops will stand to "attention" during the Salute, after which they will "Stand easy" and cheer as His Majesty approaches & passes.

Cheering will be independent & spontaneous. All men will remove their head-dress.

One yard interval will be observed between units.

5. ACKNOWLEDGE

A.L. Copland Lt. & Adjt.
5th Gordon Hrs.

6.12.18.

Appendix No. 2.

SECRET.

5th Battn. The Gordon Highlanders.
OPERATION ORDER No. 1.

Reference 1/40 000 map
and Brussels 1/100,000.

16th December, 1918.

1. The 15th Division is moving to the NIVELLES - BRAINE-LE-COMTE Area, commencing 13th December.
The 5th Gordon Highlanders will move to SOIGNIES to-morrow 17th December.
Route:- CHIEVRES - BRUGELETTE Station - CASEE - Road Junction 1 mile South of SILLY - SOIGNIES.

2. Starting Point. Farm at U.3.b.9.5.
Time. 0902 hours.
The Battalion will parade in the GRANDE PLACE in Close Column of Companies, facing the Town Hall, ready to march off at 0830 hours.
Order of Coys:- Battn.H.Q., "D", "A", "B", "C", Transport. All Battn.H.Q. personnel (less Signallers, Runners, Orderly Room Staff and Officers' Servants), Q.M. Stores, Tailors and Shoemakers will parade with their Companies.

3. Throughout the move to the new area, the following distances will be maintained:-
Between Battalions .... 20 yards.
Between Companies .... 10 "

4. Halts will be from 10 minutes to, until each clock hour.
There will be a midday halt on the 17th, from 1150 till 1300 hours for mens' dinners and watering horses. Water for horses is not plentiful and buckets will be required.

5. Advanced party, consisting of 2nd Lieut. J. Keir, C.Q.M.S's, 1 N.C.O. from Battn.H.Q. and one representative from Transport, will parade with bicycles at Battn.H.Q. [illegible] at 0800 hours.
Party will report to Staff Captain at the Statue in front of the Town Hall, SOIGNIES, near the Church, at 1100 hours. They will meet the Battalion at Road Junction X.4.d.5.1.

6. Arrival in billets, falling out states and location of Coy.H.Q. will be notified to Battn.H.Q. (X.10.b.8.3) at once.

7. ACKNOWLEDGE.

Capt Adjt,
5th Battalion, The Gordon Highlanders.

Distribution:-

Copies Nos.		
1 - 4	:	O.C.Coys.
5	:	L.G.O.
6	:	R.S.M.
7	:	Q.M.
8	:	T.O.
9	:	2nd Lieut. J. Keir.
10	:	War Diary.
11	:	File.

Appendix No. 3.

SECRET.

5th Battalion, The Gordon Highlanders.
OPERATION ORDER, No. 2.

Reference Map BRUSSELS, 1/100,000. 16th December, 1918.

1. The 5th Gordon Highlanders will move to the following areas on 18th December:-

"A" and "B" Coys .... HAUT-ITTRE.
Battn.H.Q.,"C", "D" Coys. and Transport . ITTRE.

Route:-
SOIGNIES - BRAINE-LE-COMTE - RONQUIERES - CROISEAU - ITTRE.

2. Starting Point. Road Junction at Kilo 37 (½ mile N.E. of SOIGNIES Church)
Time. 0810 hours.
The Battalion will parade in column of route ready to move off at 0730 hours, in order Battn.H.Q., "A", "B", "C", "D" Coys and Transport. Head of column to be at Road Junction X.11.c.1.9, facing S.E.

3. Advanced party (which proceeded on the 15th December) will meet the Battalion at western end of RONQUIERES.

4. Arrival in billets, falling out states and location of Coy.H.Q., will be reported at once to Battn.H.Q.

5. ACKNOWLEDGE.

G.P. Geddes
Capt Adjt,
5th Battalion, The Gordon Highlanders.

Distribution:-

Copies Nos. 1 - 4 : O.C.Coys.
5 : L.G.O.
6 : R.S.M.
7 : Q.M.
8 : T.O.
9 : War Diary.
10 : File.

SECRET.

5th Battn. The Gordon Highlanders.
Administrative Instructions
issued in conjunction with O.O., No.1.

1. One blanket per man will be returned to Q.M.Stores by 1800 hours to-night, also Orderly Room boxes and Signalling Gear.
The second blanket, and officers' valises of "A", "B" and "C" Companies and Battn.H.Q., will be loaded at Q.M.Stores by 0730 hours to-morrow. Those of "D" Coy will be loaded at "D" Coy's Orderly Room.
One G.S.Wagon is being allotted to each Company for blankets and valises, and one lorry to Battn.H.Q. for blankets, valises, Orderly Room boxes, etc.,
O.C.Coys must arrange for blankets to be rolled in bundles of 10 and so labelled that each man receives his own blankets back.

2. Officers' Mess kits will be collected by the Transport Officer at 0730 hours.

3. Billets must be left scrupulously clean and ready for inspection by the 2nd in Command by 0800 hours.

4. 2nd Lieut. Strenach will remain behind for one hour after the Battalion moves off in order to collect claims.
He will report to the Adjutant at 1900 hours to-night for instructions.

5. Every precaution must be taken for the prevention of fire in the new billets.

6. Inventories must be taken and carefully checked before vacating billets.

G.P. Geddes
Capt Adjt,
5th Battalion, The Gordon Highlanders.

APPENDIX No 4

5th Battn. The Gordon Highlanders.

SECRET.

OPERATION ORDER No. 3.

Ref. Sheet 39. 21st December, 1918.

1. The 5th Gordon Highlanders will move to NIVELLES to-morrow, 22nd December.
Route. Road Junction I.33.a.9.8 - HAUT-ITTRE - CHAPEL I.30.a.9.3 - NIVELLES.

2. Starting Point. The Battalion will pass the Starting Point (Entrance to Battn.H.Q. Mess, No. 11 Billet) as follows:-

Battn.H.Q. .... 0930 hours.
"B" Coy .... 0931 "
"C" " .... 0933 "
"D" " .... 0935 "
"A" " .... 0937 "

The Battalion will march in Sections of Threes as practised to-day.

3. Transport. Will pass the Starting Point at 0830 hours, and proceed by the following route:- Road Junction I.33.a.9.8 - Road Junction LE DOYEN, I.22.b.6.3 - NIVELLES.
Transport will wait for the battalion at the Chapel I.30.a.9.3.

4 Billetting Party will meet the battalion at Road Junction P.25.b.2.2.

5. Arrival in billets, falling out states and location of Coy.H.Q. will be reported at once to Battn.H.Q.

6. ACKNOWLEDGE.

(Signed) G.P.Geddes, Capt, Adjt,
5th Battalion, The Gordon Highlanders.

Distribution:-

Copies Nos. 1 - 4 : O.C.Coys.
5 : L.G.O.
6 : Q.M.
7 : T.O.
8 : R.S.M.
9 : W.D.
10 : File.

Administrative Instructions.
Issued in Conjunction with Operation Orders No. 3.

1. Reveille .... 0600 hours. Breakfasts .... 0700 hours.

2. Officers Valises of Battn.H.Q., "C" and "D" Coys, blankets of Battn.H.Q. and Orderly Room boxes will be piled at Q.M.Stores at 0730 hours. The blankets of "C" and "D" Coys will be loaded on the G.S.Wagons now at their disposal, by 0800 hours. Valises and blankets of "A" and "B" Coys will be piled in Coy. areas by 0830 hours Two men per Company to be left in charge as these will be carried in the second journey.
Mess kits will be ready for loading at Coy.Messes by 0800 hours.

(Signed) G.P.Geddes, Capt Adjt,
21/12/18. 5th Battalion, The Gordon Highlanders.

Ref.Map:- BRUSSELS 6. 1/100,000.

44th Brigade No. G.6. 14:12:18.

4/5th Black Watch.
8th Seaforth Highrs.
5th Gordon Highrs.
44th L.T.M.Battery.
B.T.O., 44th Bde.H.Q.
Signal Officer, 44th Bde.H.Q.
No. 2 Coy Train (for information).
46th Field Ambulance. (for information).

1. The billeting arrangements in TEMPORARY AREA (West of NIVELLES) are as follows:-

44TH BRIGADE H.Q.	FM. 1 mile due South RONQUIERES Church.	
5TH GORDON HIGHRS.	H.Q.	ITTRE.
	2 Coys	ITTRE.
	2 Coys	HAUT ITTRE.
4/5TH. BLACK WATCH.	H.Q.	HALTE, 1½ miles N. of RONQUIERES.
	4 Coys.	Factories at HALTE and PIED D'EAU.

(14 Officers and 2 Coy Officers' Messes in RONQUIERES).

8TH SEAFORTH HIGHRS.	H.Q.	RONQUIERES.
	2 Coys.	RONQUIERES.
	2 Coys.	HENRIPONT.
44TH L.T.M.BATTERY.	QUESNOY just S.E. of RONQUIERES.	
46TH FIELD AMBCE.	Eastern outskirts of NIVELLES.	
No.2 COY TRAIN.	BILOT.	

2. Following advanced parties will leave Brigade H.Q. 0800 on morning of 15th, and proceed to RONQUIERES, the lorries returning to ATH the same day:-

Each Battn.	13 ~~12~~	all ranks.
Brigade H.Q.	3	do.
T.M.B.	2	do.

3. The above parties will be billetted in RONQUIERES until the arrival of the Brigade ~~on the evening of~~ about 1100 hours 18th, making their own arrangements for reconnoitring their respective areas.

4. The Brigade will march into the area along the road BRAINE LE COMTE - RONQUIERES - CROISEAU - ITTRE, in the following order of march:-

Brigade H.Q.
5/Gordon Highrs.
4/5th Black Watch.
8/Seaforth Highrs.
46th Field Ambce.
No. 2 Coy Train (less baggage sent in).

5. Guides from advanced parties will meet units as follows:-

8/SEAFORTH HIGHRS. At P of PONT du JOUR (HENRIPONT).

OTHER UNITS. At western end of RONQUIERES.

6. Care must be taken that the column is not checked while the kits of the advanced parties of those units billetted beyond RONQUIERES are being picked up.

F. Fickle [signature]
Major,
Brigade Major,
44TH. INF.BDE.

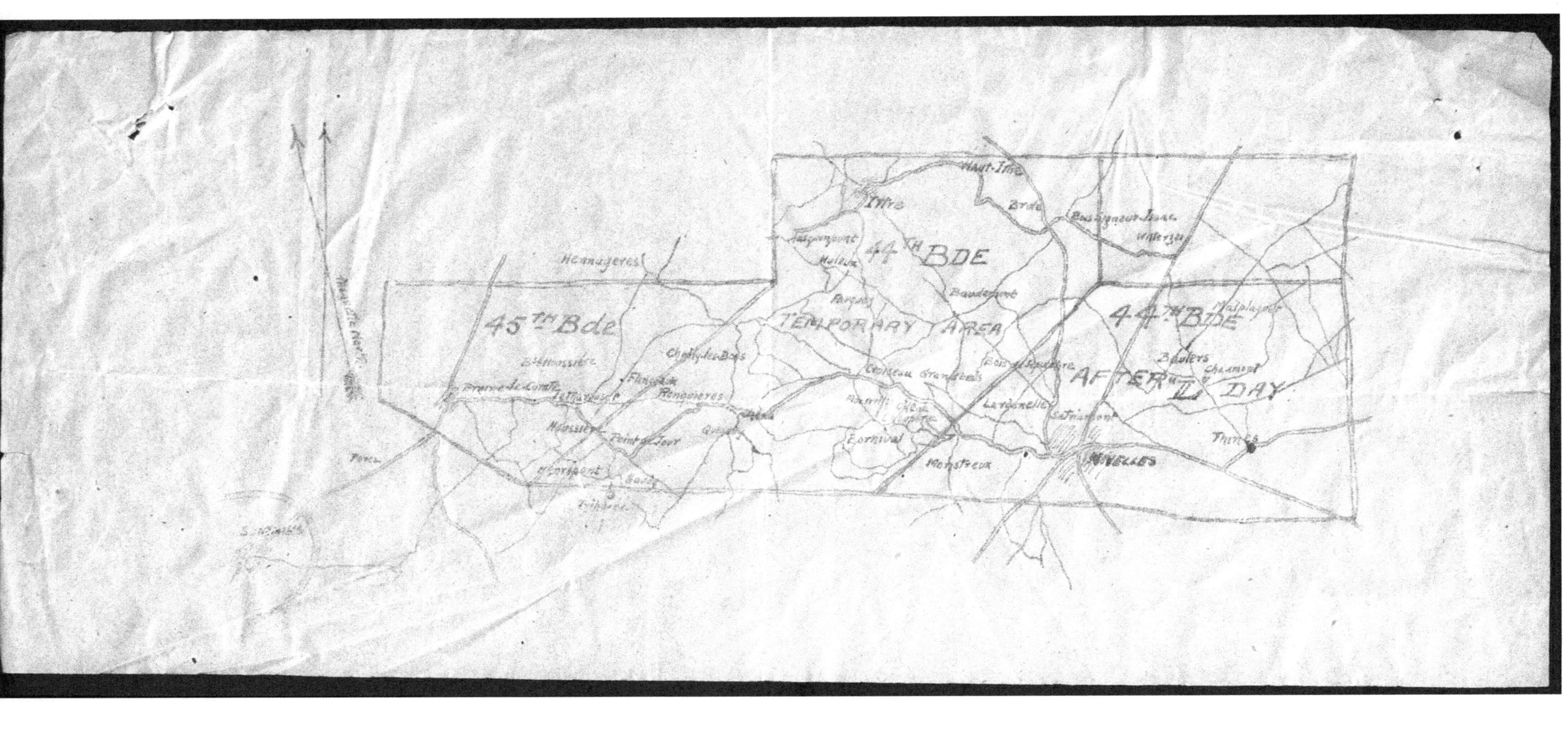
45TH Bde
44TH BDE
TEMPORARY AREA
44TH BDE
AFTER "Z" DAY
Ittre
Haut-Ittre
Baudemont
Monstreux
Nivelles
Thines

15

<u>CONFIDENTIAL.</u>

Vol 47

W A R   D I A R Y

J A N U A R Y

1 9 1 9 .

V O L U M E.

4 5.

D. G. Gordon. Lieut_Colonel,
Commanding 5th Battalion, The Gordon Highlanders.

1st February, 1919.

Instructions regarding War Diaries and Intelligence Summaries are contained in F. S. Regs., Part II. and the Staff Manual respectively. Title pages will be prepared in manuscript.

WAR DIARY
or
INTELLIGENCE SUMMARY.
(*Erase heading not required.*)

Army Form C. 2118.

Place	Date	Hour	Summary of Events and Information	Remarks and references to Appendices
NIVELLES	1/1/1919		Being New Year's Day the Battalion was given a holiday. No special functions were indulged in.	A.D.C.
NIVELLES	2/1/19 – 12/1/19		During this period, the usual work was carried on. Football & Rugby matches were arranged and played. In the evenings, Concerts, etc were arranged & were well attended by all ranks	A.D.C.
NIVELLES	13/1/19 – 14/1/19		Preparations for the 44th Brigade dance, to be given on the 15th, were commenced. Fatigue parties were supplied by the battalion to assist in decoration of the Hall etc. Otherwise, the usual parades were carried out.	A.D.C.
NIVELLES	15/1/19		During the day, the usual work was carried on. The 44th Brigade Officers Dance was held in the Brigade Hall. About 250 to 300 attended	
Do	16/1/19		The usual training & education was carried out, and baths were attended.	A.D.C.

A6945 Wt. W11422/M1160 35,000 12/16 D. D. & L. Forms/C./2118/14.

Instructions regarding War Diaries and Intelligence Summaries are contained in F. S. Regs., Part II. and the Staff Manual respectively. Title pages will be prepared in manuscript.

WAR DIARY
or
INTELLIGENCE SUMMARY.
(Erase heading not required.)

Army Form C. 2118.

Place	Date	Hour	Summary of Events and Information	Remarks and references to Appendices
NIVELLES	18th 12/19		To day, the Battalion marched to WATERLOO. They were shown the Panorama there, and the officers pointed out the battlefield to the men. Dinner was taken on the field, after which the Battalion returned to billets	ASC
Do	19th		Divine Services were held.	ASC
Do	20th/21st		Usual training & education carried out	ASC
Do	22nd		Company Route marches were carried out.	ASC
Do	23/24th		Usual parades.	ASC
Do	25th		Company Route marches carried out.	ASC
Do	26th		Usual Church parades. The pipers and drums represented the battalion at ~~the~~ a review of British troops in BRUSSELS by H.M. The King of the Belgians	WHL
Do	27th/30th		Usual training and education parades were carried out. Weather intensely cold, much frost and snow	WHL
Do	31st		Usual parades.	

D. D. & L., London, E.C. (10340) Wt W5300/P713 750,000 3/18 E 2688 Forms/C2118/16.

Instructions regarding War Diaries and Intelligence Summaries are contained in F. S. Regs., Part II. and the Staff Manual respectively. Title pages will be prepared in manuscript.

WAR DIARY
or
INTELLIGENCE SUMMARY.

(Erase heading not required.)

Army Form C. 2118.

Place	Date	Hour	Summary of Events and Information	O	OR	O	OR
28 12 18			Effective Strength	~~47~~	~~883~~	47	883
Increase							
Joined from 15th Div. Recept Camp.				–	3		
Decrease							
Transferred to U.K. (Sick) Lieut J.M. DOULL				1			
Demobilized					18		
Evacuated Sick					1		
				1	19		
Difference between Increase + Decrease						1	16
4. 1. 19			Effective Strength			46	867
Increase							
Joined from U.K. A/Capt. J. Lynn. M.C				1			
" " Div Recept. Camp				–	6		
				1	6		
Decrease							
Demobilized :- Lieut L. Bain + 2nd Lieut A. Munro				2			
" :- Other Ranks					35		
Evacuated Sick					2		
				2	37		
Difference between Increase + Decrease						1	31
11. 1. 19			Effective Strength			45	836
Increase							
Joined from 15th Divisional Recept. Camp.				–	5		

Summary of Events and Information	O	OR	O	OR
Decrease				
Demobilized :- Lt J.W. Kay + S.M. Muir	2			
" :- Other Ranks	–	33		
Evacuated Sick	–	3		
	2	36		
Difference between Increase + Decrease			2	31
18.1.19 Effective Strength			43	805
Increase :- Nil				
Decrease :-				
2/Lt. J. E. S. Tollemache, struck off strength	1			
Demob :- 2/Lts F.J.J. Bower + S.M. Barron	2			
" :- Other Ranks		57		
Evacuated Sick		7		
Over 7 days in F.A.		5		
	3	69	3	69
25.1.19 Effective Strength			40	736
Increase				
Joined from Div Recept Camp	–	5		
Decrease :-				
Demobilized :- Lt A.D. Copland	1			
" :- Other Ranks	–	62		
Evacuated Sick	–	2		
	1	64		
Difference between Increase + Decrease			1	59
1.2.19 Effective Strength			39	677

D. D. & L., London, E.C.
(A8004) Wt. W1771/M2·31 750,000 5/17 Sch. 52 Forms/C2118/14

Original

WO 95/13

(6392) Wt. W6192/P875 1,500,000 4/18 McA & W Ltd (E 2815) Forms W3091/4. Army Form W.3091.

Cover for Documents.

Nature of Enclosures.

CONFIDENTIAL

War Diary of

5th Bn. The Gordon Highlanders.

FROM:- 1st FEBY. 1919. TO:- 28th FEBY. 1919.

VOLUME 46.

Notes, or Letters written.

ORIGINAL

Instructions regarding War Diaries and Intelligence Summaries are contained in F. S. Regs., Part II. and the Staff Manual respectively. Title pages will be prepared in manuscript.

WAR DIARY
or
~~INTELLIGENCE SUMMARY.~~
(*Erase heading not required.*)

Army Form C. 2118.

5th Battn GORDON. HIGHRS

Place	Date	Hour	Summary of Events and Information	Remarks and references to Appendices
NIVELLES	FEB 1st		Being Sunday the usual divine services were held in the battalion. Capt G. Cowper died at 3rd (Australian) C.C.S. HAL of influenza	WL
	2nd		The Battalion became duty battalion for the brigade, finding the usual guards and working parties. Routine as usual.	WL.
	3rd		Training and Education were carried out. The burial of Capt G. Cowper took place. C Company provided the firing party. A large number of officers in the brigade attended	WL.
	4th/5th		Usual parades and education classes were carried out.	WL.
	6th		Usual training and education classes were carried out. Lt Col. The Lord D. G. Gordon. D.S.O. relinquished command of the battalion, on proceeding to England for demobilization. Major A. D. GREENHILL GARDYNE assumed command of the battalion.	WL.
	7th		Routine as usual	WL.
	8th		Divine Services were held.	WL.
	9th		The Pipes and Drums of the battalion, 3 officers and 120 men attended the presentation of ~~Co~~ colours to the 8th Seaforth Highlanders in the town today.	WL.
	10th		The usual parades and education classes were carried on.	WL.
	11th		The Battalion became duty Battn for the brigade. The usual guards and working parties being found.	WL.

D. D. & L., London, E.C.
(A8004) Wt. W1771/M2 31 750,000 5/17 Sch. 52 Forms/C2118/14

Instructions regarding War Diaries and Intelligence Summaries are contained in F. S. Regs., Part II. and the Staff Manual respectively. Title pages will be prepared in manuscript.

WAR DIARY
or
~~INTELLIGENCE SUMMARY.~~
(Erase heading not required.)

Army Form C. 2118.

5th Battn Gordon Highlanders

Place	Date	Hour	Summary of Events and Information	Remarks and references to Appendices
NIVELLES	12th/14th		The usual routine was carried out. Parades and Education Classes. The numbers of the Education Classes, having fallen so low in the Battalion they were amalgamated with other Battalions in the Brigade and formed into Brigade education classes.	W.L.
	15th		The usual Divine Services were held. A warning order was received at 1300 hrs. to the effect that the battalion was to hold itself in readiness to proceed to GERMANY on the 20th to join the 62nd Div.	W.L.
	16th/17		The usual routine was carried out Preparations were in progress for the move to Germany	W.L.
	18th		The battalion tug of war team pulled in the Finals of the Divisional Tug of War but were beaten after a very hard pull	W.L.
	19th		The battalion received orders to proceed at once to HALLE by motor lorries. at 1530 hours The usual billeting parties proceeded them All men who were eligible for demobilization were left behind in NIVELLES as a detachment to be attached to one of the other battalions in the Brigade The Battn was billeted in the 15th Div Reception Camp in HALLE. All the Battn equipment and vehicles were taken, but only 9 animals	W.L.
HALLE	20th		The Battn commenced loading at 0900 hrs. and left HALLE station at 1400hrs The train accomadation was good. Before leaving a draft of 6 officers and 237 OR's of the 9th (PIONEER) Battn joined this Battn. for the Army of Occupation The ~~route~~ followed was, Brussels, LOUVAIN, TIRLEMONT. LIEGE	W.L.

(A8004) Wt. W1771/M2 31 750,000 5/17 Sch. 52 Forms/C2118/14

Instructions regarding War Diaries and Intelligence Summaries are contained in F. S. Regs., Part II. and the Staff Manual respectively. Title pages will be prepared in manuscript.

Army Form C. 2118.

WAR DIARY

or

~~INTELLIGENCE SUMMARY.~~

(Erase heading not required.) 5th Battn. GORDON HIGHLANDERS

Place	Date	Hour	Summary of Events and Information	Remarks and references to Appendices
MECHERNICH	21st		The Battn arrived on the frontier at WELKENSRAEDT and crossed to HERBESTHAL in GERMANY at 0730 hours and detrained at ~~to~~ MECHERNICH at 1400 hours. The Battn spent the night in this village	WL.
ROGGANDORF and STREMPT	22nd		The Battn marched from Mechernich to the villages of ROGGANDORF and STREMPT where they took over the billets of the 2/4th Duke of Wellingtons (West Riding) Regt. The accomadation was found to be bad and the companies were very ~~much sepa~~ far apart.	WL.
"	23rd		Sunday. The day was given to cleaning up generally, after the train journey	WL.
"	24th		All money was collected from the battalion and taken to the field cashier to be changed into German Currency.	WL.
	25th		Parades under Company arrangements	WL.
"	26/28th		Usual Company parades were carried out. The weather during this period was very wet and cold	WL.
			Strength during month of February. APPENDIX I.	WL.

J.M[illegible] Major
for Lieut Colonel
Comdg 5 Gordon Highlanders

Appendix I

Army Form C. 2118.

Instructions regarding War Diaries and Intelligence Summaries are contained in F. S. Regs., Part II. and the Staff Manual respectively. Title pages will be prepared in manuscript.

WAR DIARY
or
~~INTELLIGENCE SUMMARY.~~
(Erase heading not required.)

Strength [illegible] Month of Feb 1919.

Place	Date	Hour	Summary of Events and Information	O	OR	O	OR
1. 2. 19			Effective Strength			39	677
Increase							
Major A D Greenhill Gardyne from HQ 44th Inf. Bde				1	-		
Joined from 15th Div. Reception Camp				-	3		
				1	3		
Decrease							
Demobilized - Lt Col. Lord Dudley Gordon DSO				1			
" 2/Lts Kerr, Pirie and A B Smith				3			
Captain G. Cowper died in the 1 CCS				1			
Demobilized				-	19		
Evacuated Sick				-	1		
To Base Commandants Office. Etaples				-	2		
				5	22		
Difference between Increase + Decrease						4	19
8. 2. 19			Effective Strength			35	658
Increase							
Rejoined from Hospital				-	5		
Decrease							
Lieuts A MORRISON & A P CRANNA demobilized				2			
2/ " J M McKENZIE, M.M. + T W B KNIGHT demobilized				2	~~22~~		
Other Ranks Demobilized				-	82		
To School of Cookery, Etaples				-	8		
Evacuated Sick				-	2		
				4	92		
Difference between Increase + Decrease						4	87
15 2 19			Effective Strength			31	571

Summary of Events and Information	O	OR	Remarks and references to Appendices O	OR
15 2 19 Effective Strength			31	571
Increase				
Joined from 9th Bn. Gordon Highlanders	7	234		
" " 15th Div Recept Camp	-	8		
T M B Personnel retaken on Strength	-	5		
	7	247		
Decrease				
Evacuated to U K 17.2.19 2/Lt A G MOWAT	1	-		
Demobilized 20.2.19 Lieut R.W. YOUNGSON, M.C.	1	-		
Other Ranks - Demobilized	-	63		
Evacuated Sick	-	5		
Over 7 days in F A	-	7		
	2	75		
Difference between Increase + Decrease			5	172
22. 2. 19 Effective Strength			36	743
Increase				
Taken on Strength from 9th Gordon Highrs	-	6		
Decrease				
Men left at NIVELLES for demobilization	-	135		
Demobilized whilst on Leave	-	22		
Demobilized 27 2 19	-	3		
	-	160		
Difference between Increase + Decrease			-	154
1. 3 19 Effective Strength			36	589

D. D. & L., London, E.C.
(10540) Wt W5300/1773 750,000 3/18 E 2688 Forms/C2118/16.

www.ingramcontent.com/pod-product-compliance
Lightning Source LLC
Chambersburg PA
CBHW080901230426
43663CB00013B/2598
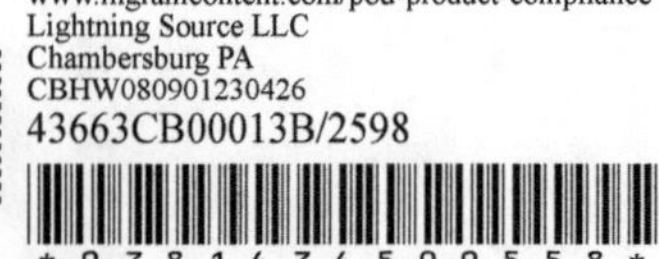